Marianne Heasly

Marianne Heasly

SUSTAINABLE ARCHITECTURE
AND URBANISM

Dominique Gauzin-Müller

with contributions by Nicolas Favet

SUSTAINABLE ARCHITECTURE AND URBANISM

CONCEPTS, TECHNOLOGIES, EXAMPLES

BIRKHÄUSER
Publishers for Architecture
Basel · Berlin · Boston

The following sections of the text were written by the architect Nicolas Favet:

- pages 76-78, "Amsterdam, Netherlands, GWL district";

- pages 79-82, "Helsinki, Finland, Viikki district";

- pages 160-165, "Housing in Viikki, Helsinki, Finland";

- pages 184-189, "Notley Green primary school, UK";

- pages 208-211, "Cultural and visitor centre, Terrasson, France";

- pages 224-229, "Avax headquarters building, Athens, Greece";

- pages 230-233, "iGuzzini headquarters building, Recanati, Italy".

Nicolas Favet also assisted in drawing up the bibliography.

Design: Richard Medioni
Cover design: Alexandra Zöller
Translated from French by: Kate Purver
Lithography: F.A. Publicité
Printing: Rotolito Lombarda, Italy

This book is also available in a German language edition
(ISBN 3-7643-6658-3)

A CIP catalogue record for this book is available from
the Library of Congress, Washington, D. C., USA

Die Deutsche Bibliothek - CIP-Einheitsaufnahme

Sustainable architecture and urbanism:
concepts, technologies, examples /
Dominique Gauzin-Müller. With contributions by Nicolas Favet.
[Engl. transl.: Kate Purver]. - Basel; Berlin; Boston: Birkhäuser, 2002
Einheitssacht.: L'Architecture écologique <engl.>
Dt. Ausg. u.d.T.: Nachhaltigkeit in Architektur und Städtebau
ISBN 3-7643-6659-1

© 2002 Birkhäuser – Publishers for Architecture,
P.O. Box 133, CH-4010 Basel, Switzerland
A member of the BertelsmannSpringer Publishing Group
© 2001, Groupe Moniteur, Editions du Moniteur, Paris,
for the original edition
Printed on acid-free paper produced from chlorine-free pulp. TCF∞

Printed in Italy
ISBN 3-7643-6659-1

9 8 7 6 5 4 3 2 1
http://www.birkhauser.ch

The French edition of this book was published under the title
"L'Architecture écologique" at Editions du Moniteur,
17, rue d'Uzès, 75108 Paris Cedex 02, France.

CONTENTS

Every book is an adventure, marked
by discoveries and encounters, moments
of enthusiasm and discouragement,
and new challenges.

My thanks to all those, both near and far, who
have provided their help and support, in particular:
Frédéric Lenne, director of Editions du Moniteur,
for his confidence in me;
Valérie Thouard, my editor, for her professionalism,
her involvement and the reassuring participation
which keeps us working together from one book
to the next;
Pierre Haïat and Thierry Kremer, editors,
for their contributions to the book's progress;
Richard Medioni, for the enthusiasm he brought
to the preparation of the book's design and
for his friendly and ever-helpful co-operation;
Nicolas Favet, architect and journalist,
for the fascinating discussions whose content
has enriched the book;
Pierre Lefevre, tutor at the Paris - La Villette school
of architecture, who generously shared with me
some of his experience with sustainable architecture
and building;
Bernard Reinteau, journalist at the *Moniteur
des Travaux publics et du Bâtiment*, for his friendly help
and contacts;
Michelle and Raoul Gauzin, for their advice
and encouragement.

My thanks also to the architects, engineers
and developers of the projects described, and to
representatives of local and city authorities, for their
assistance and their enthusiastic support for the book.

Thanks to all those who read the manuscript
and contributed their professional expertise:
Yves Moch and Hubert Despretz of ADEME,
Christophe Gobin of GTM Construction,
Jean-Claude Guy, Michel Perrin and Benoît Reitz
of the CNDB,
Ekhart Hahn, expert in sustainable urban renewal,
Alain Lorgeoux, head of architecture and urbanism
at the Rennes department of architecture,
urban planning and property management,
Michel Sabard, tutor at the school of architecture
at Paris-La Villette,
Serge Sidoroff from the Iceb,
Marie-Christine Triboulot of Enstib,
Hans-Otto Wack, expert in sustainable water
management.

Above all, my thanks to Jean-Yves Barrier,
who gave me both the initial idea for the project
and the motivation to complete it.

I am delighted that Birkhäuser Publishers has adopted
my book. Our work together greatly enriched it,
and I would like to offer my cordial thanks to:
Henriette Mueller-Stahl, my editor, for her expert
supervision and consistently friendly approach;
Kate Purver whose commitment was far greater
than can reasonably be expected from a translator.

To Florence and Thibaut

*In the hope that this book will convince
those who are willing to hear
of the need to protect this earth
that we bequeath to our children.*

Editorial note

The preparatory work for this publication was originally
planned as a project looking at sustainable architecture and
urbanism in France. Because of the importance of the theme
and growing international interest in it, the author's extensive
research has produced a book that offers a comparative view
of the subject matter involving many European countries.
This European focus forms the basis of the systematic sections
and also the selection of representative examples from the
fields of urban development and architecture.

The details about energy consumption for the 23 examples
in the third part of the book are given in as much detail as
the available information on the subject permitted. It was only
possible to give values that had actually been measured in rare
cases, as measurements are very labour- and cost-intensive,
so that as a rule only readings that are taken as part of a study
are subsequently verified.

FOREWORD

If we are to ensure that future generations can enjoy a satisfactory quality of life, a sustainable approach towards use of the earth's natural resources is now vital. The application of this idea to architecture, urbanism and land use requires the participation of all parties: policymakers, developers in both the public and private sectors, urban planners, architects, engineers, landscape designers, checking authorities, contractors and builders. The spread, and the success, of environmental quality in the building sector is linked to close collaboration between these different sections of the industry, and the use made of each one's expertise. The involvement and commitment of users is also an essential element.

Consideration of environmental issues in construction projects has economic, ecological and social implications. It must be put in an overall context and undertaken in an objective and rational way. This book aims to provide some answers to those seeking points of reference, to help them realise their desire to build in a different way.

The book's first part sets out the issues in sustainable development and describes the different trends towards environmental architecture. It looks at the different ways in which these trends are evolving within Europe, and at their possible future development, both in industrialised countries and in the developing world.

Sustainable architecture is only really effective when set in an urban planning context which itself is based on sustainable principles. The second part explains theoretical aspects of sustainability, and describes the ways in which these have been put into practice over recent decades in various European towns and cities.

If environmental quality is to be rapidly achieved, buildings must be constructed both to use less energy and using non-hazardous, renewable materials. The 23 recent European projects described in the third part show that environmental and social aims can be successfully reconciled with economic realism, looking not only at initial capital investment but at long-term running and maintenance costs. Rather than looking at spectacular, big-budget showpieces, we have concentrated on smaller projects, built on modest budgets but to a high architectural standard. Examples of all types of building are included: private and social housing; public cultural, educational and sports facilities; offices and other commercial buildings. The examples chosen offer easily reproducible solutions, which can be implemented with no significant departure from developers' normal practice.

From Finland to Greece, via (among others) France and Germany – the projects presented were built to suit a wide range of situations, climates and budgets. The diversity of the results shows that the environmental approach can be applied in any context. It must now become an integral part of our thinking, an essential element for us all.

Dominique Gauzin-Müller

9

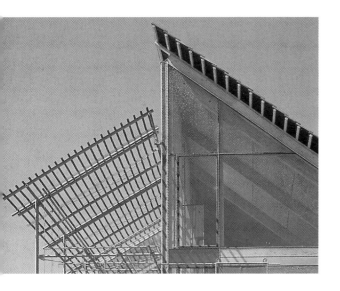

THE ENVIRONMENTAL ALTERNATIVE
ISSUES, PRACTICE AND PERSPECTIVES

The quest for environmental value in architecture, for a harmonious balance between man and his surroundings, is not new. For centuries, and particularly in domestic and vernacular architecture, people adopted this approach out of necessity. Since the industrial revolution, it has been increasingly abandoned in favour of man's belief in his own omnipotence and ability to draw unrestrainedly on the earth's resources.

Today, the effects of climate change which first became evident in the 20th century are becoming increasingly apparent. Faced with these dangers, public and policymakers alike are becoming conscious of the need to protect our natural environment. One response to these issues, as raised at international summit meetings, is to approach architecture and urbanism in a way which respects the environment. A growing number of professionals in Europe are successfully adopting this approach.

ISSUES IN SUSTAINABLE DEVELOPMENT

At the beginning of the 1990s, the United Nations' Rio Earth Summit alerted the general public to the consequences of man's pillage of natural resources, the worrying rise in global warming and the rapid and spectacular destruction of ecosystems. The agreements reached at Rio have been translated into numerous measures affecting industry, transport, energy use and waste management. These measures are also aimed at encouraging people in industrialised nations to conserve resources, with potential consequences for the way they live.

Environmental damage

For several decades experts have been warning of irreversible damage being done to the planet, with correspondingly serious consequences for the human race. This is linked to four major issues:
- rapid population growth
- squandering of natural resources and fossil fuel reserves
- decline in air, water and soil quality
- volume of waste.
The world's population has grown from around 1.5 billion in 1900 to 6 billion in 2000. This impressive rise in the numbers of humans sharing the planet raises the questions of availability to all of food, shelter and quality of life – particularly in disadvantaged regions, where population growth is unchecked. Over the same period, the use of natural raw materials and fossil fuels has increased to such an extent as to pose a real and present threat to future generations. Existing reserves of oil are expected to be exhausted in around 50 years, natural gas in 70 years and coal in 190 years from now. The decline in air and fresh water quality, particularly in the urban areas of industrialised countries, is endangering health. The waste generated by these countries piles up in town and country alike, polluting soils, with disastrous results for agriculture and the quality of food supplies. Recent scandals have highlighted this worrying situation.

Climate change

The phenomenon of global warming, as observed by climate specialists, was at first treated with scepticism. However, at the UN's second conference on climate change, in Geneva in 1996, experts confirmed that "the frequency of significant natural disasters has quadrupled over the past 30 years". The Intergovernmental Panel on Climate Change (IPCC) estimates that during the 20th century, the earth warmed up by between 0.3 and 0.6°C, while sea levels rose on average by 15 to 25cm. It predicts a sharp increase in these phenomena over coming decades. Unless effective steps are taken in the near future, the 21st century is likely to see temperature increases between 2 and 5°C and rises in sea levels leading to the destruction of several cities.
Climate change has wide-ranging implications, of which the public is beginning to be aware. Melting of the polar ice-caps, floods, reduction of land to desert, mudslides and cyclones are among them. Such natural catastrophes, and the destruction they bring, have a major impact on the GDP of the often poor countries where they occur. In certain regions, disastrous consequences are already apparent: displaced populations, famine and epidemics.

The greenhouse effect

The earth's atmosphere is a gaseous layer consisting mainly of nitrogen (78 % by volume) and oxygen (21 %). Various other gases, present only in small quantities, are however important due to the contribution most of them make to the greenhouse effect. Radiation reaching the earth from the sun is partly re-emitted by the earth as infra-red rays; in turn, part of this is reflected back towards earth by the atmospheric gases. This natural phenomenon, which favoured the development of life on earth, has over the past half-century increased sharply. Experts believe that global warming is essentially linked to this growing greenhouse effect.

According to a report produced by a French government commission on the greenhouse effect, the Mies, the atmospheric concentration of carbon dioxide (CO_2), which accounts for around 60 % of the greenhouse effect, has increased by 30 % since 1750. This date, marking the beginning of the industrial age, serves as a reference point for studies of changes in atmospheric composition due to human's activities. Until then, the composition of the atmosphere was fairly stable on a planetary scale, as shown by data obtained from the "glacial archive", the tiny quantities of trapped gases detectable in cores taken from the polar ice in Greenland and the Antarctic.

The burning of fossil fuels currently releases more than 21 billion tonnes of carbon dioxide into the atmosphere each year. Other gases linked to human activities aggravate the situation: methane (CH_4); nitrous oxide (N_2O); chlorofluorocarbons (CFCs), banned by the Montreal protocol due to their destructive effect on the stratospheric ozone layer; and their successors, hydrochlorofluorocarbons (HCFCs), which the EU intends to ban from 2015 due to their similarly destructive potential.

Sustainable development

Environmental damage and current climate change are directly linked to human activity. The economic blueprint for industrialised societies was first publicly questioned in 1968 by the newly-founded international think-tank, the Club of Rome. In 1972 members of this group published the now-famous report, "The Limits to Growth", putting forward the idea that economic development must be combined with environ-

mental protection. The first UN summit on man and the environment took place the same year, in Stockholm; most countries' ministries of the environment were created at around that time. Following international consultations, the then Norwegian prime minister, Gro Harlem Brundtland, produced a report entitled "Our Common Future", which was discussed at the 42nd UN congress in 1987. This document introduced the notion of sustainable development. It emphasised that global environmental problems are rooted to a large extent in the impoverishment of the greater part of the world's population.

At the 1992 Rio Earth Summit, heads of state committed their nations to exploring ways of achieving "development which fulfils current needs without compromising the capacity of future generations to fulfil theirs". This concept of sustainable development is based on three principles:
- consideration of the "whole life cycle" of materials;
- development of use of natural raw materials and renewable energy sources;
- reduction in the materials and energy used in raw materials extraction, product use and destruction or recycling of waste.

The notion of sustainable development is based on an awareness of environmental risk. However, it is also a social project which seeks to reconcile ecological, economic and social factors. It goes hand in hand with the basic principles of environmental law:
- precaution
- prevention
- remedy at source
- "polluter pays"
- use of the best available technology.

Agenda 21

The principles of the Rio Declaration are connected with the formulation of a development plan for the 21st century, known as Agenda 21. This recommends an integrated, creative approach so as to ensure sustainable development. The agreements reached have both social and economic dimensions, with measures aimed at combating poverty, controlling population growth, improving health, modifying current consumer lifestyles, and promoting a viable urban model in developing countries. They also allow for the integration of environmental concerns into the decision-making process.

Hungarian pavilion, Hanover Expo 2000 on sustainable development. Architects: Vadasz + Partners.

Japanese pavilion, Hanover Expo 2000 on sustainable development. Architect: Shigeru Ban.

The recommendations give weight to both environmental conservation and sensible use of natural resources:
- protection of the earth's atmosphere;
- integrated land-use planning and management;
- combating deforestation;
- preservation of fragile ecosystems;
- promotion of sustainable development in a rural and agricultural context;
- maintenance of biodiversity;
- an environmentally rational approach to biotechnology;
- protection of the oceans and coastlines;
- protection of water supplies and quality;
- environmentally acceptable treatment of waste, including toxic chemicals, radioactive and other dangerous waste, solid waste and waste water.

Since 1992, many regional authorities in Europe have produced their own Agenda 21 plan. In Germany, the Hanover Expo in 2000, with its theme of "man, nature and technology", served as a platform for a number of projects. In France, initiatives are drawn together by Comité 21, an umbrella body consisting of government and regional authorities, industry and other organisations.

The Kyoto agreement

After Rio's emphasis on the social and the cultural, the Kyoto summit in 1996 was designed to achieve more concrete measures. Under the Kyoto protocol, participating nations pledged to bring average greenhouse gas emissions over the period 2008 to 2012 back to 1990 levels. For France, this means a reduction by 16 million tonnes of carbon-equivalent (tce), of which 16.6 % will come from the building sector. To keep to this agreement, the industrialised countries need to make progress in three areas:
- reductions in energy consumption;
- replacement of energy from fossil reserves by energy from renewable sources;
- carbon storing.

In 2000, representatives of 180 countries met in The Hague to resolve the details of the Kyoto protocol, which sets levels of reductions in CO_2 emissions and five other greenhouse gases for 38 of the industrial nations. The conference ended in failure, due among other things to disagreements between Europe and the US on the question of carbon sinks (see p. 15). A fresh round of talks, entitled "Rio + 10", is to be held in Johannesburg in 2002.

THE POLITICAL AND ECONOMIC CONTEXT

The environmental movement was born in the late 1960s, initiated by a generation that rejected the excesses of the consumer society and called for an end to unrestricted economic growth. During the 1970s and 1980s it moved towards policies concerned with environmental protection, safeguarding quality of life and fighting social exclusion. Since the 1990s, the Green movement has gained some power in various European countries at local, regional and in some cases national level, with elements of their policies being taken up by more mainstream political parties.

Ecology and economy

For most environmentalists, growth and profit became more acceptable with the emergence of the idea of sustainable development, linked as it is to a more equitable distribution of benefits and less damaging exploitation of natural resources. This shift is described in "Factor Four", a report produced by the Club of Rome, which since its foundation has brought together the most advanced environmental thinkers. Written by Ernst Ulrich von Weizsäcker with energy specialists Amory B. Lovins and L. Hunter Lovins, it was first published in German in 1995 and has since been translated into English, French and several other languages. This report opens up new perspectives on the prospects for future generations, developing concepts of economic policy designed to combine profits with environmental protection. Using examples, the authors develop their theory of a quadrupling of resource productivity: doubling wealth while halving resource use, and hence significantly improving quality of life. Among other things, they posit an optimisation of existing technology, aimed at improving production efficiency without increasing costs; limiting wastage in the transport and sale of manufactured products; a move towards lower fuel consumption cars, and buildings which are both more energy-efficient and more comfortable.

With currently available technology, it would be possible to reduce by around half our consumption of energy and drinking water and the volume of waste we produce. Noise pollution, air-borne and water-borne toxins could be reduced by still more. Such changes would come at a price, but would themselves generate overall savings in both the short and long term. A study by the Federal Protection Agency (Wicke 1988) estimated that in Germany, the cost of environmental damage and its consequences, notably in public health, came to DM103.5 billion (approx. €53 billion) in 1986. And this figure continues to rise.

Implications for industry

In the industrial sector, sustainable development is already an economic reality. Markets are growing rapidly; demand is likely to be sustained. The big companies have realised that applying environmental principles can help improve industrial processes, boost brands and allow them to stand out from the competition.

For several years, the oil sector has been investing in solar and wind power, with the aim of generating more than 50 % of energy from such renewable resources by 2050. Other companies have become involved in the creation of carbon sinks, composed of plants and growing trees which absorb greenhouse gases. One hectare of managed forest can fix 3 t of carbon per year in temperate climates, and 5 t per year in the tropics. In July 1999 the Peugeot-Citroën group and the ONF together agreed upon a programme for the planting of 10 million trees in deforested areas of the Amazon.

Shortly after this, the Sydney stock exchange launched a CO_2 market, whereby polluters can invest in forest plantations and carbon sinks so as to reduce the "eco-tax" they must pay.

Following from the principles of the international quality standard ISO 9000, the International Organisation for Standardisation produced a set of environmental management standards, ISO 14000, to which increasing numbers of companies are signing up.

In France, GTM Construction was the first building construction company to become certified simultaneously by the AFAQ under the quality standards ISO 9001 and 9002, the safety standard BS 8800 and the environmental standard ISO 14001. This voluntary move towards sustainable development clearly gives companies a competitive advantage in terms of winning work which has environmental protection aspects. In the environmentally-sensitive waste treatment sector, Séché-Ecoindustrie was the first group to obtain ISO 14001 certification.

Implications for the service industries

Companies in the service sector have been investing in environmental measures for several years, and have built some successful brands as a result. An international organisation, The Natural Step, provides support and advice to groups wishing to develop successful and profitable sustainability-based strategies. Among others, this group has worked with Scandic, the Scandinavian hotel chain, which has been training its 5,000 employees in sustainable principles since 1994. Between 1996 and 2001, Scandic reduced water and energy consumption in its hotels by around 25 %. With customer co-operation, around half of the waste produced is sorted, by category, at source; whilst 97 % of furnishing materials (wood, wool and cotton) used by the group are recyclable.

In the finance sector, a number of banking groups also moved into this area early on. Both Ökobank in Germany and Triodos in Belgium have committed themselves to sustainable development, investing exclusively in projects with environmental and social dimensions without abandoning profit.

Implications for the building sector

Implementation of the measures agreed at Kyoto has wide-ranging implications in terms of land use, urban planning and architecture. The attempt to reduce consumption of energy and natural resources, bring down greenhouse gas emissions and produce less waste will have a particularly significant impact on the building and civil engineering sectors.

Across Europe, around 2 million building sector companies, with 11 million or so employees, create and maintain the surroundings of a population of 380 million. Both the construction and subsequent use of buildings have major environmental impacts; together these account for 50 % of natural resources consumption, 40 % of energy and 16 % of water use. Building construction and demolition produces more waste than the combined volume of household waste. In France, where a significant proportion of electricity is "clean" electricity from nuclear power stations, the building industry accounts for 17.5 % of CO_2 emissions and 26.5 % of total greenhouse gases. In Germany, where most electricity is generated by conventional power stations, an environmental protection strategy document (the

Self-build youth centre,
Stuttgart-Wangen, Germany.
Architect: Peter Hübner.

Arcosanti, Arizona, USA.
Architect: Paolo Soleri.

Klimaschutzkonzept) produced by the city of Freiburg im Breisgau put construction's share of CO_2 emissions at 30 %, more than transport and other industries combined.

The application of sustainable development principles to building is one of the most efficient responses we have to the need to reduce the greenhouse effect and the destruction of our environment. Such a response is based on three complementary, closely-linked tenets:
- social equity
- environmental caution
- economic efficiency.

The idea of "environmental quality" has profound social implications for professionals in the building sector. Sustainable building must be affordable; that is, available to the masses. This gives a new, civic dimension to the creation of the built environment. It also raises questions about the productivity of the industry. Affordable sustainable development calls for both close co-operation between designers and other professionals, and an involvement of end-users in design and management. Only this will allow the right balance to be struck between architecture, technology and cost.

Implications for architecture and urbanism

In June 1996, the second UN Conference on Human Settlements (Habitat II) in Istanbul put forward ways of applying sustainable principles in building. Meanwhile, the publicity surrounding the international summits, along with various scandals over the health risks associated with certain building materials (notably asbestos), raised the public profile of these issues. Public opinion began increasingly to focus on environmental protection and the need for a healthy, safe environment. Professional and industry bodies are beginning to respond to this cultural shift. In France, new forms of contracts and declarations of intent are appearing among professional institutions and property developers. Those groups whose ethical or commercial strategies have already put them one step ahead in this market have a clear advantage.

Several European countries have already adopted environmental measures via standards, regulations or financial incentives. First Scandinavia, then Germany and France have adopted the thermal performance standard RT 2000 (*see p. 98*), which sets out stringent new rules aimed

at significantly reducing the energy consumption of buildings. Even more stringent standards, such as Germany's Passive House standards (*see p. 100*) or the Swiss Minergie (*see p. 99*), are finding increasing favour amongst developers.

TRENDS IN ENVIRONMENTAL ARCHITECTURE

Although widespread awareness of these issues dates only from the Rio Summit, the need for an environmentally-friendly architecture has been appreciated for several decades. Over this period, conflicting approaches have emerged: in particular, the high-tech and the low-tech.

The pioneers of low-tech

As early as the 1970s, following the first oil shock, environmental alternatives were proposed by a number of pioneering idealists, mostly in housing and small-scale cultural and educational buildings. In the wake of the anti-authoritarian movements of May 1968, some architects rejected what they saw as the stiffness and coldness of modernism and began to encourage the involvement of end-users in the design, and sometimes the construction, of more "friendly" buildings. This was the philosophy behind the social housing of Joachim Eble in Germany; the Vandkunsten studio's Tinngarden housing projects near Copenhagen; the Belgian projects of Lucien Kroll; and the self-build youth centres and schools of Peter Hübner around Stuttgart. Most of these projects used timber, a naturally warm, light and easily-worked material.

Over the next decade architects began also to use other natural materials. The Norwegian Sverre Fehn, and the French partnership Jourda & Perraudin, completed projects using earth. Some designers incorporated turf roofs or planted facades. However, the most notable exponent of the low-tech – or indeed the "no-tech" – remains Paolo Soleri, a former follower of Frank Lloyd Wright who at his prototype town Arcosanti, in Arizona, is putting into practice his own concepts of "arcology", or architecture consistent with ecology.

The stars of high-tech

High-tech architecture is symbolised by the towering office buildings and dramatic steel and glass structures of today's international "superstar"

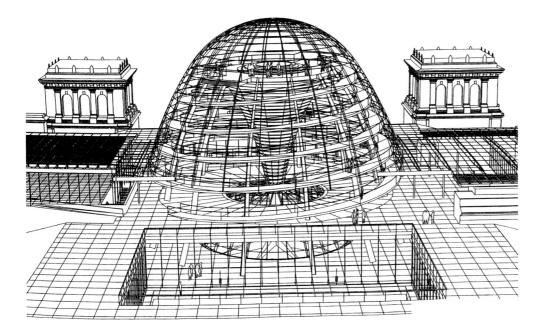

The dome of the remodelled
Reichstag, Berlin 2000.
Architect: Sir Norman Foster.

architects. Some of them, including Norman Foster, Renzo Piano, Richard Rogers, Thomas Herzog, Françoise-Hélène Jourda and Gilles Perraudin, came together to form the Read group – Renewable Energies in Architecture and Design. The group received official recognition in 1993 at the Florence conference on solar energy in architecture and urbanism, and gained EU backing.

The landmark buildings of the "eco-tech" are the Commerzbank tower in Frankfurt and the dome of the remodelled Reichstag in Berlin, both Foster projects. However, international architecture's use of advanced technology to achieve sustainability is not always convincing – particularly in the areas of temperature control in summer and energy-saving in winter. The media coverage of these highly visible projects has nonetheless had a positive effect, as others follow in their wake. Various techniques used in these projects, such as double skin glazed façades, have been applied to other, smaller projects with considerable success.

Environmental humanism

Between these two extremes of high and low tech architecture, parts of Europe are increasingly seeing the emergence of a middle way. This is set apart from low-tech architecture mainly by its contemporary image, achieved through a well-considered combination of traditional materials and innovative industrial products.

As early as the 1970s, Günter Behnisch was producing work in a luminous, colourful, free-form architectural style which owed much to his humanist philosophy. Even his urban projects are characterised by the landscaping treatment of their surroundings, which creates a favourable

and natural relationship between green spaces and their users. The influence of the practice Behnisch, Behnisch & Partner is widely felt in Germany, particularly in office buildings and educational and sports facilities. The spa pool at Bad Elster (see pp. 202-207) and the Forestry and Nature Research Institute at Wageningen in the Netherlands (see pp. 218-223) are the most recent examples of a meticulously-drawn style, whose relaxed atmosphere, far from occurring by chance, is carefully and deliberately created.

Stefan Behnisch sums up his practice's approach with typical good sense: "There are basically two schools of sustainable architecture. The Norman Foster school, where environmental problems are solved by bringing in technology; and the Soleri school, which rejects technology. We fall somewhere between these two; but my sympathies are more towards Soleri. I don't want to go back to the stone age, or to change the way we live now – but so long as we are prepared to accept that we will be warmer in summer and cooler in winter, then I am convinced that we can achieve an acceptable level of comfort by following the laws of nature."

Social and democratic environmentalism

The development of democratic environmentalism, with an emphasis on social responsibility, is another trend which has appeared in Germany, the Netherlands and Scandinavia. Peter Hübner's self-build housing (see illustrations p. 18) project at Gelsenkirchen is in the spirit of his 1970s work. This project is part of the Einfach und Selbstgemacht ("simple and self-made") programme, and

Primary school, Stuttgart-Neugereut,
Germany 1977.
Architects: Behnisch & Partner.

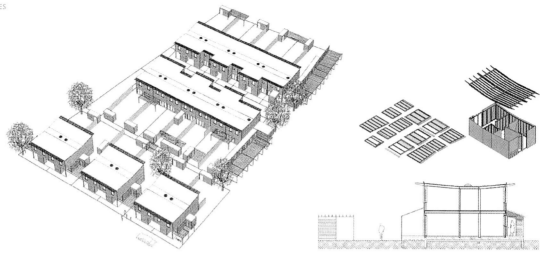

Self-build housing, Gelsenkirchen, Germany 1999. Architects: Plus + Hübner Forster Hübner. Perspective, exploded view and section.

School self-build project, Gelsenkirchen, Germany 1999. Architects: Plus + Hübner Forster Hübner. Children with their model.

received backing in the context of the IBA held at Emscher Park. By actively working on the project from initial design through to completion, low-income families can acquire one of 28 environmentally-friendly houses at minimal cost.

Awareness of social responsibility on the part of both designer and developer has also led to greater use of local materials and traditional techniques. For the Salvatierra housing block (see pp. 166-171), Jean-Yves Barrier and the construction co-operative opted for the moulded earth blocks traditionally used in the Rennes region. In their house at Essertines (see pp. 122-125), as for many of their buildings, Atelier de l'Entre focused on local timber, using small sections.

In other, less exemplary cases the use of low-energy materials can risk a tendency towards cliché, with an approach based directly on traditional models but without sufficient integration into the contemporary natural or built environment. The future must lie in a mix of materials, combining environmental quality with a contemporary feel.

Environmental minimalism

Over the past few years a new generation of architects and engineers has emerged. Less militant and more pragmatic than the pioneers of the 1970s, they use computer technology and innovative products to create buildings whose minimalism places them firmly in the modern age. Energy-saving and other environmental features are integrated into the designs without fuss or ostentation. Strong ideas and precise design are combined to respond appropriately to the site and the project brief, while familiar principles and techniques are used with pure, unadorned materials. Frequent use is made of prefabrication in order to reduce construction time and cost.

Around Lake Constance, the environmental building movement has generated a number of impressive and innovative projects. Buildings by the German architects D'Inka + Scheible, Kauffmann Theilig, Mahler Günster Fuchs, Glück & Partner and Schaudt Architekten, the Austrians Baumschlager & Eberle and Hermann Kaufmann, and the Swiss Metron practice all provide examples.

EUROPEAN PRACTICE

Since the Rio Summit, the application of environmental principles to architecture and urbanism has proceeded across Europe with varying degrees of efficiency and speed. The European Union is a driving force behind the establishment of ecological alternatives, through community-wide standards and various experimental programmes. Currently run through the European Commission's Energy and Transport department (DG XVII), these include the EC 2000 programme on environmental comfort and energy, the Sunh programme on solar energy, and Cepheus. As well as financing projects, these programmes facilitate communication between professionals in different countries, encouraging the development of common design tools and methods.

The international context

The search for environmental alternatives in the building sector can be seen in the context of international thinking on the subject. The ACE contributed to the green design handbook "The Green Vitruvius", while the UIA produced a "Declaration of Interdependence for a sustainable future". The organisation Green Building Challenge has developed a communications network grouped around shared research projects, conferences and publications, with its own system of assessment, the Green Building Tool. 14 countries are involved, including the US, Canada, the UK and the Netherlands.

In France, training programmes run by the Gepa highlight the risks of global warming, the exhaustion of natural resources and social exclusion. This group sees the environmental movement as a "historic opportunity" for architects, and encourages them to develop the expertise necessary to be at its forefront.

Different approaches to achieving sustainability

In western and northern Europe, environmentalism is already a cultural phenomenon with genuine political and economic influence. As public opinion becomes more conscious of environmental quality, backed by a growing spirit of civic responsibility, the relation between man and his surroundings has become central to the thinking of planners and architects.

In Germany and Austria since the late 1980s, the different sectors have combined to take an empirical approach. In France, the UK and Scandinavia, tools measure a building's performance against a range of defined objectives. Most assessment methods are continually updated to take account of empirical results as more data is gathered. Whatever the approach, the success of the sustainability movement relies on a real will on the part of developers, combined with the ability of architects to assemble and lead a competent design team.

German pragmatism

Thirty years ago, environmentalism in Germany was still on the "hippy fringe"; its application to building, along with its "woolly jumper brigade" exponents, was regarded with a certain condescension. Since then, sustainable development has moved beyond ideology into economic reality. For many companies today, it is the force behind a modern and innovative image.

This change is closely linked to the rise of the Green party. Since the late 1970s, the Greens in Germany gained political power at a local, later regional, and finally national level. Their influence

House at Lochau, Austria, 1998. Architects: Baumschlager & Eberle.

House at Constance, Germany, 1999. Architects: Schaudt Architekten.

Switch house, Donaueschingen, standard unit housing for allergy sufferers. Germany 1995. Architects: Werk Gruppe Lahr.

Municipal workshops, Hohenhems, Austria. Architect: Reinhard Drexel; design engineers: Merz Kaufmann Partner; contractor: Kaufmann Holz AG.

is behind much of the environmental legislation passed by the government since the 1980s, including measures on energy conservation, waste sorting and water management. Since Rio, the sustainability movement has gained even more ground. The global need to tackle the greenhouse effect has made sustainable alternatives a central issue in Germany for developers, architects, engineers and contractors alike.

The move into the mainstream is also linked to changes in thermal performance regulations, and the introduction of the Low Energy (see p. 98) and Passive House standards (see p. 100). The approach that has emerged in Germany, based on ideas of optimising form, material, use and maintenance, applies over the long term, and is seen in most public and private projects. Cities such as Freiburg im Breisgau (see pp. 69-75) and Stuttgart (see pp. 63-68) were among the first to embark on urban environmental programmes; educational syllabuses already include reference to sustainable principles, now undisputed by most people. Manufacturers of prefabricated housing units have for some years been offering Bio-Häuser, low-energy houses and "healthy dwellings" for those affected by allergies.

With annual market growth estimated at over 30%, interest in sustainability has become a powerful economic force. According to opinion polls, 58% of Germans believe that not enough is being done to combat climate change, while 94% of potential home-builders would be willing to spend more to achieve a more environmentally-friendly result.

Simplicity in Vorarlberg

Vorarlberg is a densely-populated region of western Austria, whose population of 350,000 is divided between urban areas and villages. Here, designers and planners have developed new architectural and urban models aimed at making the most economical use of land, energy and materials.

These initiatives sprang from ideological differences between the Austrian Order of Architects and a group of young designers, who in 1980 came together under the name Vorarlberger Baukünstler, or Vorarlberg Building Artists. With an emphasis on refined simplicity, they expressed a desire for realistic architectural and technical solutions. Their work seeks a balance between

the technically achievable and the socially justifiable; between the structurally rational and the aesthetically desirable. Their motto "simple is not always best, but the best is always simple" is borrowed from the German architect Heinrich Tessenow.

The success of this project lies in the proficiency and pragmatism of the architects, engineers and contractors. Co-operation between the different disciplines from the earliest stages allowed specific constraints to be taken into account at each site, to produce ingenious and innovative solutions. The Ölzbündt project at Dornbirn (see pp. 142-147) is an example. Using experimental construction techniques and energy concepts, it combines industrial products with craftsmanship to achieve a contemporary result appropriate to its social environment.

Environmental assessment in Britain; BREEAM

In the UK, it is estimated that building (energy consumption and the building materials industry) accounts for almost half of CO_2 emissions. Since the 1980s, experts in high-tech architecture have worked with the BRE on environmental alternatives. This British equivalent of the French CSTB has carried out extensive research in this area, and in 1990 produced its own Environmental Assessment Method, or BREEAM. This is a tabular system using a number of criteria, and was originally intended for use in office projects. Specific versions are also now available for housing, the service sector, commercial and industrial buildings. Buildings are rated according to a series of benchmarks relating to the following areas:
- management
- health and well-being
- energy (consumption and CO_2 emission)
- transport (distances travelled and CO_2 emission)
- water consumption
- environmental impact of materials
- land use (areas of planting, water-impermeable areas)
- environmental treatment of the site
- air and water pollution.

The combined score then gives the building a rating of Fail, Pass, Good, Very Good or Excellent. Aimed principally at designers, BREEAM is now widely used; in 2000, around 500 UK projects were completed with its help.

Waterside housing for two families, Ecolonia, Alphen aan den Rijn, Netherlands 1997. Architect: Peter van Gerwen.

Environmental assessment in Holland; the DCBA method

In Holland, the city of Rotterdam was the first to set benchmarks with its environmental buildings plan at the end of the 1980s. In 1992, Amsterdam's regulations and recommendations for new buildings included a list of alternative, more environmentally-friendly materials. The government showed its commitment to sustainability with the publication in 1995 of its "Sustainable Building Plan: Investing for the Future". This was accompanied by funding initiatives and various manuals, issued between 1995 and 2000, on specific themes such as housing, industrial and commercial buildings, management and urban development. While the ambitious aim of these measures − that by 2000, 80 % of buildings would be built using sustainable criteria − was not achieved, the result is still impressive: these criteria are now substantially integrated into procedures throughout the building sector.

The environmental assessment tool in general use in the Netherlands is the DCBA method. This sets out different levels of intervention, with four categories of objective and result:

A: "autonomous" situation, with near-zero environmental impact

B: little environmental impact

C: conventional construction but with reduced environmental damage

D: conventional construction.

To facilitate sharing of information and conclusions, in 2000 the Netherlands organised an international conference on sustainable building in Maastricht, attended by delegates from 45 countries. By 2002, Holland aims to reduce the energy consumption of new buildings by 25 %, water consumption by 10 % and greenhouse gas emissions by a significant amount.

The Scandinavian approach

The rigours of climate, along with strong architectural traditions, have given the Scandinavians a long-standing awareness of the relationship between humans and their natural surroundings. The first summit on the environment was held by Sweden in Stockholm in 1972, while it was the Norwegian prime minister, Gro Harlem Brundtland, whose report first put forward the concept of sustainable development. Scandinavia is facing up to the growing dangers posed by environmental damage with admirable realism. Policies of environmental protection are based both on strict laws and on ideas of individual responsibility, symbolised by the Swedish concept of *allemansrätt*, or the right of all to benefit from the natural environment.

In the mid-20th century, Scandinavia saw the emergence of a modernist style of great originality and warmth, characterised by the work of Finnish architect Alvar Aalto. During the 1970s, however, there was a rejection of modern architecture, with

HQE:
the 14 target areas

EXTERNAL ENVIRONMENTAL IMPACT

Environmental construction
- relationship with immediate surroundings
- integrated choice of construction materials and methods
- low-nuisance construction processes

Environmental management
- energy management
- water management
- waste management
- maintenance policy

SATISFACTORY INTERNAL ENVIRONMENT

Comfort
- humidity
- acoustics
- visual
- olfactory

Health
- sanitary treatment
- air quality
- water quality

---

the appearance in its place of a more traditionalist, environmentally-minded trend. In Sweden, while some neo-regionalism remains, Stockholm and Malmö (see p. 37) in particular now boast a number of interesting examples of urban sustainable building.

The SBI has published its own software, known as Building Environmental Assessment Tool or Beat 2000. It contains a database of values of environmental variables such as material lifecycles, energy sources, greenhouse gas emissions and so on.

In Finland, there is a growing tendency towards the integration of modern lifestyles with environmental imperatives. Direct democracy, strong communal initiatives and the development of builder-resident co-operatives all help to create a framework that favours control of energy consumption. Environmental efficiency has become an important aspect of building design and systems, and Finnish clients increasingly require architects to carry out environmental assessments. In response to this demand, most consultants now use the Granlund LCA-Tool software, which gives data on the whole life cycle of the building. Another environmental assessment tool, Pimwag, produced by the Helsinki planning department together with the Finnish Environment Ministry, has also been used for the first time in the Viikki area of Helsinki (see pp. 79-82).

France; the HQE scheme

The most widespread system in use in France is that of the HQE denomination. Unlike the tools in use in the UK and the Netherlands, this is not an assessment so much as the application of ideas within an overall framework. HQE is voluntary and continuously-evolving; it links concepts of environmental comfort and quality with the management principles and co-operative structures needed for their application to a project.

The scheme is based on 14 target areas, grouped into four themes: environmental construction, environmental management, comfort and health. This table of targets, as defined by the HQE Association (see on the left), aims to define a group of objectives corresponding to quantifiable aspects of sustainable development. Intended for use by clients, planners and design teams, and depending for its application in practice on contractor and industry involvement, it requires all parties to re-

think conventional methods. By 2001, around 20 HQE buildings were in use, with another 250 under construction or in the design phase.

In the 1970s and 1980s, the main aim of environmentally-friendly architecture was to save energy by applying bioclimatic principles. By contrast, HQE brings a more complete approach, though one which is correspondingly more complex and difficult to apply. The table of targets is fairly theoretical in nature, and makes no distinction between objective and more subjective goals. There is also no distinction between "everyday" measures to be applied by all architects and innovative approaches requiring specialist advice.

The system has the merit of allowing a project to be seen as a whole, rather than as a set of separate sub-contracts, encouraging communication between external consultants such as acoustic or thermal specialists, quantity surveyors, etc. Co-operation between disciplines from early in the design process strengthens the client and design team in their aims, and is the first step towards accomplishing environmental quality.

There is some apparent ambiguity in the conditions attached to HQE denomination. In fact, while there is no formal regulatory standard or certificate attached, for a building to be HQE-denominated all the target areas must have been rigorously taken into account. An environmental management system must also be in place, led by specifically-trained professionals.

Other French assessment tools

The 1990s saw the appearance in France of several other, software-based environmental assessment systems for buildings, as follows.

Escale, designed by the French building research institute, the CSTB, with Savoie university, is a method for assessing environmental quality throughout the design phase. It defines eleven main criteria: energy resources, other resources, waste, global pollution, local pollution, suitability to the site, comfort, health, environmental management, maintenance, and adaptability. The results are expressed as numerical scores.

Equer, developed at the Ecole des Mines university in Paris, is a life-cycle assessment tool that uses Swiss and German materials databases, linked to an energy analysis programme, Comfie. It takes into account twelve environmental indicators, and gives output in the form of an environmental profile, with options for introducing modifications. Papoose, produced by the engineers Tribu, is designed to assist clients in the decision-making process. It covers the various design phases, examining a dozen different areas. Particular attention is given to energy and user comfort, and economic aspects are also taken into account. The results are presented in numerical and graphical form, with performances expressed as a percentage.

Team, developed by Ecobilan, is a building-specific variant of the Team Life Cycle Assessment software.

A further tool, in the form of an array of 24 sustainable development criteria, has also been developed by the CSTB, ADEME and the construction company GTM. With GTM's co-operation, its methodology has been adopted at the international level by the CIB, and is the subject of a guide published by the FFB. The document is entitled *Pour une meilleure prise en compte de l'environnement dans la construction*, ("Towards a better integration of environmental issues in construction"), and is in two volumes: *Bonnes pratiques de la filière construction* ("Good practice in the construction industry") and *Manuel d'application des réalisateurs* (Constructors' guide).

All these initiatives demonstrate the building sector's commitment to improving environmental quality. However, the small-scale application of many different methods is not in itself helpful to a movement which emphasises partnership and the sharing of expertise. For a more efficient result, harmonisation of approaches and exchange of information are vital. The dearth of precise data from French industry is another reason for difficulties with materials life-cycle evaluation, an essential part of environmental quality assessment; easier access to such information is needed before environmental alternatives can become widely adopted.

Switzerland; the Minergie standard

Switzerland has set itself a target of a 10 % reduction in CO_2 emissions by 2010. This has led to the development of Minergie, a trademark registered by the cantons of Zurich and Berne. Rights to the use of the trademark are controlled by the Swiss confederation, 25 cantons and around 50 companies, associations and schools. Minergie aims to promote rational use of energy, the use of renew-able energy sources, enhanced quality of life, economic competitiveness and reduced pollution and environmental damage; these aims are quantified via maximum values of heating and electricity consumption (see p. 99).

The Swiss building sector's use of energy breaks down as follows:
- heating, ventilation and air-conditioning 65 %
- construction 15 %
- hot water consumption 10 %
- electricity consumption 10 %.

Minergie projects use only around 35 % of the energy consumed by a conventional new-build project.

The Minergie label has been intensively promoted. Initially it applied principally to housing, particularly individual houses. In 2000, the Swiss government announced its application to all federal buildings and state-subsidised projects. Several cantons have also made the label compulsory for local government buildings, and offer financial assistance for other Minergie projects, while some banks offer reductions of approximately 1 % on building loans during the first two or sometimes even five years of repayment.

TIMBER IN SUSTAINABLE DEVELOPMENT

The increased use of timber in building is seen by most European governments as an important part of the effort to reduce greenhouse gas emissions. The conference for the protection of European forests, held in Helsinki in 1993, defined a number of courses of action, corresponding to the major issues on which commitments were made at the Rio Summit:
- sustainable management of European forests
- reduction in wastage in the timber industry
- exploration of biomass energy use in order to conserve fossil fuels
- increased use of timber in construction.

Timber as a weapon against the greenhouse effect

One way of combating the greenhouse effect, which is due largely to the increase in carbon dioxide in the atmosphere, is through a significant increase in the amount of timber used in construction. As trees grow, they absorb CO_2 and convert it into cellulose and lignin. The carbon is assimilated and fixed by the photosynthesis process, and the oxygen is released. The use of timber in construction delays the release of this fixed carbon, which will occur with combustion or decomposition of the wood.

The French timber development body, the CNDB, estimates that for every tonne of timber used in building there is a 1.6 t reduction in atmospheric CO_2. If at the end of the building life cycle the wood is burned, the stored CO_2 returns to the atmosphere. Thus the contribution of the timber itself to global warming can be seen as effectively nil; while that of other construction materials (steel, concrete, glass and plastics, for example), whose production requires significant energy and corresponding CO_2 emissions, is always positive.

European forest management

In most European timber-producing countries, forests have long been managed in a sustainable manner:
- felling is kept below new growth levels;
- future supply is safeguarded by maintaining capacity for growth;
- biodiversity considerations are taken into account.
European forests are currently under-used; timber reserves are expected to grow in coming decades, thanks to the significant reforestation which occurred after the 1939-45 war. In France, barely two-thirds of annual growth, of around 85 million m^3, is utilised. The focus is therefore on developing new uses for available indigenous timber.

The huge storm which devastated large parts of Europe in December 1999 was seen by many as a taste of climate change to come. While it would be wrong to term this an environmental disaster, many forestry companies ran into financial difficulties as a result.

Several comparable, though more local, storms had been seen in Europe in the preceding years: in the Massif Central in 1982, in the UK and Brittany in 1987 and in southern Germany in 1990. What set the 1999 event apart was the wide area affected and the vast number of trees felled by the wind in a few days. In France, 140 million m^3 of timber, or around 1$^{1/2}$ years' growth, was destroyed. However, the international abundance of timber as a commodity was demonstrated by the fact that this had no significant

effect on its cost or availability for construction in Europe.

Tropical forest management

The rise in the use of timber in construction during the 1990s was in France partly due to the popularity of tropical hardwoods (iroko, ipe, doussie, okoume, padouk and basralocus, amongst others), particularly for fittings and exterior use. Other European countries, led by Germany, have since the 1980s banned the use of tropical hardwoods in an attempt to protect the tropical rainforests. In fact, a report by the FAO estimated that such applications account for only 6 % of deforestation.

While 13 million hectares of tropical forest is lost every year, this is largely due to agriculture. Forest is destroyed for economic reasons, to create either grazing land for cattle or plantations of coffee, cocoa, sugar cane or oil-palm – all destined to produce products for export to the industrialised world. Deforestation also results from "slash and burn" subsistence farming, and is thus directly linked to the problems of poverty and overpopulation in developing countries. The solution is the establishment of a forestry industry which would allow these countries to exploit their hardwood resources more profitably, by exporting not logs, but value-added products such as sawn timber or panels.

Sustainable management of tropical forests is made more difficult by the variety of species and the complexity of the fragile ecosystems involved. However, those wishing to employ tropical hardwoods for their appearance, colour or natural durability can now obtain products from sustainably-managed forests where logging of particular species is carefully controlled within defined areas.

Environmental certification

In 1996, the then WWF launched the Forest Stewardship Council (FSC) label, a guarantee to consumers that products came from sustainably managed forests where biodiversity was protected and certain social responsibility criteria were met. These forests are generally over 100,000 hectares in area and are mainly in Asia, Russia and Canada. By 2001, 20 % of Canadian forests were FSC certified, with 1,400 companies worldwide subscribing to the FSC. In France, the buyers group ProForêts was formed in 1999 to promote use of the label. At the same time, European forestry groups established the Pan European Forest Certification Council (PEFC) scheme for the smaller, 3-7 hectare forests of western Europe.

Environmental forestry certification schemes have also been set up in various countries in Asia, Central America and Africa. The French timber company Isoroy helped established the Eurokoumé label for forests in Gabon planted with okoume, a species used in plywood. This scheme also has the support of Pro-Natura International and of Biofac, a group of experts from the CNRS national research centre and various universities which is looking at biodiversity protection in the tropical forests. These forests are home to many animal and plant species about which little is currently known, and which may yield substances beneficial to science or medicine.

Timber construction in Europe

In many European countries, the use of timber is considered to be a useful tool for controlling CO_2 emissions. With government encouragement, it is seeing increasing use in structure, cladding, exterior fittings and even civil engineering. There has been a particularly sharp rise in its use in the housing sector.

The Netherlands (a country with no native forests to speak of) established a plan to increase timber's share of the building industry by 20 % between 1995 and 2000. In Germany, it is estimated that in the short term 20 % of individual houses will have timber structures. In Belgium, economic conditions and political will have combined to favour a strongly-growing market; over the past five years timber's share of the individual house market has risen from 5 % to 15 %. In France, around 5 % of houses have timber structures, but demand is increasing rapidly; market research carried out by the CNDB indicated that 10 % of households would like to build in wood. Unfortunately architects and the building industry are not currently able to respond fully to this demand. Other industrialised countries also build in timber. In the US and Japan, wood accounts for around 90 % of the market in individual houses. However, building techniques are very different. In the US, most houses are built of a framework of thin 5- by 10-cm studs, according to

one of two systems known respectively as balloon-frame and platform-frame construction.

In some countries, notably Finland, where around 90 % of houses are built in timber, recent changes to fire regulations have allowed structures of three or four levels. The result is a number of low-rise housing blocks with timber frames, which in Scandinavia are more economical than their concrete equivalents.

Timber construction in France

Following other European countries' example, the Mies proposes to increase timber's share of the building market by a quarter between 2000 and 2010, taking it from 10 % to 12.5 %. This would represent a reduction in CO_2 emissions of around 7 million tonnes, or 14 % of the French commitment, under the Kyoto agreement, to reduce annual emissions by 50 million tonnes by 2010.

In December 1996, the passing of a French law on air and rational use of energy demonstrated growing political awareness of environmental concerns. Five years later, article 21-V of this law, which deals with the use of timber in construction, came into effect at the end of 2001. The law is a somewhat watered-down version of the original draft, with requirements for the use of wood in public buildings replaced merely by an obligation to make public the quantity used.

The framework document "Bois-Construction-Environnement", signed in March 2001 by representatives of client bodies, architects and building companies, may allow the establishment of a proper development plan. This agreement comprises a charter, with the commitment of the 18 signatories to put it into practice. It defines ten priority aims, under five headings: communication, markets, competitiveness, research and training, and regulation and standardisation.

Timber in HQE projects

Despite the glut of available timber in France, early HQE projects often ignored it. Thanks notably to the CNDB, this tendency has subsequently been reversed; in several recent projects the use of timber has gone hand in hand with HQE from the initial project brief onwards. Unsurprisingly, areas where forestry is a local industry have shown particular enthusiasm for timber as an indicator of environmental quality. Beyond its environmental

Bi-coloured hardwood structure in koto and dark red meranti, Aquitaine Department of Cultural Affairs, Bordeaux 1994. Architects: Brochet, Lajus, Pueyo.

advantages, increased use of timber has social and economic merits: it creates employment in often disadvantaged rural areas, and brings a return on the significant investments made in forestry by both public and private sectors.

In the Vosges region of France, where 48 % of land is covered by forest, the timber industry accounts for approximately 25 % of jobs. In 2000 the regional council signed a three-way, seven-year agreement with the technical university Enstib, and the regional research centre Critt-Bois, providing notably for the acquisition of equipment to encourage technology transfer. The regional council will give financial support to local authorities or companies for building projects where timber represents over 30 % of the cost of the works. The Vosges also plans the construction of two HQE colleges, at Mirecourt and Senones, which will use 1,300 m³ of timber. In Aquitaine, another heavily-forested region, the French timber research institute CTBA has extensively explored the use of wood in buildings in its new centre in Bordeaux.

**Headquarters of the French timber research body CTBA, Bordeaux 2000.
Architect: Philippe Pascal, Art'ur.**

RATIONAL USE OF ENERGY

Over 30 years, global energy consumption has doubled. Electricity, hot water, heating and transport, those essential features of daily life, all depend on the earth's natural resources. Oil and gas reserves are dwindling rapidly and becoming more difficult to extract. A reduction in consumption of fossil fuels, so as to limit the greenhouse effect and combat global warming, is one of the main resolutions of the Rio Summit.

But to maintain, or indeed enhance, our current quality of life while at the same time conserving natural resources will require a fundamental shift in energy strategy, along with strong political will and financial incentives.

While some EU nations have already put significant measures in place, others currently have little more than good intentions. Meanwhile at the international level, renewable energy is an expanding market, growing in some countries by as much as 40 % per year.

EU resolutions

The EU has acted within the context of the Rio agreements, and against a background of rapid change in international energy markets as electricity markets are deregulated. The European Commission has attempted to combine support for renewable energies with efforts to use less energy in the building sector. The 6th Environmental Action Programme for 2001-10, published in January 2001, gives priority to a reduction in European greenhouse gas emissions of 8-12 % by 2008-2012.

The use of renewable energy sources varies widely between countries. In Sweden, 30 % of consumer electricity and heat comes from renewable sources (primarily hydro-electricity and biomass); this figure is above 15 % for Austria, Finland and Portugal, but only 1 % for Belgium. The EU directive of December 2000 calls for 21 % of electricity to be generated from renewable sources by 2010. To meet this target different countries are focusing on hydro-electric, wind, solar or biomass energy, according to their various geographical characteristics, industrial policies and political strategies.

French energy strategy

In France, the energy agency ADEME aims to help the renewable energy sector become economically viable by providing financial support in various ways:

grants of up to 30 % for research and development of the most promising technologies;

subsidies of 20-30 % for "flagship" projects using ideas already tested on a small scale;

financial aid for larger scale projects using proven technologies to allow these to enter a competitive market.

In 2001, approximately 16 % of French electricity came from renewable sources. For this to reach the EU target of 21 % by 2010, production would have to increase by 35-40TWh. The planned breakdown of this ambitious figure is as follows:
- 70-75 % wind energy
- 15-20 % biogas and timber energy
- 10 % small-scale hydro-electricity
- 3 % geothermal energy
- 3 % photovoltaic solar energy.

Although energy-saving measures are relatively easily applied on their own, such a sharp rise in renewable energy requires investment on a national scale. For systems linked to the national electricity network, it also presupposes that the electricity supply companies will be prepared to purchase green energy.

Legislation passed in February 2000 allows larger electricity consumers to choose their supplier, and provides for the purchase of non-polluting energy by EDF, the national supply company. The price of such purchases is a determining factor in the growth of renewable energy. In June 2001 an agreement was signed on the cost of wind energy, setting this at €0.07/kWh over 15 years for the first 1500MW of installed capacity – a rate which is likely to give a considerable boost to the wind energy industry. Fairly satisfactory rates have also been set for biomass energy, small-scale hydroelectrics, incineration and geothermal energy. However, the rate fixed for photovoltaic energy in France is low: €0.15, compared to €0.53 in Germany.

German energy strategy

Germany has the largest population in Europe, and makes a correspondingly high contribution to CO_2 emissions. After the steady 20-year rise in the political power of the Green party, the "green socialist" government which came to power in 1998 fulfilled a campaign promise when it pledged to close down all nuclear power stations, which produce around 15 % of German energy, by 2020. In 2000 the government set a target of a 25 % reduction of CO_2 emissions on 1990 levels, or 35 million tonnes, by 2005. By the end of 1999, a reduction of 15.3 % had already been achieved.

Energy-saving measures in both new and old buildings were combined with rapid development of renewable technologies, such as wind, biomass and solar energy, and co-generators, which generate electricity and heat water simultaneously. These measures were supported by successive strengthening of thermal performance regulations (see p. 97).

Three-quarters of German houses were built before 1979, when the first energy-saving measures were introduced. Since bringing existing housing up to the new standards is costly, grants have been made available for property-owners who decide to modernise their heating systems, make use of renewable energies, install better insulation or high thermal performance windows. This renovation programme, or CO_2-Gebäude-sanierungs-Programm, aims to reduce annual CO_2 emissions by at least $40kg/m^2$ of habitable area.

Public finances have also contributed to experi-mental projects such as those using the Passive House label (see p. 100), which provide an arena for testing innovative technologies in the hope that they will rapidly gain a strong position in a fast-growing market.

Thermal solar energy

The solar radiation reaching the earth's surface consists of both direct radiation and more diffuse radiation, which reaches us through clouds. In central Europe the annual solar energy incident on a $1m^2$ flat area is 1,000kWh, or the equivalent of 100 litres of heating oil. Around half of this is in the form of diffuse radiation; thus, although it generates less heat in winter than in summer, solar heating can be used all year round.

In Belgium, the Walloon regional authority has put in place an action plan entitled Soltherm, whose target is installation of $200,000m^2$ of solar collector panels by 2010, or the equivalent of 5,000 – 7,000 domestic water heaters per year. The plan is accompanied by financial incentives. In Germany, the slogan Solar, na klar ("clearly solar") in 1999 kick-started a 3-year campaign to encourage the use of solar energy by households, busines-ses and local authorities. Its target of 2.5 million m^2 of solar panels by 2003, or $400,000m^2$ each year, is the equivalent of a reduction in carbon dioxide emissions of 75,000 t, a significant contribution. An unusual element of the campaign is a partner-ship initiative between public bodies and profes-sionals to train operatives in solar panel installation in new-build and refurbishment projects, creating many jobs as a result. 400,000 solar panels were already in use by the end of 2000.

Photovoltaic solar energy

Germany has also applied its environmental poli-cies to the photovoltaic cells industry. These cells, which convert solar radiation into electricity, are now manufactured in several facilities in Ger-many. At Shell Solar's factory in Gelsenkirchen in the Ruhr, automated fabrication has lowered pro-duction costs by almost 20 %. As production vol-umes rise, the price of photovoltaic panels is expected to halve between 2000 and 2010. In terms of capacity linked to the national grid, Ger-many's stated aim is 100,000 photovoltaic roof panels by 2004, or an installed capacity of 300MW. The federal budget for this, of DM1.1 bil-lion (€562.421 million), includes an allowance for

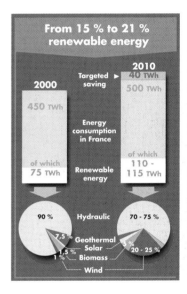

Breakdown of renewable energies in France, 2000-2010.

highly favourable financing terms for those installing cells: zero-interest loans, with no repayments for the first two years; loans available at five days' notice, and exemption from the tenth annual payment if the panels are still functioning after nine years. These incentives come in addition to other subsidies available from the regional authorities in some Länder.

In the Netherlands, the national target is one million roof panels by 2020. A project has recently been completed at Etten-Leur comprising around 50 "zero-energy" houses, which thanks to a photovoltaic cell canopy produce more energy than they consume. In Switzerland, consumers in Zurich may opt, at a price, for "green" electricity from a photovoltaic generation plant. France is not currently actively seeking to link photovoltaic sources to the national supply, but there are a number of private initiatives, such as the Phoebus project, which has financial backing from the EU. Progress in France is only modest as yet: 22 houses were equipped with panels in 1995, 40 in 1997, 150 in 1999. However there are a number of photovoltaic cell production plants, including that of Total Energie in the Lyon suburbs.

Wind energy

Wind energy in Europe is showing particularly strong growth. In 1999 Europe already represented 67 % of global wind power generation, with a capacity of 5,000MW. By 2000 this had increased to 12,000MW, including 6,100MW in Germany (mostly in the north of the country), 2,300MW in Denmark and 2,250MW in Spain. Current estimates predict capacity of 60,000 to 85,000MW by 2010. Installations range from single turbines – supplying farms, for example, a common practice in Denmark – to arrays of several dozen turbines which generate power for a residential area or industrial estate. According to the German Wind Institute (DEWI), 1,495 turbines were built in Germany in 2000, bringing the total installed base to 9,360 turbines, which function for an average of 2,000 hours per year, supplying power of 12TWh.

France has the second highest potential wind energy capacity in Europe, after the UK. In 2000, installed wind power capacity in France was only 70MW. However, the Eole programme, set up in 1997 by EDF and the ADEME, aims to increase total capacity to 360MW in 2005. France is counting on the development of wind energy to help meet EU targets for "green" electricity. The target is ambitious: 10,000-12,000MW by wind energy by 2010. At the current cost of €1,100/kWh, this is equivalent to investment of €11 billion. Initial projects are concentrated in the most wind-exposed parts of the country, particularly Languedoc-Roussillon and the Nord-Pas-de-

View of the Amorbach area of Neckarsulm, Germany, showing the 7,500m² of solar collector panels installed.

Wind farm at Fellbach, Germany.

Calais region. Nine 300kW generators have been installed along the Canal des Dunes near the port of Dunkirk.

Offshore wind power generation represents potential European capacity of 9,000MW. Exploitation of this resource is hampered by concerns over the impact it could have on bird life and fishing. In 2001 work began on construction of the largest offshore installation to date, 12.5km off Knokke-Heist on the Belgian coast. The first phase of the project consists of 60-100 turbines with rated power of 1.6MW; this should be operational in 2004, with capacity reaching 400MW in 2010.

Energy from timber

Biomass energy is derived from wood and biogas. Its share of European energy is set to rise from 45 million tonnes of oil equivalent (toe) in 2000 to 135 million toe by 2010, thanks to strong EU support. In a number of countries, the timber energy sector is developing through new outlets in the under-exploited forestry industry and use of the high stocks of available timber (due in part to the results of the storm of December 1999).

In France, timber represents 4 % of energy consumption and is the third largest energy resource, behind nuclear and hydro-electric energy. France aims to increase its annual consumption, which is currently stable at 10 million toe (around 42 million m^3) despite the fact that volumes of available timber are increasing: stocks currently stand at 39 million m^3. In 2000, there were 1,000 wood-fuelled industrial heating plants and nearly 500 urban heating plants nationwide. The Bois-Energie programme, which along with local development schemes provides 10 to 60 % project financing, aims to see 2,000 such installations by 2006. To promote timber as an energy source, and reduce atmospheric pollution, a seven-year framework agreement for the construction of a number of wood-fuelled heating plants was signed between the ADEME and the Vosges regional authority.

The heating plant at Autun, in the Morvan region, is an example of a local authority engaging in global sustainable thinking. Built in 1999, the 8MW wood-fuelled boiler provides 70 % of local urban heating needs, equivalent to 3,500 households. The plant replaces two oil-fired heating plants, and has allowed significant reductions in

emissions of both CO_2 (11,000 t/year), and sulphur (280 t/year). It is fitted with noise-reduction equipment to reduce local environmental impact, and was the first such plant in France to receive ISO 14001 certification.

Biogas

Exploitation of biogas from organic material both limits greenhouse gas emissions and allows recycling of a proportion of household, industrial and agricultural waste. With annual production of 150,000 toe, biogas currently represents less than 0.5 % of natural gas use in France, but has the potential to meet 5 to 10 % of needs. Energy is extracted by conversion to heat through combustion, or into electricity via thermal motors or gas turbines.

Europe's most up-to-date biogas plant is at Neubukow in north-eastern Germany, and converts organic waste and manure from the surrounding agricultural region into electricity and heat. Each year this plant utilises 80,000t of a gas which contains 65 % methane, converting, via co-generators, the 3.25 million m^3 of this produced into electricity for 2,000 households and heating for 1,500 households, distributed through the local networks. After fermentation the resulting organic material is used as a fertiliser, more easily tolerated by plants and soils than the untreated manure.

In developing countries, biogas can provide solutions to both environmental and health issues. A project in Nepal, financed by the German ministry of economic co-operation and development, will see the installation of 100,000 small-scale biogas plants using bovine excrement. 65,000 of these were in service by the end of 2000, producing gas in external underground reservoirs to fuel lamps and household cookers. The project has created some 2,000 jobs, with the establishment of around 50 small businesses. As well as providing a brake on deforestation, it has also improved local quality of life considerably through the removal of the daily chore of gathering fuel and the reduced incidence of smoke-related respiratory ailments.

Hydro-electric energy

Most European countries use hydro-electric power, which is relatively easy to exploit. In France, 90 % of electricity from renewable

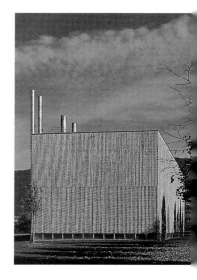

Timber heating plant, Bière, Switzerland 1998. Architects: Pierre Bonnet and Christian Bridel.

sources (which makes up 15 % of the total) is from hydro-electric plants. As well as an industrial capacity of 1,800MW, there are 1,700 smaller-scale plants with capacities below 8MW, most of which are rated at less than 1MW. These smaller installations currently supply 1 % of French energy consumption, or around 7TWh. The EU target of 21 % of energy from renewable sources by 2010 calls for an additional 4TWh from hydro-electricity, requiring new hydro-electric capacity of 1,000MW. This calls for heavy investment, depreciable over around 20 years.

Small-scale hydro-electric developments generally opt for partnership solutions, combining public and private financing. Alongside construction of new plant, turbines on some older industrial sites are being updated. In Belgium, the renewable energy agency Apere is looking at former water-mill sites with a view to their renovation.

EXPERIMENTAL PROGRAMMES

Aside from central government financing, which is generally determined by strategies linked to national energy policy, there are various ministerial, regional or local initiatives supporting experimental projects in the areas of social housing and public amenities.

In northern and central Europe, pilot projects are seen in the context of a long-term development framework, and designed to be reproducible; they thus have a social purpose and their usefulness is not in dispute. In other EU countries, particularly France, failure to transfer knowledge gained through such experiments is holding back progress. Innovation is left to the brave few who are willing to take risks in using materials and techniques which, though they have been extensively tested in neighbouring countries, do not have the official approval necessary for the standard ten-year guarantee.

EU pilot projects

Set up under the EU's Thermie programme, the Cepheus project aims to reduce CO_2 emissions at the domestic level. The project consists of 250 housing units, built between 1999 and 2001 in five European countries. Its purpose is to show that by radically cutting the amount of energy used for heating, fossil fuel consumption by households can in time be reduced to zero, all energy

Block of 17 flats with timber structure, Ingolstadt-Hollerstauden, Germany 1998.
Architects: Ebe + Ebe.

needs being met instead by non-polluting renewable alternatives. The buildings conform to the Passive House standards (see p. 100) set out in the early 1990s by Wolfgang Feist, who has overseen the technical aspects of the Cepheus project. The project also aims for cost efficiency: the overall capital cost and the running cost, normalised over 30 years, must not exceed that of a conventional building. The only French contributor to the programme is the Salvatierra building in Rennes (see pp. 166-171), which comprises 40 passive housing units with earth and timber walls with hemp insulation.

The Thermie programme has various other strands. The EC 2000 (Energy and Comfort 2000) strand has funded various projects, including research into energy saving and user comfort at the Avax headquarters in Athens (see pp. 224-229). The Sunh programme focuses on innovative, reproducible solutions in the areas of energy saving, solar power and green construction. Sunh projects include the housing blocks at Viikki in Helsinki (see pp. 160-165).

Various pilot housing projects using solar energy have been subsidised through the renewable energy study group Read. The Solar Quarter in Regensburg consists of 500 houses designed by several architects to a master plan drawn up by Norman Foster. In Linz, Austria, the last of four phases of solarCity, developed from a concept by Norman Foster and Thomas Herzog, should be completed in 2003.

This ambitious project comprises 1,500 housing units in the form of flats and terraced houses, built by twelve different developers. Different parts of the project focus on the use of environmental materials, such as timber structures, reduction in thermal losses and passive and active use of solar energy.

The timber social housing programme in Bavaria

In the context of the commitments made at various international summits, several German Länder have come up with their own pilot projects in the housing sector. In 1992 the Bavarian interior ministry launched a programme entitled *Mietwohnungen in Holzsystembauweise*, or rental housing built in timber. While France had seen several initiatives encouraging timber building in the 1980s, this was the first such initiative in Germany.

The Bavarian programme, which took in around 900 housing units on 22 sites, aimed to boost the social housing sector by showing that costs could be reduced without loss of either comfort or architectural quality. Total programme budget was DM60 million (€30.7 million), and project costs were limited to DM1,800/m² (€920/m²). Projects were undertaken by six German and international architects, who developed proto-types of different building systems using timber structure and cladding. The housing block at Nuremberg-Langwasser, designed by the Danish architects Vandkunsten, was one of the first projects to be completed, in 1993. The most recent is Ebe + Ebe's 1998 building at Ingolstadt-Holler-stauden, which comprises 17 flats on four levels, with internal walls and floors in nailed laminated timber.

Since the completion of these projects, the use of timber construction in multi-storey housing blocks has increased rapidly. Several studies have been carried out in Germany, Austria and Switzerland into ways of optimising conformity of such structures to acoustic and fire resistance regulations.

HQE projects in France

In France, the only experimental pilot programme to have received national backing remains the 13 REX HQE projects, funded by the Plan Con-struction et Architecture. Launched at the 1993 Batimat exhibition, these consist of 700 social housing units in 22 regions, which meet a list of 25 defined environmental targets. Unfortunately these projects did not provide a sufficiently impressive example, either in terms of architec-ture or of environmental credentials, to have any real effect on the social housing sector, and subse-quent buildings have seen no notable modifica-tions as a result.

Through regional initiatives, ADEME provides HQE projects with both technical support and funding. Grants are available of up to 50 % of the cost of research into environmental performance, carried out by external consultants (such as design engineers or checking authorities). These grants are made to developers and management compa-nies of public and service sector buildings; research may concern environmental management, energy control, the use of renewable energy or waste management. The AMO-HQE scheme, which

provides support to developers, forms part of the ADEME-funded sustainability studies.

Funding initiatives at regional and departmental level are aimed mainly at public buildings. Public projects under the HQE scheme appeared first in areas where environmentalists have political influ-ence: the Nord-Pas-de-Calais region, for example, was among the first to build HQE schools, includ-ing those in Caudry, by Lucien Kroll, and Calais, by Isabelle Colas and Fernand Soupey (see pp. 196-201). For the latter project, the additional capital costs of around 8 % were met by the regional authority.

THE FUTURE OF GREEN BUILDING

In Europe today, increasing numbers of buildings are being designed with the aims of balancing opti-mum user comfort with conservation of natural resources and ecosystems. However, there is still often a gap between environmental and architec-tural quality.

As with any new approach, environmentally-friendly construction requires motivation and commitment from developers, designers and contractors. All parties must look again at stan-dard practice. However, the inevitable invest-ment in time spent on this, and in developing new responses, will bring rapid rewards.

The construction of green buildings is a necessary, but not sufficient, condition for meeting the EU's ambitious targets for reduction in CO_2 emissions and energy conservation. Environmental consid-erations must also be applied to the planning pro-cess; on an urban and regional scale, but with the human dimension always in mind.

This book describes the approach of six local authorities who have integrated environmental thinking into their planning processes. It also pre-sents 23 individual building projects that were designed and built according to environmental principles. A wide range of project types is cov-ered, including private houses, social housing, pub-lic buildings, business and service buildings. Their relevance to environmental issues, their formal and technical quality and the variety of solutions they provide constitute proof that the environ-mental alternative is not only desirable, but feasi-ble, within reasonable budgets and in the context of contemporary architecture.

URBANISM AND SUSTAINABLE DEVELOPMENT

6 European examples

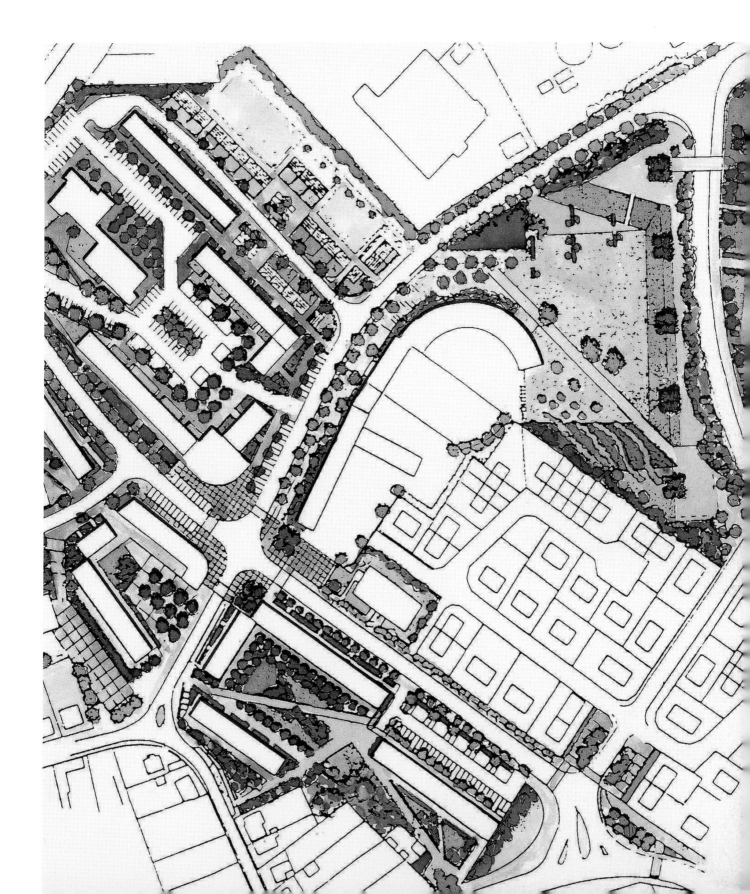

With the global communications revolution, and the growing awareness of the threats to the earth's environment and hence its population, our lives have taken on a new dimension. Besides new energy strategies and an environmental approach to building design and construction, the beginning of the 21st century finds us faced with important social choices.

TOWARDS GLOBAL SUSTAINABLE DEVELOPMENT

Environmentalism goes well beyond architecture. Environmental ideas are applied through a global, interdisciplinary strategy, beginning with urban planning and land use. All aspects of our lives are affected:
- infrastructure
- energy strategies
- industry and manufacturing
- use of natural resources
- education
- health
- social structures.

Sustainable development of our towns and cities aims to improve living conditions for their three billion inhabitants, through a balance between technological progress and improvements in health, economic and social conditions. At issue are both the requirement to meet basic needs in the developing world, and enhancing quality of life in the industrialised nations.

The urban explosion

The past 100 years have seen a population explosion unprecedented in human history. In 1900, only around 14 % of the world's population, or about 200 million people, lived in cities. At the beginning of the 21st century, 50 % of people world-wide are city-dwellers. For more than 70 % of inhabitants of the EU, quality of life already depends on the urban environment. However, the bulk of future urban population increases will be in developing countries. The World Bank predicts that by 2025, 80 % of the population in these countries will be living in cities. Such uncontrolled growth often results in the destruction of arable land vital for food production, with the spread of vast shanty towns which for a significant proportion of the world's population provide their first and only experience of urban living.

Over the past 200 years, the average population of the world's 100 biggest towns has risen as follows:

1800: 200,000
1900: 700,000
1950: 2,100,000
2000: 5,000,000.

By today's standards, a city of 200,000 inhabitants is a medium-sized town. Such has been the vigour of urban growth that in the space of 30 years man has built as much as in his entire preceding history. It has been estimated that over the next 40 years, further development will be needed equivalent to a thousand cities, each with 3 million inhabitants – most of this in developing countries.

This perspective brings an urgent reality to the need to build tomorrow's world on sustainable principles. Professionals and policymakers in the industrialised countries must focus on ways of improving quality of life in cities which are already seeing rampant unemployment, ethnic, religious and social intolerance, and violence.

Sustainable development is a long-term project, with at its heart an awareness of the human and economic cost of social breakdown in the cities. The cost of reversing the damage done by development in the industrialised world, and controlling that now emerging in developing countries, is impossible to evaluate. Clearly it will be huge. But the longer we wait, the higher this cost will be.

Urban environmentalism

One of the first advocates of urban environmentalism was the German academic Ekhart Hahn. In his 1987 paper *Ökologische Stadtplanung* ("ecological urban planning"), he set out the issues involved in sustainable urban development, and proposed a first set of measures though which it might be achieved. A subsequent international project, which looked at theoretical research and case studies, resulted in the 1990 report *Ökologischer Stadtumbau* ("ecological urban restructuring"). This defines eight areas of consideration:
- ethics and respect for the individual
- participation and democratisation
- structuring through networks

- a return to the natural world and sensory experience
- controlled urban density and mixed development
- respect for the *genius loci*, or spirit of place
- ecology and economy
- international co-operation.

These considerations can be applied through a strategy of local environmental development, with the establishment of "ecostations", to function as centres of information, communication, activity and culture. With a series of measures spread over three levels of intervention *(see table below)*, they form the framework for environmental urban development.

Sustainable urbanism depends on both responsible politics and the professional capabilities of policymakers, planners, architects and the building and civil engineering industry. It makes best use of the built and natural environments, to the economic and social benefit of the community. It has positive consequences for daily life:

- a cleaner, less noisy and less polluted city
- traffic priority given to pedestrians and cyclists
- more welcoming public spaces
- enhanced community life and sense of civic pride.

For a city to be sustainable – that is, viable in the long term – its harmful impact on the environment must be limited, and living and working conditions for its inhabitants must be pleasant.

Application of a sustainable development policy requires both political strength and commitment on the part of central authorities.

At present, the most active local authorities in this area are those where population is rising rapidly, such as Mäder in Austria *(see p. 60)*, and those such as Stuttgart *(see p. 63)* which have the financial resources to put in place far-reaching measures. Freiburg im Breisgau *(see p. 69)* and Rennes *(see p. 83)* are examples of rapidly-growing university towns where sustainable policies have been initiated by committed environmentalist politicians.

**Measures for sustainable urban development,
divided into three sectors**

Urban design and technologies	Communication on environmental matters and local democracy	Economics and environment
Architecture and environmental building	Participation and responsibility of individuals concerned	Energy tax
Heat and electricity supply	Information and consultation on the environment	Pollution tax
Water management	Decentralisation of administrative and decision-making powers	Payment according to consumption
Journey management	Environmental training, consultancy and qualifications	Environmental accounting for businesses and institutions
Waste reduction and recycling	New models for co-operatives and property development and marketing	Modifications to planning tools, building standards and legislation
Green spaces, protection of the natural environment	Creation of ecostations, local centres for communication on environment and culture	Financial assistance and incentives
Urban climate, air quality	Creation of energy, water and waste agencies	Environmental strategies for the industrial, commercial and craft-based sectors
Protection of soil and water	New housing and neighbourhood development models	Creation of environmental services, commercial and activity centres
Protection against noise		Employment creation in the environmental sector
Food supplies and health		

(Source: Ekhart Hahn, *Ökologischer Stadtumbau, Theorie und Konzept*)

SUSTAINABILITY
IN EUROPEAN CITIES

Political commitments to sustainable development have been made first at international level, at the various UN summits, and then at European level. National strategies have been formulated to meet these commitments, and implemented via regulations and legislation on such issues as air and water pollution and waste management. Once these national targets have been set, regional authorities have the task of meeting them at the local level, through application of environmental criteria to decisions on urban planning, social housing, transport and public amenities.

Even with legislation and regulations in place, the sheer inertia of central governments faced with the new environmental, economic and social realities can often militate against their swift and efficient application. Thus regional authorities and local developers have a key role to play in sustainable development. Since the Rio Summit, more and more initiatives have emerged, with increasing numbers of regions, cities, towns and villages setting up their own Agenda 21 programmes. Measures put in place encompass land use, green spaces, soil quality, journey management, energy, water and waste management, and social measures. Although comparing measures on air and water pollution is relatively easy, it is more difficult to draw overall comparisons between projects, since subjective criteria complicate the measurable indicators. However, more and more European towns and cities now merit the label "sustainable".

European networks

At the first sustainable cities conference in Aalborg, Denmark, in 1994, a total of 84 local authorities committed themselves to drawing up their own Agenda 21 programmes. Besides the application of sustainable principles, the conference document called for exchange of data, the setting up of networks for collaborative working, promotion of flagship projects and the establishment of a set of urban indicators.

At the same time, the 700 member authorities of the Climate Alliance (*Klimabündnis*) agreed on measures intended to reduce CO_2 emissions to 50 % of 1988 levels by 2010. The small Austrian town of Mäder (*see pp. 60-62*) joined the Alliance in 1993. In order to meet its ambitious objectives,

in 1998 Mäder set up Austria's first environmental school, and has promoted the use of renewable energy in public buildings.

Dialogue and teamwork are key elements of an Agenda 21 programme. Successful application of regulatory and fiscal constraints, while taking into account technological progress and growing public environmental awareness, requires co-operation. The aim is to arrive at a consensus in which responsibility is taken by both individuals and institutions: industry, local authorities, other groups and the public at large. Solutions will be different for each context; comparison of experiences will be a first stage in the emergence of a common culture between different communities. This will support the creation of a Europe-wide strategy aimed at a new balance between quality of life, protection of the environment and economic development.

The West must also take responsibility for the developing world. As western democracies develop their environmental strategies, they become more able to pass on technology and expertise to developing countries. Protection of ecosystems, energy conservation, water and waste management, for example, can be effected through direct co-operation between local communities.

The Dutch pioneers

The Netherlands' pioneering attitude to sustainable development may be explained by that country's high population density, creating as it does considerable pressure on the environment. Moreover, some experts have predicted that the rise in sea level due to global warming in the 21st century could wipe out several Dutch towns.

In 1993, Rotterdam introduced environmental priorities into development plans; since 1992, Amsterdam's regulations and recommendations for new buildings have included a list of alternative, more environmentally-friendly materials. Several authorities have built new developments along sustainable lines.

As early as 1988 the Netherlands Energy and Environment Agency, Novem, launched an experimental low-energy housing project: Ecolonia, in Alphen aan den Rijn, built from a master plan by Lucien Kroll.

The project used the DCBA environmental assessment method (*see p. 21*), with choice of materi-

als, energy consumption, water management, waste treatment and planting all being determined using environmental criteria. The data gathered and expertise gained at Ecolonia were contributory factors in the decisions to embark on other such projects during the 1990s, such as Kattenbroek in Amersfoort, Ecodus in Delft, and the GWL district of Amsterdam (see pp. 76-78). Nieuwland, in Amersfoort, was the first new development to apply sustainable development principles on a large scale, with 4,700 homes built between 1994 and 2001 (see above).

Scandinavian projects

Scandinavia was also quick to concern itself with urban ecology, with the first international conference on the subject being held in Denmark. In Finland, the environmental assessment system Pimwag was tested on the experimental development at Viikki, in Helsinki (see pp. 79-82). In Sweden, sustainable principles have been applied to projects in Malmö and in the redevelopment of central Stockholm.

During 2001, Malmö held an international exhibition on the theme of the sustainable city in the long term. The expo dealt with urban development on brownfield sites, greenfield site development, transport strategies, and environmental quality of buildings, and resulted in the construction of an experimental development on a spur in the Öresund channel. This project comprises 26 housing blocks, built of timber on two to four storeys, to house 500 people, along with educational facilities and office and commercial buildings. Landscaping includes two parks, a canal and a waterside leisure area.

Urban ecology in Germany

The German town of Freiburg im Breisgau (see p. 69) has long been an international benchmark for environmentalism. Stuttgart (see p. 63) also provides examples, with the application since the 1980s of an energy management policy for public facilities and social housing.

The various levels of subsidy accompanying the international horticultural exhibitions (IGA), such as the one held in Stuttgart in 1993, and architecture exhibitions (IBA, or Internationale Bauausstellung) have enabled far-reaching projects to be completed on a district and regional scale. The best example of these is the Emscher valley development in the Ruhr (see p. 44).

In Berlin, the 1980s saw the beginning of several "soft renovation" community projects, whose objectives were both environmental and social. The most well-known of these are the refurbishment of the Ufa-Fabrik complex in the Tempelhof district, and Block 103 in Kreuzberg. Since the fall of the Berlin Wall in 1989, the authorities have concentrated on sustainable reconstruction of the former East Berlin. Some private investors have led the way: the new DaimlerChrysler headquarters building in Potsdamer Platz, designed by Renzo Piano, comprises 44,000m^2 of offices, flats and commercial premises using solar energy and rainwater recovery systems (see p. 51).

"London as it could be"

London, whose industrial smogs remain notorious, is one of the least sustainable European capitals. Between 1970 and 2000 a decline in the quality of life, linked in particular to air pollution, led to central London losing around 30 % of its

"London as it could be":
sketch for Richard Rogers
Partnership's proposed
pedestrianisation of the banks
of the Thames near Somerset
House, 1986.

population, with a corresponding 20 % fall in jobs. The population moved out to the suburbs, which continue to extend.

In 1986, the architect Richard Rogers produced a scheme for restructuring the city centre, entitled "London as it could be", bringing together architecture, environment, transport and social integration. Subsequently the new city authority developed a Spatial Development Strategy. A product of the European Spatial Development Perspective, a consultative document produced by the EU, this "London Plan" covers economic and social solutions within a sustainable development framework, with issues to be addressed at borough level.

In his "plan for the millennium", Rogers proposed a shift in the focus of central London towards the river Thames, with increased public access to the river banks. Some of his recommendations, including new bridges and riverside walks, are now reality. The largest element is Millennium Park, a new public space of almost 20 hectares on the Greenwich peninsula. Built on previously contaminated land, this provides a "green framework" for a regenerated area.

Sustainable urban projects in France

By the end of 1999, 51 Agenda 21 projects had been submitted to the French Environment Ministry. These programmes are required to meet criteria of social equity, economic efficiency and improvements to the environment. To meet these aims, 25 % of local authorities took an "organisational" approach, through training and the creation of specific structures; while the remaining 75 % chose an approach by sector (housing, energy, urbanism or landscape). Strasbourg, through its public transport policies, and Angers, with measures to control noise pollution, provide examples of sustainability strategies which go back several years. However the Nord-Pas-de-Calais region was the first to implement more wide-ranging initiatives, in particular in Dunkirk and Lille.

Dunkirk has seen both a partnership agreement between industry and local people for extension of its port (see pp. 44-45), and the construction of France's first wind farm. Its Agenda 21 programme also includes two HQE housing projects: ten social housing units built in two new blocks near the coast, and refurbishment of 104 homes

at Grande-Synthe. These two projects have shared aims:
- to improve the social environment and minimise deterioration, through close liaison with residents;
- to reduce energy consumption, thus reducing charges and hence non-payment problems;
- to invest for the long term in high-quality, environmentally-healthy materials.

In Lille, the 1997 development master plan for the city called clearly for future urban development to be within a framework of sustainability. The policy of urban renewal focuses on reconstruction of existing districts within the existing city envelope, rather than new development beyond it, with priority given to 21 areas suffering from economic, social or environmental deprivation. In the Sainte-Hélène district, the community chose to put sustainable principles into practice: preliminary analysis, and a study led by the city development agency, was followed by a feasibility study looking at financial and other aspects of environmental urbanism. The principles that emerged served as a reference both for the restructuring of other districts and the creation of new development zones.

Eastern European cities

In his study of "urban ecological restructuring", Ekhart Hahn (see p. 34) looks at four case studies, including Bratislava and Krakow. He paints an alarming picture of the situation in Eastern Europe. Bratislava is in one of the most polluted areas of Slovakia, while Krakow has been recognised as an environmental danger zone. In both cases air, water and soil pollution, along with the destruction of forests, have reached worrying levels. Besides a lack of environmental protection measures, there is apparent disregard for basic safety precautions in the nuclear industry and at toxic waste dumps. Pollution-related illnesses such as bronchitis, allergies, leukaemia and cancers are 30 % more common in these areas than in the surrounding country.

Eastern Europe's environmental problems are essentially rooted in the economic and energy policies of the former communist powers. Subsidies to the energy industry, which kept prices artificially low, also encouraged wastage, reduced productivity and increased pollution. Although the democratic regimes which came to power after the fall of the Berlin Wall in 1989 put in place new policies, most Eastern European cities still lack the financial resources necessary for adequate environmental measures. The introduction of energy conservation measures brings some hope. However, financial aid and co-operation from the European Union, with a focus on locally-adapted strategies, is vital if there is to be a rapid and lasting solution.

SUSTAINABLE DEVELOPMENT AND URBAN PLANNING

The long-term future of our towns and cities cannot be left to the vagaries of the international market. It must be directed by the local authorities, through policies of genuinely user-oriented, sustainable development.

Preliminary requirements

For a town to develop along sustainable lines, certain conditions must be in place:
- commitment on the part of the elected authorities and administration;
- willingness of all parties to work together – including businesses, local associations, schools and colleges;
- active participation of residents;
- and a marshalling of professional expertise, including that of architects, engineers, urbanists, landscape designers, elected officials and technical services.

The involvement of specialists can often result in simple and ingenious solutions, which meet both popular concerns and budgetary constraints. For elected authorities wishing to improve quality of life for their electorate, the environmental approach is a pragmatic one, aimed at ensuring that projects are both successful and economical.

Aims

In terms of application of sustainable principles to land development and urban planning, strategic aims are broadly the same throughout Europe, as follows:
- equilibrium between urban development and preservation of agricultural land and forest, as well as green spaces for leisure use;
- preservation of soils, ecosystems and natural landscapes;
- diversity of use in urban areas, with a balance between living and working space;

- socially mixed areas (residential and otherwise);
- journey management and control of vehicular traffic;
- protection of water and air quality;
- reduction of noise pollution;
- waste management;
- control of natural and technical risks;
- protection of exceptional city sites and conservation of our urban heritage.

For this wide range of objectives to be met by a local community, they must be defined in precise terms in the local context. With all parties working together, goals can be modified and refined as specific needs develop.

Methodology

Before drafting an Agenda 21 programme, or more generally an urban plan defined within environmental parameters, there must be an analysis of the situation and its context. With the participation of local associations, businesses and residents, the local authority then defines the major strands of the project. For each of these strands
- existing measures are studied;
- aims are defined, with acceptable limits or thresholds set for quantifiable variables;
- specific action is proposed;
- the parties concerned are assigned the appropriate responsibility.

There should then be a policy of following up and evaluating initiatives within the community, in order to learn from them and increase their reproducibility, both within the area concerned and in terms of potential transfer to other areas or countries.

In France, the CSTB and the consultants La Calade have produced an assessment table designed to help local authorities draw up their programmes. By matching objectives to sustainable principles, this system helps define aims appropriate to the particular context of a town or district.

Funding

Sustainable urbanism is a long-term project. Its overall costs include construction, renovation and maintenance those for both building and infrastructure; it aims to optimise both initial investment (including demolition costs) and operating costs. A sustainable approach has cost benefits, particularly for developers who retain responsibility for building management, which is generally the

case for local authorities. Running costs can be reduced by adopting sustainable measures from the outset:
- integrating energy conservation systems from initial design stage (particularly for social housing and pubic amenity projects);
- choosing low-maintenance materials, technologies and architectural concepts;
- establishing rational systems for rainwater and waste management.
For the sustainable construction of a school in Calais (see pp. 196-201), the Nord-Pas-de-Calais regional authority estimated its initial investment at 8 % above that for a conventional building, but with running costs 25-30 % lower. Similar reductions in running costs have been demonstrated in Stuttgart over a 15-year period.
The high initial costs are explained by:
- the necessity to conduct new research and trials for each project;
- the current high costs of innovative materials and techniques which are not yet used on a mass scale;
- the need for the involvement of the relatively few professionals qualified in these areas.
In those countries where application of sustainable principles is becoming more widespread, increasing numbers of companies are entering the market and materials and technology prices are falling rapidly. German companies in particular are gaining strong positions in this market, which looks set to be one of the most fast-growing of the 21st century; this should therefore have considerable positive impact on the German economy over the next decades.

The French legislative framework

In France, the basic aims which will create a framework for sustainable development to take place are defined in a 1998 report entitled *Demain la ville* ("The city tomorrow") written by Jean-Pierre Sueur, and in various legislative documents – notably the Voynet report, issued by the Land and Environment Ministry in May 1999, and the SRU (*Solidarité et Renouvellement Urbain*) law of 13 December 2000.
The Voynet document sets out the following aims:
- restraint of urban expansion
- concerted and united management of assets and resources
- efficient and responsible use of collective assets

- reduction of environmental damage and risks
- combating social exclusion
- combating the concentration of wealth and business within small areas.
The SRU law takes a broad approach to urban policy, introducing measures favouring social heterogeneity and support: administrative areas within conurbations of over 50,000 inhabitants must contain at least 20 % social housing. The law defines new urban planning documents, with local urban plans (PLU) replacing the former land use plans (POS). The new documents must be compatible with regional land use plans (SCOT) for the whole conurbation or area.

LAND USE AND MANAGEMENT

The effective implementation of a sustainable urban plan assumes that the local authority controls a certain amount of land, acquired strategically over the long term.
At present, environmental urban development projects are mostly in the areas of refurbishment of old city districts, regeneration of former industrial land and in enterprise development zones (known in France as Zac).

Property policy

A strong position in the local property market is a prerequisite for proper urban planning – particularly so when an authority decides to adopt an environmental approach. Such a position enables the authority:
- to designate land for public projects in good time;
- to apply environmental regulations and measures more easily;
- to acquire land at more favourable prices;
- to plan for the future, with possible alternative uses for given areas.
A truly efficient property policy will look ahead in order to make better strategic choices, and take opportunities as they arise, whether or not they fall within the normal regulatory framework. When possible, land will be acquired independently of its definitive future use, and purchases will have legal protection clauses attached as appropriate.
The environmental, social and economic need to conserve land is becoming increasingly evident. In Rennes (see p. 41), where property strategies are

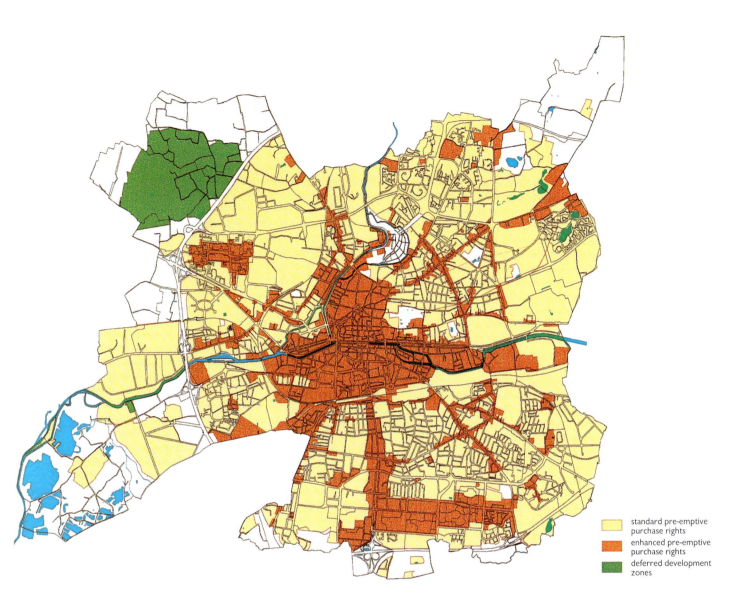

standard pre-emptive
purchase rights

enhanced pre-emptive
purchase rights

deferred development
zones

a key part of urban planning policy, the authorities recognised early on the dangers of allowing the city to spread further. Instead, development has focused on the city itself, through a number of strategies – remodelling of public spaces, development of vacant infill sites, regeneration of industrial sites, increased density in poorly or sparsely-developed areas – which have allowed the "green corridors", the pockets of rural landscape, to be preserved.

The compact city

The radical, deliberatist urbanism of the 1960s and 1970s saw cities extending into the formerly agricultural land which surrounded them. The new towns and districts which sprang up as a result met immediate needs, but failed to take into consideration the long-term effects on the population and the environment.

Sustainable development rejects such expansion, in favour of the reclamation of urban identity and culture through redevelopment of the existing

city: renovation of older districts, regeneration of former industrial and military zones or docklands. A basic principle of sustainability as applied to urban development is increased density. A first step towards this is a move away from the detached house, set in its own plot of land at the edge of the city. Property prices, particularly in densely-populated areas, are a major influence on this.

In a compact city, the proximity to each other of housing, jobs, services and amenities can make for optimum use of space, with economical use of natural areas and efficient public transport. The challenge is to ensure a sufficiently attractive, vibrant environment relative to the rival attractions of a house and garden in the suburbs, and thus prevent families from moving out of the inner city as soon as they are able. Sustainable urban planning also allows synergy to be developed between, for example, businesses, research facilities and higher education establishments on a single site.

Local authority strategic property purchase plan, Rennes.

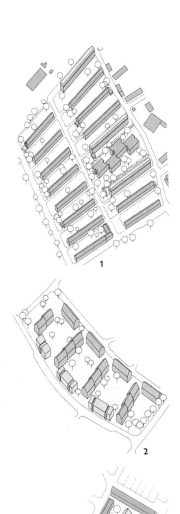

Three examples of increased housing density in existing districts in North Rhine-Westphalia, Germany:

1. Neurath development, Höhenhaus, Cologne: upward extension of three housing blocks;

2. Von-Witzleben, Münster: completion of city blocks by construction of three new buildings;

3. Viersener, Neuss: two new buildings within existing city blocks.

Housing densification

A building's impact on its surroundings depends on its position, shape, structure, materials and energy needs. For a housing block, these factors can be expressed per housing unit. When the site, residents' requirements and the local urban plan make it appropriate, grouping together several units in a simple, compact volume can bring considerable environmental and economic benefits (*see table below*):
- use of less land
- a smaller building envelope
- lower volume of materials used
- reduced energy consumption
- lower construction costs.

The simplest way to bring this about is by building multi-storey housing blocks. Where inhabitants' preference is for houses rather than flats, an intermediate solution may be appropriate. Some experimental "intermediate housing" developments were built in France in the 1970s. In the Burgholzhof district of Stuttgart (*see p. 67*), one such project comprises two superimposed terraces of ten apartments, each on two levels.

If urban spread is to be prevented, there must also be some densification of older city districts. Depending on the structure of existing buildings, it may be possible to add one or two floors to them — usually in timber, given its relatively low weight. With very large city blocks, construction of a new building within the enclosed courtyard space is sometimes a possibility. U-shaped blocks may be completed by the addition of a fourth side, thus creating a more private space.

Low-rise, high-density housing

Low-rise, high-density housing is one response to the problems of rising urban population, and can be a useful solution where the preference is for houses rather than flats. In Germany, where land prices in urban areas are very high, there are increasing numbers of environmental housing projects consisting of low energy consumption terraces. Local authorities, mostly with financial backing from the Länder, are setting aside plots of 200-300m² for terraced housing aimed at young families buying their first property. Similar schemes exist in Austria and Switzerland, under the Energy 2000 *Nachhaltiges Bauen* (sustainable building) programme.

The Bavarian regional government in 1996 launched the most ambitious of these pilot projects, known as the *Siedlungsmodelle,* or housing models. This consists of around 7,000 housing units, or up to 20,000 inhabitants, within twelve administrative districts. Most of these are terraced or semi-detached houses which fulfil the Low Energy House (*see p. 98*) or Passive House criteria (*see p. 100*). No one material is imposed, although much timber is used, often in association with steel and concrete. The new housing has been developed in close co-operation with the local

Comparison of surface areas, heating energy consumed and construction costs for eight housing units, in different configurations: eight separate houses; two terraces of four houses each; and a block of eight flats.

	8 separate houses (ground floor plus basement)	2 terraces of 4 houses (ground floor plus basement)	block of 8 flats (2 storeys plus basement)
Site area	100 %	70 %	34 %
Envelope surface area	100 %	74 %	35 %
Heating energy	100 %	89 %	68 %
Construction costs	100 %	87 %	58 %

(Source: H.R. Preisig et al., *Ökologische Baukompetenz*, Zurich 1999, pp. 109)

authorities, with the aim of respecting environmental and social criteria while also reducing costs.

As part of this scheme, in 1996 the town of Ingolstadt ran an ideas competition for new urban development, on the theme of "new ways towards economical and environmental social housing". The first of these projects to be completed is by Werner Bäuerle, consisting of 54 timber-framed terraced houses (*see illustration, right*). The high density of this development and its linear geometry are successfully mitigated by the landscaping treatment of the external space, with timber canopies and small, enclosed private gardens.

Sustainable development in residential districts

For most urban dwellers, daily life is framed by the neighbourhood in which they live. For large sections of the population – children, older people, the economically inactive – life takes place almost exclusively within it. The scale of such districts is an appropriate one at which to apply sustainable urbanism projects, enabling them to address at a local level such issues as energy and water use, noise, refuse collection and sorting, as well as problems of social exclusion.

A number of development zones have been created in Europe along sustainable lines, with mixed success in architectural, environmental and urban planning terms. All are based on integrated ideas of mixed use and social heterogeneity; some have also proposed environmental transport solutions and the use of non-hazardous, renewable and recyclable materials. Landscaping aims to fit in with local surroundings and preserve biodiversity. Most of these areas have received local authority funding, either through one-off grants for experimental projects or subsidised land prices.

One of the first "green neighbourhoods" was Ecolonia in Alphen aan den Rijn, followed on a larger scale by Amersfoort (*see p. 37*). In 2000, several were being completed in Germany: Burgholzhof in Stuttgart (*see p. 67*), Sonnenfeld in Ulm, and a group of developments as part of the international exhibition at Emscher Park in the Ruhr (*see p. 44*).

Two of the most successful projects are in Freiburg im Breisgau: the new Rieselfeld district at the edge of the city, and Vauban, an inner-city area on the site of a former French army barracks (*see p. 70*). Successful pilot projects often inspire

further development: after completion of the Salvatierra building (*see pp. 166-171*) under the EU's Thermie programme, Rennes in 2001 launched a new phase of the Beauregard development zone, which requires developers and architects to integrate environmental protection measures (*see pp. 88-89*).

Urban renewal

Sustainable urban redevelopment combines energy and water conservation, waste management, noise abatement and creation of a pleasant living environment, with improvements to the microclimate achieved by external planting. This must go hand in hand with social measures: residents and users must have a say in both design and management decisions, if not construction strategies.

Of the European capitals, Berlin has the most experience in this area. The city's particular circumstances – with West Berlin literally walled in within a foreign country until reunification in 1989 – have demanded a particular response. The city applied sustainable principles to its renovation during the 1980s of residential and former industrial areas, and has continued to do so for the new government, administrative and business centres (such as Potsdamer Platz) built after 1989.

In the context of the IBA architecture exhibition, Berlin's urban renewal agency, Stern, was working as early as the 1970s on "soft" redevelopment of disused urban sites. The first example of this was Kreuzberg's Block 103 (*see p. 44*), containing 332 housing units, 41 businesses and 18 educational, cultural and social facilities. The project sprang from a political clash, when in 1981 a group of protesters began squatting in a block of buildings due to be demolished to make way for an expressway. A residents' co-operative was formed, and led eventually to the introduction of various then-experimental technologies such as photovoltaic cells, heating via a gas co-generator, and green roofs, with collected rainwater used for irrigation and grey water for toilet flushing. Now privatised, Stern is currently working on renewal projects in Prenzlauer Berg in the former East Berlin.

Sustainability in industrial areas

In 1990 the town of Dunkirk, France's third largest port and home to 15 "high-risk" industrial facili-

Timber-framed terraced housing at Ingolstadt-Hollerstauden, 1999. Architect: Werner Bäuerle.

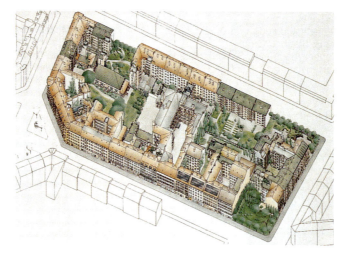 

"Soft" renovation of Block 103 in Kreuzberg, one of Berlin's first environmental regeneration projects.

ties, committed itself to sustainable development through the signing of an environmental quality agreement between the urban community, the port and various local institutions. In 1993, an "industrial environment scheme" was put in place addressing the location of industrial sites, their management and associated environmental problems and hazards (see p. 45). This is one of the country's best examples of co-operation between industry and local communities to increase sustainability.

In Rotterdam, the 1993 Rijnmond land and environment plan was drawn up after consultation between the local administration, businesses and regional and national authorities. The plan aimed to reconcile an expansion of the port, with new industrial plants and accompanying infrastructure, with protection of the environment and quality of life for the city's million inhabitants. To ensure a sustainable framework for the 1,500 hectare port development, a number of principles were laid down:
- extension of the port onto reclaimed land in the estuary, rather than expansion onto hitherto undeveloped land (despite the higher cost of land reclamation);
- measures to improve traffic circulation around the port zone and inland;
- restrictions on pollution-generating industry close to residential areas;
- reduction of road traffic through more use of rail and river transport and pipelines;
- regeneration of former industrial sites vacated following sea-front redevelopment;

- protection of the natural environment, including existing green spaces and recreational areas;
- protection of rural landscapes.
These principles have been applied to a total of 50 separate projects now in progress.

Urban renewal on a regional scale: Emscher Park

The huge areas of derelict industrial land, disused railway sidings or docks which exist within or on the outskirts of many cities present an opportunity for sustainable development on a larger, sometimes regional scale. The most dramatic example of such brownfield development is in the Emscher valley, in Germany's Ruhr basin. This region, with a population of 2.5 million and encompassing 16 local administrative authorities, saw a late but precipitate industrial transformation, with no attention paid to environmental or urban quality.

Since the decline in the steel industry and the closure of the mines in the late 1980s, the North Rhine-Westphalia authorities have focused on regeneration of the area, with the emphasis on reviving the Emscher valley, restoring the landscape and creating the conditions for sustainable economic renewal. To this end, the Land administration and the local authorities together initiated a one-off IBA expo.

The Emscher Park IBA covers an area of 800km² and is intended to take place over 20 years. All areas of activity are affected, through around 85 projects which by their scope have created the inter-community dynamic vital to the region's

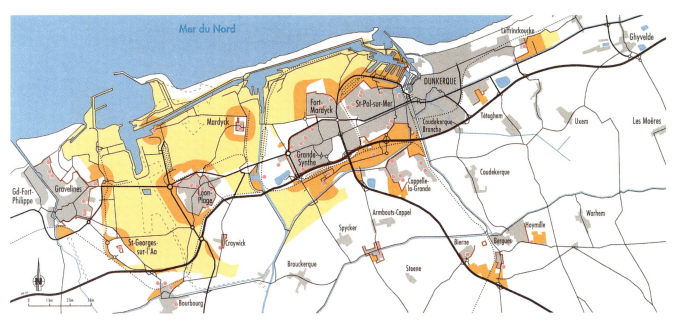

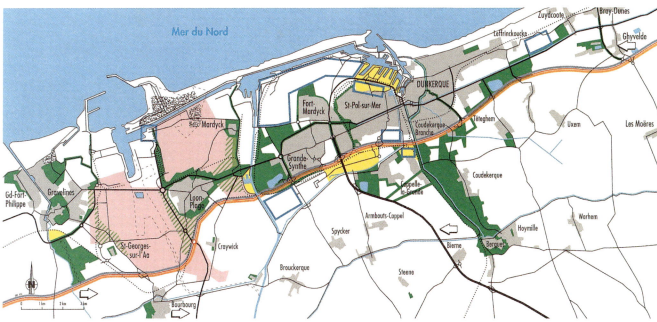

Maps showing the industrial
areas around Dunkirk.
Above, businesses moving into
the orange zones are asked
to consider the problems arising
from the proximity of industrial
areas (yellow) to the town (grey).
Below, landscaping principles.
(Source: Agur-VDB)

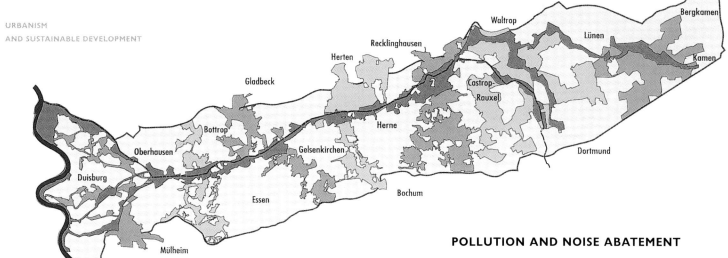

Site plan of Emscher Park.

**Environmental treatment
of polluted watercourses
of Emscher Park:**
- complete culverting
- canal with concrete outfall
- urban watercourse with wastewater
  collector
- natural watercourse and wastewater
  collector.

social and economic regeneration. There are five main project types:
- 19 landscape projects, covering some 30km², to interlink and preserve open spaces which were fragmented and polluted by industry, making them viable areas once more;
- ten ecological renewal programmes along the 350km of the Emscher and its tributaries, repairing the damage done by heavy industry through restoration of the river banks and construction of high-performance water purification plants;
- seven projects to restore derelict industrial sites, of which several are listed as being of historical interest;
- 22 business zones and technology parks, using a combination of public and private investment;
- 26 housing projects, covering 3,000 new and renovated homes.
The Emscher Park IBA strives to achieve high-quality architecture, good environmental design and a successful application of social principles to development. The regeneration has been financed through existing subsidy schemes at Land level, along with federal government funds for structural development and European Community aid. Around DM2.5 billion (€1.278 billion) has been injected into the projects in total; around two-thirds of this is public funding, with the remainder coming from the private sector.
The Herne-Sodingen training centre by Jourda & Perraudin (see p. 102), and the conversion of the former Zollverein XII colliery buildings at Essen-Katernberg into a cultural centre, are two of the best-known projects. However the expo also includes many interesting housing developments, among them various "garden village" projects; the Küppersbusch development by Szyszkowitz + Kowalski; and Peter Hübner's low-cost, ecological self-build terraces in Gelsenkirchen (see p. 18) and Lünen.

POLLUTION AND NOISE ABATEMENT

Noise, polluted air and poor-quality water: city-dwellers are subjected daily to nuisances that can have severe consequences for both physical and psychological health, including respiratory diseases, allergies and cancers. Since the late 1990s, increasing numbers of measures have been introduced in order to meet new national and European standards.

Water pollution

In some areas of Europe, groundwater and watercourse pollution levels reached alarming levels in the late 1990s, due largely to the presence of nitrates and phosphates in agricultural fertilisers and animal manure. New laws were introduced as a result. Given the risks involved, these will oblige the agricultural sector to reconsider its practices and look at other ways, or indeed the necessity, of increasing yield.
The European Parliament's Water Framework directive no. 2000/60, passed in October 2000, is designed to prevent further deterioration in water quality and to strengthen protection of aquatic ecosystems. The directive calls for sustainable water use, taking into account the basic principles of environmental law (precaution; prevention; remedy at source; "polluter pays"; and use of the best available technology).
The directive defines three sets of objectives concerning inland surface waters, coastal waters, transitional waters and groundwater – although it does not oblige member states to meet these objectives, rather to put in place the instruments enabling them to be met. The directive indicates that the cost of such environmental measures should be included in the price of water.

Noise

Urban noise derives largely from road traffic and from industry. Growing volumes of traffic, especially heavy lorries, has led to a corresponding

increase in noise levels. To counter this, various measures are possible:
- limiting emitted noise, through quieter engines and anti-noise road surfaces;
- reducing transmitted noise, by screening roads
- sound insulation of buildings.

In the Netherlands, noise is considered the primary environmental problem for urban residents, and road traffic is seen as the principal cause. In a 1994 survey, 25 % of respondents stated that they suffered "serious disturbance" from traffic noise. The law on noise abatement which came into effect in 1982 was one of the first pieces of environmental legislation. A revised law is due to take effect in 2003, under which responsibility will be devolved to regional and local authorities; noise abatement plans must be put in place, to reduce levels to below 55dB in sensitive areas.

Air pollution

Each year, European municipal authorities respond to air pollution "peaks" with a variety of measures, such as journey rationing, which have met with varying levels of success in terms of both effectiveness and compliance. These summer pollution alerts are attributable to a combination of traffic and industrial emissions. The alarming rise in air pollution levels in recent years has led to a need for increased monitoring of urban air quality. In France, the budget for such monitoring has tripled since 1995, to over €38 million in 2001. Pollution levels are measured in all cities of over 100,000 inhabitants and via some 680 fixed monitoring stations, recording levels of sulphur dioxide (SO_2), the oxides of nitrogen (NO_x), carbon monoxide (CO), lead and ozone. More recent pollutants, such as benzene and heavy metals, are also tracked.

By 2004, the EU programme "Pure Air for Europe" should bring tangible measures to meet the objectives of the 6th Environmental Action Programme – in particular, removal of the most dangerous atmospheric pollutants such as microparticles and tropospheric ozone. Application of European standards on cleaner fuel, combustion and car exhaust emissions is perhaps more likely to have significant effects than closing city centres to traffic. However, there is no doubt that a fundamental re-thinking of car use in cities is required.

JOURNEY MANAGEMENT

Environmental urbanism calls for a shift in attitude toward the city in general, and our manner of moving about it in particular. Journey strategy is a factor in both the quality of life and the economic vitality of urban areas. In France, local transport plans or PDUs, which were introduced as a result of 1996 air pollution legislation, set out organisational principles for public transport, traffic and parking. All towns of over 100,000 must draw up such a plan.

Increasing mixed use of central and inner-city districts, particularly in development zones, is essential to the reduction of distances travelled between home, workplace and services, encouraging a better balance between motor vehicles, bicycles and pedestrians.

Car traffic

50 years ago, the world's population of 2.6 billion drove 50 million cars. In 2000, 6 billion people between them used 500 million vehicles, with this number set to reach 1 billion by 2050. If urban air pollution is to be limited, behaviour must change; in particular, individuals must no longer automatically use their cars even for short journeys.

Car traffic is responsible for air pollution, greenhouse gas emissions (particularly CO_2), tiredness and accidents. Many towns now have transport and parking policies designed to promote the use of public transport over private cars. Other solutions include car-sharing, which is increasingly popular in some European cities.

Improvements to engine design, with a reduction in toxic exhaust gases, can also minimise noise and pollution. Some local authorities have set an example by opting for biofuel (as used in Paris) or solar-powered vehicles for their service fleet.

Public transport

Expansion of public transport services such as buses, metro systems and trams is clearly a vital part of the drive to protect the environment and preserve air quality and quality of life in the cities. A variety of interconnected factors can increase public transport use:
- better ring roads to keep traffic out of city centres
- a closely-spaced urban network
- well-designed timetables and tariff structures
- an improved service, with updated vehicles and better safety and security.

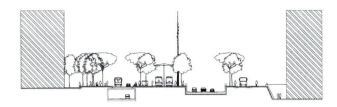

Section on the Vivier-Merle esplanade, Lyon. Architect and urban designer: Alexandre Chemetoff.

Cycle tracks between road and pavement, Copenhagen.

Cycle track and footpath in a Helsinki park.

Cycle parking next to a pedestrianised area, Copenhagen.

In several countries, "park and ride" schemes have been operating for many years and have proved very successful. Visitors leave their cars at out-of-town car parks built adjacent to bus or train stations, and use these services to reach the city centre, or other mass-attraction sites such as a sports stadium or exhibition centre.

Strasbourg's tram system, begun in 1989 with the last two lines coming into operation in 2000, has demonstrated its use not just as a means of transport but as an urban management tool. The tram network has linked and revitalised the different city areas, and changed the perception of city streets, with less space available to cars. The grassed areas and planted strips between the tracks have also lessened water run-off problems. Other French towns such as Grenoble, Nantes and Orleans have also opted for tram systems. In Part-Dieu, the business district of Lyon, a remodelled road system allows space for cars, buses and trams, with wide pavements and central reservations for safer pedestrian access (see section above).

Bicycles

The streets of Amsterdam, Copenhagen, Helsinki, Freiburg im Breisgau and Tübingen are already full of bicycles. In Germany, and to an even greater extent in the Netherlands and in Scandinavia, urban cycle paths are commonplace, usually on each side of the road. In Copenhagen, the cycleways are slightly raised with respect to the roadway, but lower in their turn than the pavement. This system of different levels makes for a clear and safe separation of road, cycle and pedestrian traffic.

Widespread bicycle use in cities raises the issue of cycle parking, which can be problematic particularly around public buildings, housing blocks and bus and train stations. A number of practical and secure solutions have been developed in Scandinavia, where there are large cycle parks in front of department stores, schools and colleges, cultural and sports centres and adjacent to pedestrian-only areas.

Various Scandinavian towns have free bicycle loan schemes, aimed at encouraging cycle use by both residents and visitors. Copenhagen has a coin-release system, as for supermarket trolleys, where the coin is returned when the bicycle is put back; the bikes' distinctive livery, bright yellow with solid wheels, and use of non-standard parts

mitigates against their disappearance. A similar scheme, using electronic cards, was introduced in Rennes in 1998 (see p. 87).

Pedestrianisation

In many European countries, people are encouraged to make more city-centre journeys on foot through the development of a network of pedestrianised streets, creating pleasant and safe routes for walkers. Residential areas are improved by redesigning traditional streets as "urban courtyards", with much reduced road traffic. This may be achieved through a number of measures:
- closing the road to through traffic
- giving right of way to pedestrians and introducing "dead slow" (10km/h) speed limits
- making the streets safe for children to play
- limiting parking.

In Delft, there have been such streets since the 1970s, with residents working with the appropriate local authority departments on their redesign. This has given rise to a more personal appropriation of communal space; neighbours tend the planted areas adjacent to their homes, and the urban space acquires a warmer, more community-based feel.

ENERGY MANAGEMENT

The building sector is one of the biggest energy consumers. Energy is consumed throughout the construction cycle:
- in fabrication and transport of materials
- during construction on site
- during the building's life, in heating, air-conditioning, hot water, lighting and power to appliances
- in demolition and removal of rubble.

Choices in European energy policy are discussed in the first part of this book, which sets out the issues involved in sustainable development. Passive and active measures designed to reduce fossil fuel consumption in construction are dealt with in more detail in the third section.

The potential for energy conservation

In urban planning, several factors can help reduce energy consumption:
- urban density (a compact housing block uses around 20 % less heating energy per home than does a terrace of five houses, and around 40 % less than a detached house);

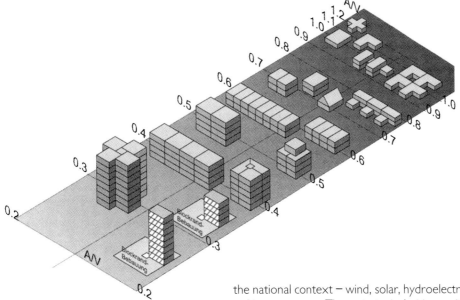

Comparison of the ratio of building envelope area to useable space, as a function of building shape. The lower the value, the more energy-efficient the building.
(Diagram by Solarbüro, Dr. Peter Goretzki, 1997)

- site design to make best use of passive solar gain: ensuring sufficient incident sunlight by limiting shadows from adjacent buildings, site topography and planting;
- optimum roof slopes and orientations to allow best use of solar collectors and photovoltaic panels;
- a rational energy supply strategy.

The computer programme Gosol, developed by Dr. Peter Goretzki as a tool to increase passive solar energy use in urban planning, allows all these factors to be modelled and optimised. The resulting total energy savings reach 5-15 % on average. Town and city authorities are in a position to set an example in this area, by applying these principles to all publicly-funded buildings. To encourage their spread to the private sector, local authorities may create incentives or indeed take more coercive measures:
- encouraging higher densities in new developments and existing residential areas (see p. 42);
- subsidising energy conservation measures in new and existing buildings (increased thermal insulation, low-emissivity double glazing, more efficient heating systems, solar water heaters, etc.);
- introducing regulations on optimising new building layouts for best use of active and passive solar gain, as in Burgholzhof, Stuttgart (see p. 67);
- contractually linking the sale of public land for development to construction of low-energy buildings, as in Freiburg im Breisgau (see pp. 69-75).

Local heating plants

Each European country has defined its own strategy, and introduced the accompanying legislation and financial backing, to encourage development of the renewable energy sources best suited to the national context – wind, solar, hydroelectric or biomass energy. These strategic decisions, with the corresponding implications for land use and development, must then be replicated at regional level.

Regional measures include the construction of urban heating plants which use domestic waste, such as those in Paris and Rennes. Berlin uses heat from gas co-generators, a highly efficient technology which produces little pollution. Plants are built on a small scale, such as for a refurbished city block or a new housing development, to avoid large energy losses in transit.

Historically, energy conservation measures have been largely restricted to housing. In recent years, some authorities have been exploring new energy management models for public and service buildings. In the environmentally-conscious town of Mäder in Austria, the heating plant is fed by wood from tree pruning, while community buildings are supplied with electricity from photovoltaic cells.

Sustainable housing projects

Cities in Europe are increasingly looking towards low-energy, environmental housing projects. Some combine subsidies for energy-saving measures in existing buildings with grants for low-energy housing, such as for the Low Energy House label. In an effort to change consumers' habits, authorities have also taken on the role of information provider and advisor, through exhibitions, pamphlets and presentations at public meetings and schools.

Recent years have seen a steep rise in solar energy housing, particularly in Germany and the Netherlands. These have generally had financial assistance at local level, often backed by regional, national and European funding. Sir Norman Foster and Thomas Herzog's solarCity, in Linz, con-

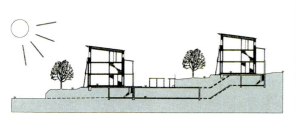

The Sonnenfeld "solar quarter"
in Ulm. Architects: Kottkamp
& Schneider, 1999.
Section and general view.

tains 1,500 homes; Ulm, in Germany, built 113 Passive House solar-powered homes in 1999, in fulfilment of its commitments to the Climate Alliance. As part of the Hanover Expo in 2000, the architects Kottkamp & Schneider designed a project consisting of 13 semi-detached and terraced timber-framed houses, laid out so as not to shade each other and hence to make best use of solar gain (see above).

ENVIRONMENTAL WATER MANAGEMENT

For a local authority, a sustainable water management policy must have several strands:
- protecting groundwater and surface water;
- reducing consumption of drinking water, a natural resource in increasingly short supply, and ensuring its quality;
- minimising the volume of wastewater to be treated, thus bringing down costs associated with water treatment, such as expansion of overloaded networks and construction of new sewage stations;
- environmentally-friendly water treatment processes;
- improving surface drainage (retaining permeable ground areas) in order to reduce risks of flooding;
- creating reservoirs within green spaces, thus improving air quality and the social environment.

Reducing flood risk

Increasingly frequent floods in Europe over recent years have demonstrated the disastrous consequences of the destruction of hedges and thickets, culverting of watercourses, lack of maintenance of riverbanks and the general spread of

concrete and tarmac that has led to an overall loss of soil permeability. Radical solutions are called for, both to protect human life and property and to reduce the waste which is responsible for so much environmental pollution.

The most basic flood prevention measure is prohibiting development on flood plains. There must also be a natural restructuring of river banks, replanting of trees and shrubs and a regeneration of the grid of hedges and banks which formerly retained much run-off water. This policy was adopted by Mäder in the 1970s, in an attempt to limit flooding from the Rhine (see p. 60).

In France some authorities, including Nancy and Bordeaux, have recently taken measures to collect and retain rainwater, reducing its impact on drainage systems. Along with the construction of collection tanks, areas such as car parks, stadia, courtyards and town squares may also function as temporary water retention areas in cases of heavy downpours and flooding. The Seine-Saint-Denis region has implemented a number of such schemes. In Angers, some floodwaters from the river Maine and its tributaries are retained by the Ile Saint-Aubin, a green area of 600 hectares. In the town centre, the 45-hectare Balzac Park was redesigned in the 1990s to act as a water meadow, with a system of avenues and canals planted with local species such as oak, ash, poplars and white willows, to hold flood-water and filter polluted urban run-off.

The water cycle

In Germany, environmental water management measures are set out by law and in local regulations:
- restriction of the use of drinking water to applica-

tions where this is necessary (federal and regional water legislation);
- local responsibility for rainwater management (federal and regional water legislation);
- construction of cisterns and measures to help rainwater drainage into the soil (local land use and development plans);
- rainwater collection (some local development plans).

Local authorities are able to lead the way by taking simple, low-cost steps to decrease water consumption in public buildings and social housing, as well as requiring new projects and refurbishments to include more economical installations.

Household water use in detached houses is around 50 % higher than in housing blocks. A considerable portion of this is due to garden watering, for which the use of drinking water is not absolutely necessary. The provision of rainwater cisterns in domestic gardens is a simple and economical measure which has the added benefit of heightening householders' awareness of their responsibility. Many local authorities in Germany have been promoting this strategy since the late 1980s, providing collection tanks at subsidised prices. A similar campaign was launched in Rennes in 2000.

Rainwater collection

In Germany, rainwater collection and re-use is widespread in housing, public buildings and even in the service and industrial sectors. Unlike France, it generally does not require specific authorisation. Collection is particularly economical when the water is used for year-round applications such as toilet flushing, washing machines, cleaning and production processes. A number of large businesses have installed collectors, partly to improve their "green" image but mainly to reduce drinking water consumption, which is becoming increasingly expensive (see p. 105).

A particularly good example is the *Urbane Gewässer* (urban waters) area around the DaimlerChrysler building on Berlin's Potsdamer Platz (see on the right). Combining environmental with aesthetic concerns, a network of streams and ponds forms a 12,050m² area of calm and relaxation within this otherwise dense, busy business quarter. This not only brings character to the area but also gives it a healthier and more pleasant microclimate, particularly in summer. Rainwater is dealt with in different ways: 17,000m² of

The DaimlerChrysler building on Potsdamer Platz, Berlin. Architect: Renzo Piano. Site plan showing extent of the rainwater recovery system. Designer: Atelier Dreiseitl with Hans-Otto Wack. Left, detail of one of the pools.

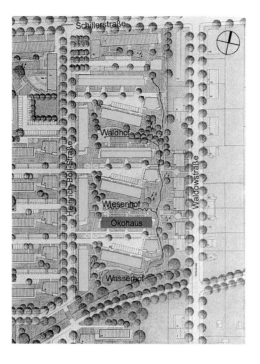

The Heinrich-Böll development, Pankow, Berlin 1999.
Architects : W. Brenne and J. Eble.

roof space (out of a total of 50,000m²) is planted, while water which is not retained by the planting is stored in cisterns with total capacity of 2,600m³. The 7,700m³ collected each year is then used for toilet flushing, plant irrigation and to feed the external pools.

The water is kept clean by bio-mechanical purification, with more high-tech equipment used only when necessary, such as during the critical summer period.

Maintaining soil permeability

Within towns and cities, management of the water cycle needs an adequate balance between impermeable surfaces, such as tarmac and concrete, and permeable areas such as grass – grey space versus green space. Recent natural disasters show how this balance has been lost in some places. To regain it, a number of proven measures can be implemented quickly and easily :

- providing grants for converting flat roofs to green roofs;
- the choice of permeable surfaces for car parks (stabilised turf, or grass and perforated paving slabs);
- promoting the creation of grassed areas in courtyard spaces.

In cities, where there are very large areas of hard surface, measures must be taken to aid rainwater evaporation and natural infiltration into the underlying ground. This should be done within each building plot, to reduce pressure on drainage systems, regulate water flows and limit the volume of waste water to be treated. In gardens and green spaces, an economical and effective solution is to divert surface water to drainage trenches, grassy ditches or small planted pools. This both allows the water to soak gradually into the soil, helping restore the water table to natural levels, and aids evaporation, which increases air humidity and improves the microclimate.

In Germany, several Länder have introduced laws requiring landowners to dispose of rainwater within their own boundaries; connection of rainwater pipes into the mains drainage system requires special authorisation. Many local authorities have subsequently attempted to do away with their rainwater drainage systems altogether, thus generating considerable cost savings. Soakaway systems enabling drainage directly into the ground, often via a pond or biotope area, are common at public service buildings and in new developments in the regions of Hesse, North Rhine-Westphalia and Baden-Württemberg. In Berlin, examples include the 1999 Heinrich-Böll development (see *illustration, left*), an experimental social housing project of 216 apartments which allies economy with environmental quality. This project is in the Pankow residential district in former East Berlin, and was built by the non-profit-making housing organisation GSW (*Gemein-nützige Siedlungs- und Wohnungsbaugesellschaft*). It uses bioclimatic principles, non-hazardous materials, energy conservation measures and a large area of photovoltaic panels; there is also a system whereby rainwater is collected and used in the landscaped areas. In each of three landscaped courtyards, water runs through cobbled channels and permeable plant-filled trenches. The rainwater tank is topped by a fountain, powered by electricity from photovoltaic cells; the movement of the water animates the space, inspiring children's games.

Green roofs

Towns and cities the world over are dominated by stone, concrete and tarmac. Tall buildings obstruct natural air movements, preventing wind from efficiently renewing the air at street level. This results in the typical city microclimate of high temperatures, low humidity and high levels of pollution.

This phenomenon can be partly countered by introducing large areas of turfed or planted roof. Evaporation of retained water from plants and soil increases the humidity of the air, cooling it and helping lay airborne dust. Such green roofs also provide thermal insulation to the building, helping reduce energy consumption and hence greenhouse gas emissions. In case of heavy rain, they retain and gradually release water which would otherwise run straight into drainage systems. Thus the overloading of these systems which has resulted from the loss in overall permeability, leading to sudden rises in watercourse levels and risks of flooding, is reduced.

In Germany, there is a local tax on drainage from impermeable surfaces into the mains system, providing a clear incentive to install green roofs or soakaways.

Many towns have established the principle that removal of potential green area at ground level should be offset by planting the equivalent area at roof level. In some areas this is compulsory and incorporated into the local development plan. Various local authorities give grants for roof greening:
- Darmstadt allows up to DM20,000 (€10,226);
- Stuttgart and Bremen, up to 50 % of total cost or DM35/m^2 (€17.90/m^2);
- Backnang and Duisburg up to 50 % of cost or DM50/m^2 (€25.56/m^2).

Others reduce the tax on impermeable surfaces when a green roof is introduced: Freiburg im Breisgau, Aix-la-Chapelle, Paderborn and Giessen reduce the tax by around 50 %, while in Hildesheim it is reduced to zero.

Green roofs, Berlin.

Similar measures have been introduced by city authorities in some other industrialised countries, notably Italy and Japan.

The Max Schmeling hall development in Berlin, with a roof area of 25,000m^2, was only granted planning permission on condition that rainwater was drained within the project boundaries. Such conditions are imposed increasingly frequently when ground conditions allow.

GREEN SPACES

As urban authorities seek to maintain quality of life in the towns and cities, they have become increasingly aware of the value of green spaces within urban areas. Preservation of open spaces, protection of plant life, biodiversity and regeneration of river banks all involve social and cultural issues. Correct environmental management of urban green spaces requires close, creative co-operation between urban planners, architects, landscape architects and engineers.

The regulating effect of green space

In surroundings where pollution and noise assault the senses, green space, while not in itself solving the problems, can have a considerable normalising effect. Green areas improve the urban environment in several ways:
- trees, through transpiration, increase air water content in the often dry city environment;
- the mass of vegetation can bring down temperature, by as much as 1-4°C during hot periods;
- photosynthesis stores carbon and releases oxygen;
- foliage traps dust and fixes toxic gases, reducing air pollution (one hectare of woodland absorbs around 50 t of dust per year).

Vegetation helps regulate and regenerate the natural water balance. It increases the ability of the ground to absorb water, and helps maintain groundwater levels as some of the water retained by plants finds its way into the soil. This water is thus naturally filtered before reaching the water table.

Green spaces also help combat noise, as vegetation absorbs sound, though the effectiveness of this depends on the density and type of planting. Other advantages include:
- positive effects on the physical and psychological well-being of inhabitants;

- provision of social and leisure space, particularly for young people;
- economic opportunities such as market-gardening, city farms and forestry-related activities;
- preservation of the natural environment, wildlife and plant conservation, and combating erosion.

Preservation of ecosystems

A town's identity is structured by the relationship between the natural and built environments. An objective measure, such as green area per inhabitant, is not meaningful without consideration of the disposal of green areas within the city – their relationship to the buildings around them, and their function (public parks, dedicated leisure areas, private gardens, allotments, woodlands, etc). The density, characteristics and species of planting is also important. To maintain or restore ecological equilibrium within a city it is desirable to plant a variety of trees and plants, based on native local species. In Germany, city authorities have taken this approach for some time; residents are encouraged by low prices to buy traditionally local tree species which would otherwise be disappearing.

In many European cities, such as Berlin and Nuremberg, destruction of green areas has led to a decrease in biodiversity. In Germany, it is estimated that one species of animal and one species of plant disappears every year. In its turn, the loss of one species threatens 10 to 20 others which depended on it in different ways. Thus it is imperative to protect these endangered species. In Stockholm, conscious of the ecological role played by "virgin forest", the authorities have created an "ecopark", an area of natural, undisturbed woodland at the edge of the city. In both public parks and private gardens, lawns are increasingly being replaced by meadow areas, containing a wide variety of wild flowers and grasses; these attract insects, creating their own, small-scale ecosystems.

Landscaping projects

Urban green spaces have many functions, depending on their size, treatment and position within the city. As one moves away from the city centre and towards its rural surroundings, the provision of open space for walking and other outdoor leisure activities becomes more important, and many areas have been designed specifi-

Green space in central Copenhagen.

A park in central Helsinki.

Landscaping at La Rocade,
Sablé-sur-Sarthe. Landscape
designer: Dominique Caire.

Courtyard planting in Ruoholahti,
Helsinki.

cally with this in mind. To ensure optimal use of existing and potential space, cities should have a "green plan", setting out present and future needs and strategies and allowing opportunities to be taken up as they arise. The first step is a detailed analysis of the current situation – climate, topography, soil conditions, human and natural environment, flora and fauna – and a definition of needs, drawn up in conjunction with residents.

At Sablé-sur-Sarthe in France (see *illustration above*), an area of five-storey housing blocks, built in the 1960s and neglected since, was renovated in the early 1990s through creation of a "green grid". The 550 existing apartments were refurbished, and new housing blocks, along with public amenities, built close by to increase density. There was also a complete remodelling and landscaping of the previously undefined public space around and between the buildings. Car parks were landscaped, an urban park of 1.5 hectares created, pedestrian routes signposted, and a planted and landscaped framework created so as to confer on each group of blocks an individual identity. Such

"residentialisation" of 1960s and 1970s housing projects, led by social landlords in partnership with city authorities and in co-operation with residents, is a useful tool for redefining the public or private nature of external spaces.

Courtyard greening

The question of treatment of internal squares and courtyard areas arises regularly in urban renovation projects. Various attempts in France have so far failed to match, in either effectiveness or scope, what has been achieved in other countries over the past 30 years in terms of reconverting grey to green space, with the aim of improving the microclimate in built-up areas.

In Copenhagen in the 1970s, a city council resolution concerning refurbishment of old housing stock and renovation of recreational areas led to the systematic remodelling of internal courtyards in the city's inner ring. As a result, around one hectare of gardens, each 800-1,000m^2 in area, were created each year in some of the most densely-built parts of the city. Design and management of the projects was undertaken free of

Courtyard greening in Block 89,
Schöneberg, Berlin.

charge by the local authority, with construction costs paid by the city and repaid over ten years by the building owners.

For 20 years or so, many German cities, among them Berlin, Stuttgart and Tübingen, have had policies of creating landscaped areas within city blocks, in co-operation with inhabitants, in their older districts. The renovation of block 89 in Schöneberg (see p. 55) in Berlin, begun in 1986, combined energy and water conservation measures, waste management and non-hazardous materials policies with creation of green roofs and courtyards. In Munich, the organisation *Urbanes Wohnen* ("urban living") persuaded the authorities to provide 50 % funding for a large-scale courtyard greening project. The resulting landscaped communal spaces often integrate such amenities as children's play equipment, bicycle racks and arrays of recycling bins. Such community projects, led by local administrators but bringing together some hundreds of households, can have real positive social impact. A total of 65 hectares of courtyard space has now been converted to green space in Munich, at a cost 50 times less than the cost of creating a new public park of this size.

Roof gardens

Urban infrastructure projects can also create opportunities for landscaping, providing both green spaces and rainwater collection systems. The Hector-Malot project in Paris (see *illustration p. 57*) is linked with the development of the Viaduc des Arts, a former railway line linking the Bastille city district with the Bois de Vincennes park, which has been converted into a landscaped walk. The project has created a 442-place, seven-level car park, surmounted by a 2,300m² garden. These "hanging gardens" consist of an upper, brick-paved square, planted with maples, and a lower terrace criss-crossed by stone pathways lined with scented, flowering plants and shrubs. Benches and fountains are integrated skilfully into the composition, and wistaria-covered pergolas lead towards the adjacent residential areas. Rainwater is collected in channels for irrigation. The maples are planted in 2m of soil, ventilated by means of perforated blocks integrated into the paving arrangement. The indirect heating of the garden slab by air from the car park below, combined with water evaporation from the channels, creates a warm, humid microclimate which

encourages plant growth – particularly that of the stands of bamboo, which are a refuge for birds.

CONTROLLING WASTE

The treatment and disposal of waste is an issue of increasing international concern. Reduction in waste volumes is one of the Kyoto targets, while recycling is one of the four priority aims of the EU's 6th Environmental Action Programme (for the period 2001-2010).

Household waste

Waste disposal is set to be a major problem for urban authorities over the coming years. The rising cost of treatment and disposal is likely to increase further in 2002, with the closure of traditional landfill sites and their replacement by more specialised depots taking only non-recyclable, stabilised waste. Faced with this change, along with increasingly draconian regulations, authorities are seeking effective methods of environmentally acceptable disposal, both for household rubbish and the even greater volumes of construction and demolition site waste (see p. 117). To prevent volumes and costs spiralling out of control, they are looking towards recycling, sorting and energy extraction.

Waste sorting

Household waste sorting was introduced in Germany in the early 1980s and is now becoming commonplace throughout Europe. It has three main aims:
- separation of toxic or dangerous waste such as medicines, batteries, items containing chemicals, heavy metals or asbestos;
- recycling of glass, metals, paper, plastic and other reusable materials;
- removal of biodegradable elements, thus reducing final waste volumes.

Sorting of non-recyclable waste allows each type to be treated in a suitable way without generating pollution. The EU aims for 30 % of household waste to be recycled after sorting, and 20 % to be utilised through biological treatment.

For waste sorting to be successful it requires the active co-operation of the population, the necessary facilities at home and in the workplace, and an adequate collection infrastructure. Provision of different bins takes up more space; in some Euro-

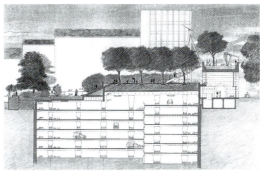

The Hector-Malot public gardens and car park, Paris 1996.
Landscaping and urban design: Christo-Foroux.
General view and section.

pean towns, households are already routinely equipped with separate bins for compostable waste, paper, packaging and non-recyclable items. There must also be a recycling industry able to cope with the volume collected, and a big enough market for the products obtained (such as recycled paper).

SOCIAL ASPECTS

Improving quality of life in cities also involves reducing social exclusion, and ensuring an equilibrium between different sections of the population living side by side. To succeed, this requires the combined efforts and genuine co-operation of politicians, professionals, technical services and local groups.

Health and comfort benefits

Quality of life may be enhanced through:
- good architectural design, which responds to the needs and wishes of users, and through the use of non-hazardous and natural materials which create a better sensory environment;
- good urban design, which allows the creation of green spaces and the reduction of noise, air pollution and other adverse factors.

Another factor is natural light. A number of studies have shown that exposure to natural light has a highly positive impact on human health and well-being, being linked to reduced rates of illness and better performance at school and at work.

Only 25 % of the light we receive is necessary for us to see by. Our bodies use the rest to regulate metabolic and hormonal balance. The seasonal depression which is prevalent in northern countries, where there is little sunlight in winter, is often treated by light therapy using special lamps whose spectrum corresponds to that of sunlight. Thus besides the economic and environmental advantages associated with better energy efficiency, taking into account incident sunlight in building design through layout and orientation can have significant positive effects on public health.

The urban and social mix

The crime and social problems seen in many urban areas, particularly the inner-city suburbs and housing estates, have shown the importance of maintaining an urban and social mix:
- mixed usage, with housing, business and commercial premises and public amenities in the same area;

**The Les Brandons quarter,
Blainville-sur-Orne, remodelled
as a garden city.
Architect: Jean-Yves Barrier.
Site plan and view of façades.**

- and social heterogeneity, combining the low-rent, social and private housing sectors.

Provision of the necessary housing without creating social ghettos calls for strategic property planning, with co-operation between city authorities, developers and architects, as in Rennes (see p. 41). The redevelopment of Les Brandons in Blainville-sur-Orne (see above), near Caen in France, provides an example. The architect Jean-Yves Barrier and the developer André Mabille, of the La Plaine property company, have transformed this formerly working-class quarter, following its original layout, into a contemporary garden city. Each of the district's three areas now consists of small, low-rise housing blocks, along with urban villas set within a park and town houses with terraces and gardens. This diverse housing provision encourages social mixity within a dense urban environment.

User participation

The implementation of a sustainable urban plan requires partnership between local groups, and the involvement of the local population at drafting stage. Residents' respect for their environment and amenities depends on their awareness and sense of ownership; there will be no such sense of civic responsibility if people are not consulted before decisions affecting their environment are made. In France, the existence of so-called *Maisons de quartier*, or local social centres, facilitates local involvement in the preservation or regeneration of their surroundings. Nonetheless, participation of residents in urban design can be a long and arduous process; it must be approached in gradual stages, with the possibility of backtracking if mistakes are made. However it is vital if sustainable urban development is to succeed. A number of urban environmental projects failed in the 1980s through not taking account of residents' priorities and behaviour; users were not sufficiently prepared for, or interested in, ideas of an environmentally responsible lifestyle.

Such projects succeed most easily in areas where there is already active participation in local democracy. One of the best examples is the creation of a new residential complex on the site of the former Vauban barracks in Freiburg im Breisgau (see p. 70). A local residents' committee, the Vauban

Forum, was formed and drew up both a community framework plan and an architectural and urban design concept. The existence of this body has encouraged community life and a sustainable social project for the area. There have been similar developments in Berlin, where the organisation Stadtforum led a number of projects during the 1980s and 1990s.

Local authorities as educators

Within a city, different local groups often have conflicting interests. Politicians, promoters, architects, finance organisations, local businesses and associations and the general public all bring their own logic and priorities to the issues — priorities which may not be consistent with sustainable development.

All these players must be brought together and encouraged to adopt changes in behaviour, such as waste sorting, rainwater recycling or more use of public transport, with a view to protecting the environment and ecosystems around us. In this, local authorities have a key role to play. For public, professionals and politicians to bring their active co-operation to a project, they must be educated and informed.

In France, the first national "Environmental Education" consultation sessions were held in Lille in 2000. These established a number of objectives:
- to bring environmental education into the social and political debate;
- to draw up education programmes at each regional level;
- to increase awareness of environmental issues for all age groups in the population as a whole;
- to widen and communicate useful expertise in the domain of environmental education;
- to establish, support and train bodies of individuals able to carry out such education;
- to facilitate putting environmental projects into action.

Some European towns are already putting these policies into practice. Mäder, in Austria, began in 1994 a project for an eco-school, aimed at raising awareness amongst young people. In Angers, France, whose council has pioneered noise abatement and waste sorting measures, the *Maison de l'Environnement* (environment centre) beside the Lac du Maine runs courses and workshops. Activities are designed for different sections of the population, including professionals, company employees, teachers and schoolchildren, who can conduct experiments in the centre's organic garden.

UTOPIA INTO REALITY

For the European Union, sustainable development is the main theme of international change. Future development of towns and cities must be conform to environmental, socially uniting principles, striking a sustainable balance between economic, social, environmental and cultural issues. This will be one of the major challenges which authorities will face in the decades to come.

However, these new challenges hold the key to the future. Environmental development opens up new perspectives, with significant potential for innovation, and brings a dynamism to individual and collective initiatives. A cleaner city, with well-designed buildings and public spaces set within well-maintained green space, is a competitive city, which will attract top-quality businesses and a renewed, revitalised population.

Protection of the environment is an element of citizenship. It can bring together individual and community initiatives, giving a sense of common purpose to the men and women who, together, make up the city. More and more towns in Europe are demonstrating their willingness to act and their ability to innovate. With wider dissemination of the information gained from their experiences, and direct co-operation between different authorities, sustainable development can become a daily reality throughout the European Union, before spreading to the Eastern European countries and the developing world beyond.

A rural town sets the standard

Location:
Vorarlberg, Austria.
Geographical context:
on the banks of the Rhine;
altitude 414 m.
Demographics:
population 786 in 1951,
3,150 in 2000.
Economic context:
40 local businesses, 800 jobs.
Sustainable development measures:
landscape regeneration programmes; environmental "eco-school"; biomass heating plant; photovoltaic electricity supply to public buildings.

Mäder is a small, fast-growing town in Vorarlberg, a melting-pot of contemporary architecture where sustainable development is put into practice at every scale. Thanks to a number of bold decisions taken some decades ago, it is now a model environmental community.

Mäder – a sustainable town

Mäder is located in the south of the economically and culturally flourishing region of Vorarlberg (*see p. 20*), where towns and villages are crowded together in a narrow plain between Lake Constance and the Bregenz forest. The expansion in recent decades of Bregenz and its satellite towns explains the similar rapid growth of Mäder. Its population has quadrupled over the past 50 years, creating a need for major public works to accommodate this expansion.

In 1991, the environmentally-aware town council decided to make Mäder a model "green" community. In 1993 it joined the Climate Alliance, an international association of local authorities working to combat increases in the greenhouse effect and contribute to global sustainable development. Alliance members aim to reduce CO_2 emissions to 50 % of 1988 levels by 2010. In 1995, Mäder was the first town in Vorarlberg to draw up its own Agenda 21. Since 1999 it has also been involved in the Energy-Efficient Towns programme set up by the Vorarlberg Energy Institute.

Protection of the landscape; the water cycle

Mäder is on the banks of the Rhine, and this proximity to Europe's "greatest river" has been a major factor influencing the town's development and the environmental measures it has put in place. Between 1700 and 1900, the Rhine burst its banks 33 times. After the first international regulation agreement in 1892, land which had previously been liable to frequent flooding became cultivable. This resulted in the early part of the 20th century in the felling of large numbers of trees and removal of banks and hedges. This change in the landscape destroyed its distinctive character, upset the region's ecological balance and had a negative effect on both climate and soil conditions. In the absence of natural windbreaks, storms regularly caused damage to buildings.

Plan of the town showing regeneration of the landscape.

1974-84

1984-94

In response to these problems, in 1973 Vorarlberg passed new regional laws on landscape protection, calling on local authorities in the region to come up with solutions. In 1974 Mäder was the first to respond, with a long-term regeneration programme involving the planting of 80,000 trees and shrubs.

Ten years later, this programme was 75 % complete. The re-planted trees and network of hedges reduce wind speeds and climatic extremes through a number of beneficial effects:
- a wind-break effect
- reduction in soil erosion by the wind, and in surface drying, thus enhancing soil quality
- provision of wildlife habitats, helping protect biodiversity
- reduced rainwater and stormwater run-off.

Hedges and banks also reduce flood risk by retaining a proportion of rainwater; part of this soaks into the soil and the rest is released only gradually as surface water, helping to regulate river flows. The planting programmes undertaken in the 1970s and 80s have also had economic benefits. Hedge trimming and tree lopping produces a plentiful and renewable supply of timber for use in the biomass heating plant, which was opened in 1994 to supply public buildings and services as part of efforts to cut CO_2 emissions. Around 700m^3 is incinerated each year, thus allowing a complete natural cycle to take place within a small geographical area.

An architectural culture

Vorarlberg is without doubt one of the areas of Europe where architecture has the highest public profile, due partly to the existence and expertise of the *Vorarlberger Baukünstler* group. It was therefore not surprising that Mäder's town council commissioned the internationally-known Austrian practice Baumschlager & Eberle to design three public buildings in the new town centre: the community hall, the school and sports complex. The community hall, completed in 1995, uses contrasting shapes, colours and materials. The entrance foyer, cloakrooms and a meeting room are grouped within a white, plastered cube. Beside it, the hall itself, a contemporary Noah's Ark in brilliant red, seats up to 470 people. Other public buildings are of similarly striking architectural quality. The steel and glass sports hall, partly sunk into the ground, extends in long horizontal lines. The

Aerial view of the new centre of Mäder, including kindergarten, library, school and sports complex, community offices and community hall.

The green roof of the kindergarten building.

**90m² of photovoltaic modules
are installed on the roof of the sports
complex.**

**Right, earth cooling tubes
are buried beneath the courtyard
of the eco-school.**

glazed band around the upper section maintains contact with the outside environment, gives passers-by a view of the activities within and also provides natural lighting, thus reducing energy consumption. Close by, the soft, curving lines of the building housing the kindergarten, nursery and library vanish into green, its green roofs arranged around a huge weeping willow tree. The eco-school *(see pp. 190-195)* is the culmination of a long-term environmental approach to public architecture.

Ecology and education

Taking the view that lasting changes in attitude will only come via the coming generations, the town decided to establish Austria's only eco-school. The school building is built on sustainable principles, and ecology and environment is a compulsory subject. Its project-based teaching aims to raise awareness of the natural environment through field work, in the many nearby traditional orchards, at the protected Sandgrube site, in the wetlands biotope area at the Brühl leisure centre and along the banks of the Rhine. The aim is to develop young people's awareness and responsibility towards their natural environment, and encourage individual initiatives. As well as courses in applied ecology, the school integrates basic sustainable development principles throughout the syllabus.

Refurbishment and energy conservation

Energy saving measures have also been applied to existing building stock. The community offices, built in 1952 as a primary school, were refurbished in 1996 along sustainable lines. A reduction in annual energy consumption from $236kWh/m^2$ to $83kWh/m^2$, or more than 60 %, was achieved through a combination of measures:
- installation of a computer-controlled heating system
- high-performance windows ($U = 1.1W/m^2K$)
- a ventilated cladding system with external insulation (140mm of mineral wool).
The resulting savings are equivalent to the net heating costs of the other public buildings. With the introduction of the biomass heating plant, annual CO_2 emissions fell from 43 tonnes to less than 2 tonnes.

Use of solar energy

To set an example, the town council opted for solar power. The roof of the school incorporates $28m^2$ of solar collectors, providing 50 % of hot water requirements; the $90m^2$ of photovoltaic modules installed in 1998 on the flat roof of the sports complex have a capacity of 10kW and annual production of 10,000kWh. Surplus electricity is sold to the municipal network, the revenues obtained being invested with the aim of doubling the area of panels in the long term. The existing PV installation was financed by the issue of 1,000 "solar cheques" each to the value of €72; this was highly successful, with sponsors including local businesses and individuals as well as larger bodies such as Liechtenstein's Propter Homines foundation. On 24 June of each year, holders of these cheques are invited to a festival. Thus while at the cutting edge of environmental innovation, Mäder strives to retain the community spirit of the country town which it has always been, and hopes to remain.

STUTTGART, GERMANY

Pragmatism for the long term

A major centre for the European automobile industry, Stuttgart is also a green city, by virtue of its high proportion of undeveloped land and the political influence of the Green party. For over 20 years the city authority's decisions on urbanism and architecture have been taken in the context of long-term sustainable development, and the city has seen a number of environmental initiatives.

Historical context

Stuttgart grew up a short distance from the river Neckar, in a narrow valley formed by one of its tributaries. The resulting distinctive topography of the city, with a variation in altitude of more than 300m, has been a determining factor in its development. During the 19th century it grew rapidly with the rise of the mechanical, automobile and electrical industries; its population rose from 21,000 in 1801 to around 175,000 by 1900. Constrained by the valley, whose eastern slopes were too steep to build on, the city expanded northward towards the Neckar and over the gentler slopes to the west. During World War II, Stuttgart's status as an industrial

centre made it a target for allied bombing; around 60 % of buildings were damaged or destroyed, and none of the city's historic buildings escaped unscathed.

The 1945 bombing destroyed 90 % of the city centre. After this Stuttgart took on a new aspect, influenced by the growing importance of road transport. The basic street plan remained, but with wider and straighter streets, and a number of historic buildings were sacrificed in the interests of traffic flow. The two main roads from the surrounding region were re-routed to pass through the city; more than 30m wide and linked by four transverse roads, these run the length of the central area, cutting it off from the rest of the

Location:
Baden-Württemberg, Germany.
Geographical context:
in the Neckar valley, at the northern edge of the Swabian Jura.
Area:
20,733 hectares, of which 44 % is occupied by buildings and roads, 17 % gardens, 15 % agricultural or vineyards, 24 % forest.
Demographics:
population 505,000 in 1950, 640,000 in 1962, 580,000 in 2000.
Economic context:
industrial and university city and international business centre.
Sustainable development measures:
compulsory roof greening; 25 % additional insulation requirement for public buildings; use of wood and non-hazardous materials in schools and sports buildings; experimental district built for the IGA gardens exhibition in 1993; pilot development on former military land at Burgholzhof; passive housing development at Feuerbach; subsidies for energy-saving measures in new and existing buildings.

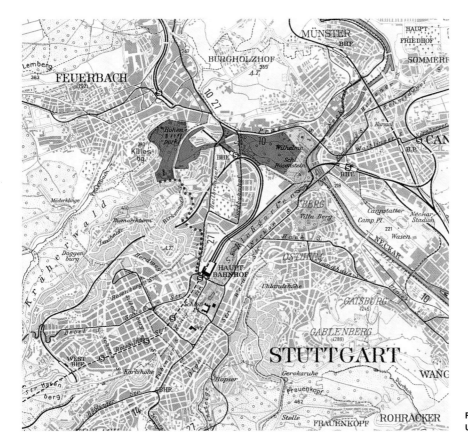

Plan of the city, showing the green U created for the 1993 IGA expo.

Right, terraced housing
with photovoltaic modules built
for the IGA 93.
Architect: Thomas Herzog.

Above, collective housing built
for the IGA 93.

city. While most southern German cities, such as Munich or Nuremberg, chose to rebuild their historic centres as they had been, the Stuttgart authorities looked instead to the principles of the 1933 Athens Charter. This applied a number of the ideals of the Modern movement, such as single-function zoning. Thus commerce and services, government and administrative buildings were concentrated in the city centre. A mixed zone outside this was surrounded in its turn by dormitory suburbs and industrial areas built up around the road network. A lack of housing resulting from steep population growth, from 505,000 in 1950 to 640,000 in 1962, led to new towns being created on greenfield sites outside the city.

The return to mixed use

During the 1960s, quality of life in central Stuttgart declined steadily, with a lack of green space and increasing air pollution and noise. The expressways effectively closed off the centre, destroying the urban structure. More and more people moved out of the city, leaving social and functional problems; the city centre was overcrowded during the working day and deserted each evening. This soon led to a re-examination of the ideas of the separation of living and working zones. In an attempt to attract residents back to the centre, the city authorities began a programme of major projects to regenerate the urban fabric:
- the creation, around the Königstrasse, of one of Europe's first pedestrianised urban areas

- a pilot project to revitalise the inner-city Bohnen-Viertel district, through regeneration of its traditional fabric of housing, workshops and small businesses.

A green awakening

Stuttgart is at the centre of one of Europe's most successful industrial regions. Its economic boom depends both on the industries established in the region a century ago, such as DaimlerChrysler and Bosch, and on the presence of international groups such as Kodak, Sony, Hewlett-Packard and IBM. The dominance of the car industry, and the city's topographical situation at the bottom of a valley, with the resulting high levels of air pollution, have both perhaps made environmental protection a particular concern for its inhabitants. For whatever reason, Baden-Württemberg in 1978 became the first of the German Länder to return Green members to its parliament. Since then the Greens have had a continuous and undeniable influence on policies at local and regional level. In the 1980s, for example, Stuttgart was one of the first authorities to make flat roof greening compulsory (see p. 106), and to introduce sorting of household waste.

A green city

With only 44 % of its total area built on, Stuttgart is one of Germany's greenest cities. There are numerous parks, and the city is surrounded by extensive woodland which is open for public recreational use. Over the past 50 years, five garden exhibitions have contributed to an increase in the number and quality of green areas. The most recent IGA expo, in 1993, enabled the city to create its "green U", an 8km uninterrupted green strip, 200 hectares in area, which begins in Schlossplatz at the heart of the old city and passes through the castle gardens, the Rosenstein, Leibfried and Wartberg parks and the exhibition area at Killesberg before reaching the forest at the city's edge. Several public projects have been built with regional and national funding, including footbridges over main roads and railways, a number of further green areas, and the compost unit at Löwentor, which takes organic waste from the nearby Wilhelma botanical gardens and zoo.

As part of the 1993 expo, 13 experimental "green" projects were set up through partnerships between the city and private developers, on the theme of "appropriate and responsible use of the natural world within the city". As part of the Housing 2000 programme, 19 semi-detached houses and seven housing blocks, containing 100 rental apartments, aimed to provide innovative solutions to the problems of pollution, noise and other urban nuisances. Most of the competition winners were pioneers in the field of environmental architecture: the German practices of Thomas Herzog and Dieter Schempp, the French partnership Jourda & Perraudin, the Austrians Szyszkowitz + Kowalski, and the Danish Vandkunsten practice. Thomas Herzog's terraced housing was one of the first projects to use photovoltaic modules.

Sustainability in public buildings

Since the early 1980s, around 30 educational buildings and sports centres have been built in Stuttgart. Thus there have been various opportunities for architects to develop ideas of what form such public buildings should take, when designed along generally "green" lines and with economy and durability in mind. The use of natural materials such as wood, brick or linoleum, and of paints without hazardous solvents, have been standard practice in Stuttgart for some time – particularly for children's buildings, such as the kindergarten in Heumaden (*see pp. 172-177*).

All these buildings have large areas of façade glazing. The sober elegance of the structure and architectural volumes is a result both of co-operation between the different parties involved, and of

precise detailing. External treatment and landscaping is meticulously executed; rainwater collected from roof surfaces is usually channelled to a biotope area. This urban architecture combines space, light and planting, making best use of materials and taking a rational attitude to structure and space. Based on humanist principles, it is not revolutionary, rather user-friendly and ecologically efficient.

The use of timber

Almost all these buildings make extensive use of wood, whose warmth and pleasant sensory aspects make it an ideal material for use in schools. Most use it for both external cladding and internal fittings. Structurally, timber is used in various ways: columns and beams in the kindergartens in Heslach (Peter Hübner, 1994) and Luginsland (Behnisch & Partner, 1990) and the Stammheim primary school (Peter Hübner, 1989); nailed laminated panels at the Heumaden kindergarten (Joachim Eble, 1998); timber and steel bowstring trusses in the Wolfbusch sports hall in Weilimdorf (Baisch & Frank, 1998). A number of sports centre buildings which combine timber and steel in their structures, such as those at Botnang (1993) and Hausen (1998), were designed by the city's own buildings departments. The monopitch roof of the French-German school sports hall (BauWerkStadt, 1999) is supported by portal frames in glulam timber. As well as the sports hall, this roof covers a cube in

Kindergarten in Stuttgart-Heslach, 1994. Architect: Peter Hübner. Perspective view.

Above, sports hall,
Stuttgart-Botnang, 1993.
Architect: Hans Repper;
Stuttgart city works department.

Right, museum of agriculture,
Stuttgart-Hohenheim, 1996.
Architect: Friedrich Wagner.

unfaced concrete containing changing rooms, lavatories and storage. The roof and gables are clad in patinated copper, which requires no maintenance. The forest and woodlands centre (see p. 93), the agriculture museum buildings at Hohenheim, and even a tram stop (in one of the city's wooded areas, see p. 67) also make use of timber. The mayor, Wolfgang Schuster, feels the choice of such a natural, renewable material is an obvious one for both environmental and economic reasons: it carries no health risks, minimises CO_2 emissions, allows extensive prefabrication, enabling shorter construction times, and can produce technically satisfactory solutions at low cost.

Energy management in public buildings

Since the 1980s, Stuttgart has taken an environmental approach to both materials and energy. The results are convincing, both in terms of cost reduction and CO_2 emissions. Experience showed that significant savings could be made through improving internal organisation and by applying clear specifications in practice. Every building is considered as a whole in order to optimise its construction, use and maintenance, in terms of both sustainability and cost. In 1997, new city regulations were introduced requiring all public buildings (among others) to have 25 % more insulation than demanded by existing national codes of practice (see p. 98), themselves considered among the most stringent in Europe. The capital cost of this measure was offset by a fall in annual heating energy consumption estimated at 30 %.

Energy conservation measures for housing

Stuttgart has been able to implement energy conservation measures by virtue of its property policies. When publicly-owned land is sold for housing, the contract demands that the buildings erected conform to Low Energy rating requirements. The Feuerbach district in 2000 saw the completion of what was then the largest development of Passive House rated housing. The 52 terraced houses use 80 % less primary energy for heating than the figure set by the thermal performance regulations. They have well-insulated and airtight envelopes, make use of solar gain through bioclimatic measures and high-performance glazing, and use two-way ventilation systems which recover heat from used air via a heat exchanger. These houses were sold at advantageous prices to young, low-income families.

Energy-saving measures have also been applied to existing housing stock, in both the public and private sector.

Home-owners or tenants installing such measures as high-performance glazing, increased insulation, solar panels or heat pumps can apply for grants from the city of 15-30 % of the cost. Grants are around DM5,200 (€2,660) on average, but can be up to DM12,000. As part of the EU programme *Save II*, the city has also set up an energy advice centre which provides guidance to private developers on updating their buildings. This centre (the Stuttgart *Energieberatungszentrum*) is "twinned" with the local energy management agency in Montreuil, France.

The *Stuttgarter Modell*

Many local authorities have been prevented from implementing sustainable development measures, which would clearly be beneficial, by lack of finance. This is exacerbated by the way in which budgets are allocated to distinct departments, and the separation between capital spending and operating budgets. Energy-saving measures incur capital costs, which must be paid for by a specified department, but their benefit is felt through reductions in operating costs. One solution which is increasingly adopted is contracting out, whereby such projects are funded up-front, often by a private contractor.

Stuttgart opted instead for its own solution, known as the *Stuttgarter Modell*. Projects are paid for by the city's department of energy and the environment. As the resulting savings feed through in the form of reduced running costs, sums equivalent to these savings are repaid to the energy department, until the total capital cost has been refunded – a sort of interest-free loan to the municipal department concerned. This allows the funding of both large-scale projects and small renovation work. The system has been in place since 1995, and has proved to be very effective.

The Burgholzhof district

Burgholzhof is a new development zone in north-eastern Stuttgart, on the site of the Robinson Barracks, a former US army site which became vacant with German reunification. The new 10.5-hectare residential district was designed with a variety of housing types, to create a social mix:
- 600 apartments in private-sector buildings
- 60 low-cost "rent-to-buy" homes for young families
- 195 rental social housing units
- 95 housing units for staff at the nearby Robert-Bosch hospital.

Work on the first phase began in 1996.

The energy policy adopted combines various measures:
- a building layout designed to make best use of solar gain;
- the obligation on the part of developers to meet Low Energy House requirements (with energy consumption 30 % below the 1995 maximum regulatory values);
- solar water heating;
- heat energy supply from a gas-fuelled urban heating plant.

The development has 1,750m² of solar panelling, one of the largest installations in Germany when it was erected in the late 1990s. This provides around 50 % of the district's hot water, producing approximately 720MWh/year. The panels are positioned on the south-facing roof pitches of three apartment blocks at the district's centre. Heated water then flows through 350m of pipes to a 90m³ capacity tank. The heating plant's three boilers meet 89 % of heating requirements.

Burgholzhof also features green roofs, grassed parking areas and a specified minimum number of trees per plot, depending on the un-built area.

Ruhbank tram stop, Stuttgart-Degerloch, 1999.
Architects: Jakob + Bluth.

Perspective view of the Burgholzhof development, showing green roofs and PV panels. In the background on the right is Kottkamp & Schneider's 20-duplex housing block, 1998.

There is a 30km/h speed limit throughout the district, which besides housing contains a school, nursery and sports hall, shops and social amenities. An analysis of construction costs for seven of the buildings (11,742m^2 of habitable space in total, for 157 housing units) gives figures for the cost of energy conservation measures:
- integral measures (such as increased insulation and high-performance windows) came to 1.7 % of building costs
- technical installations such as solar panelling and heat-recovery ventilation systems to 1 % of costs. This investment is quickly recouped through savings in heating costs.

One of the housing blocks at Burgholzhof was built in 1998 by the property company Arche Nova, which specialises in green construction. The building meets Low Energy housing standards, and consists of two superposed rows of ten duplex apartments of 100m^2 (see illustration p. 67), each with living spaces on the lower floor and bedrooms above. Access to the upper apartments is via three external staircases linked to steel walkways, separated from the main structure. This block, which has timber framed and panelled walls and solid glulam floors, was the first four-storey timber building to be built in Germany.

This building is part of a city pilot project entitled Preiswertes Wohneigentum (good value housing), aimed at assisting young, low-income families with more than one child to buy economical, sustainable homes. The price of an apartment is around DM298,000 (€152,000), around two-thirds of the market price for similar property in Stuttgart. The difference is attributable to the simple volumes, the repetitive nature of the plan, the choice of materials and finishes and the optimised services, as well as land prices which were subsidised by the city authorities to a considerable degree.

The value of example

Stuttgart's example has inspired neighbouring authorities to set up their own projects, thus contributing to the rise in sustainable development. Fellbach, to the north-east of the city, set a target in 1995 of a 20 % reduction in CO$_2$ emissions by 2000. 200 different measures were studied, and most of them implemented, including increased insulation levels, replacement of conventional light-bulbs with low-energy bulbs, optimising existing equipment and replacing older heating systems. Such simple, economical and rapidly-applied steps were complemented by larger-scale projects: a wind turbine installation, solar water heating in the new development of Rotkehlchenweg, and an urban co-generation heating plant.

The wind farm came into operation in January 2001, and comprises four Vestas V 47-660/200 turbines with a capacity of 660kW each. Projected annual output is around 4.2 million kWh, equivalent to more than 1,600 households' electricity consumption. The most dramatic project is the "solar sail" rising above the district of Rotkehlchenweg on the main approach to Fellbach. Designed by the sound and light artist Walter Giers, this 7.2m x 10.7m structure, supported by tensioned cables off a 16.7m high steel pylon, holds 50m^2 of solar collectors in the form of 260 borosilicate glass tubes. Use of solar energy has economic, environmental and in this case also artistic value.

The solar "sail" at Fellbach, near Stuttgart, 1999. Designer: Walter Giers; engineers: Schlaich Bergermann & Partner.

Freiburg deserves its reputation as the European capital of environmentalism. The city was among the first to adopt sustainable urban development policies, which it has applied intensively and effectively. With a young and motivated population, as well as 20 years of experience in the field, Freiburg is currently building two new major developments of sustainable buildings: Vauban, on a former military site near the town centre, and Rieselfeld, in the west of the town.

Environmentalism as a vector of economic expansion

In the mid-1980s, the city authorities drew up a rational energy planning strategy, in co-operation with the regional energy and water company (*Freiburger Energie- und Wasserversorgung AG*).

In 1996, the city council adopted an environmental protection plan, whose main aim was a 25 % reduction in CO_2 emissions by 2010. To meet this target, the council laid down two priorities:
- to encourage the use of renewable energy, particularly solar energy
- to encourage energy conservation measures, in both new and existing buildings.

Freiburg is a fast-growing university town, whose political and administrative authority includes a number of committed environmentalists. During the 1990s, two regional schemes brought the active participation of inhabitants to the application of sustainable development principles. At the 1999 municipal elections the Greens gained even more influence, with 20 % of the vote.

A well-developed public transport system, pedestrian and cyclist priority on the roads, household waste sorting and recycling, and constructive use of solar gain have long been part of daily life in Freiburg. More than half of journeys within the city are made by bicycle (there is 160km of cycle track), tram or the regional rail network. Positive consequences include the creation of more than 10,000 jobs in the environmental sector, while the combined efforts of businesses, the university and the city authorities to encourage the development of biotechnology industries have led to

Location:
Baden-Württemberg, Germany.
Geographical context:
in the Rhine valley, at the edge of the Black Forest.
Area:
15,306 hectares, of which 40 % is taken up by buildings, 10 % by roads and 50 % by green space (forest 42 %, parks 3 %, vineyards 5 %).
Demographics:
population 117,000 in 1950, 174,000 in 1970, 204,000 (of whom 88,000 were economically active) in 2000.
Economic context:
university town (with 30,000 students); major centre for commerce and tourism close to the French and Swiss borders; industrial centre, particularly for biotechnology industries.
Sustainable development measures:
commitment to reduce CO_2 emissions by 25 % by 2010; Low Energy House rating compulsory for new buildings; support for use of renewable energies, particularly active and passive solar energy; flat roof greening compulsory; comprehensive public transport strategy; extensive network of footpaths and cycle paths; two new "green" districts created.

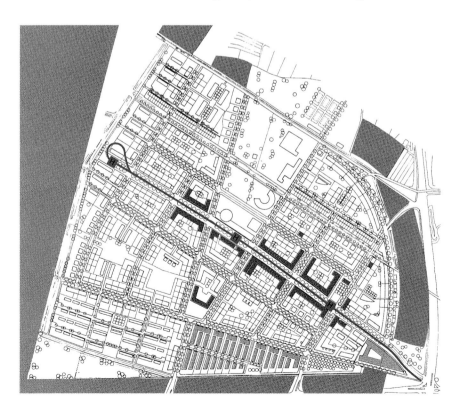

Plan of the Rieselfeld district.

**Terraced houses in the
"solar district", by Rolf Disch.**

the creation of a biotech business park. There is even a green tourist organisation, Freiburg Futour, which offers multi-lingual tours of the town's many environmental attractions.

The solar city

Freiburg is home to the headquarters of Solar-Fabrik, one of Germany's largest solar panelling manufacturer, and to the Fraunhofer Institute for applied research into solar energy. The town is thus at the cutting edge of this fast-growing sector, which is making a growing contribution to the German economy. A wide-ranging programme entitled "Freiburg – solar city" was associated with the Hanover Expo in 2000. Among the seven separate projects included in this programme were:
- the façade of the office tower above the city's main railway station, which integrates 240 vertical photovoltaic panels into the curtain walling system;
- the *Solarsiedlung* development of "positive energy" houses, which produce more energy than they consume, using photovoltaic panel cladding inclined at 45°.
This development, designed by Rolf Disch and close to the "green" district of Vauban, has seen slow progress for financial reasons.
In the Rieselfeld and Vauban developments, passive use of solar energy is standard, while many buildings also use solar collector panels and PV modules.
In Freiburg as a whole, the use of solar energy has been brought to the wider public. The renewable energy institute, the FESA (*Förderverein Energie-und Solaragentur*) brings together individuals wishing to club together to purchase PV installations.

The chamber of commerce and a professional centre provide training for apprentices and technicians in the manufacture and installation of solar panels.

The Rieselfeld district

Work on the pilot projects at Rieselfeld began in the mid-1980s, when the construction of a new regional sewage treatment station meant that the former infiltration basin site, at the western edge of the city, became vacant. The authorities decided to create a 250-hectare natural reserve area along with a 78-hectare housing development, with around 4,500 homes designed to house 10,000-12,000 people. An ideas competition for the site was held in 1991, followed by several separate architectural competitions. The erection of various different building types has allowed comparisons to be made between their different performances, particularly their energy consumption:
- small scale city blocks
- urban villas
- apartment blocks
- 2- and 3-unit town houses
- terraces and crescents.
A far cry from ghetto suburbs or dormitory towns, the new district, which is 15 minutes by tram from the city centre, is designed to contain all the facilities necessary to sustain a community, including primary and secondary schools, doctor's surgeries and shops. There are already 5,000 jobs at the nearby Haid business park, and a further 1,000 are set to be created within Rieselfeld itself.
Rieselfeld is the biggest development currently in progress in Baden-Württemberg. Various measures have been put in place to ensure that CO_2 emissions are lower than in other city districts:
- cutting journeys by locating workplaces and housing close together
- low energy construction
- a transport strategy which gives priority to pedestrians, cyclists and public transport.
One section of the district is "car-free"; residents must agree not to own a vehicle.
These measures were the subject of a study carried out as part of the ExWoSt (experimental housing and urbanism) federal research programme, looking at reducing levels of toxic substances through appropriate urban planning.

Vauban: environmental and social regeneration of a former military site

Following the fall of the Berlin Wall, in August 1992 the French troops who had been based in Freiburg departed, leaving the Vauban barracks empty. In 1994 the city purchased the 34-hectare site, and in 1995 the decision was taken to convert it into a flagship environmental and social project. The main aims were:
- a mix of housing and workplaces
- emphasis on transport by foot, bicycle or public transport
- preservation of existing trees and protection of the green area surrounding the Sankt-Georgen stream
- a social mix
- harmonious relationship between housing and external spaces
- use of urban heating plants
- low energy construction.

Three phases were planned, to be built between 1998 and 2006. The project comprises 2,000 homes, to house around 5,000 people, plus business units to provide some 500-600 jobs.
At the foot of the Schönberg hill, Vauban is set to become a vibrant and green area of the city. The first houses were completed in 1998, and the second phase began in 1999. Particularly worthy of note from an environmental point of view is the home and workplace building (see pp. 154-159).

Property planning

In Freiburg, as in Rennes (see pp. 83-89), a well-thought-out property strategy enabled the city authority to achieve its environmental and social aims, within an overall planning context and through sale of individual plots:
- increased building density
- a social and functional mix
- flat roof greening
- rainwater disposal within development boundaries.

Rolf Disch's "heliotrope" follows the sun's path, turning around its vertical axis.

Plan of Vauban.

A 220-space solar garage was built at the edge of Vauban, a "car-free zone".

In Vauban, all buildings must meet the Low Energy House requirements of annual heating energy consumption 65kWh/m^2 or less *(see p. 98)*. The city has also drawn up a further set of required measures, more stringent than national requirements. A number of terraces, oriented north-south and unshaded by adjacent buildings, are designed as Passive Houses *(see p. 100)*, using less than 15kW/m^2 per year for heating. All housing uses the urban heating plant, apart from the Passive Houses, which use independent renewable sources only.

Regeneration based on co-operation

Vauban's success is undoubtedly due in large part to the commitment of the members of the Vauban Forum, a non-profit organisation which was founded in 1994 as a way of getting the public involved with the new development.

The Forum has around 300 members; it was involved, within the Vauban working group, in planning the new district as soon as the city commission had completed its preparatory work. The Forum set out to:
- inform the public about "green architecture"
- provide practical advice on energy-saving measures
- support owner-developer groups
- and encourage alternatives to private car use.

The Vauban Forum is funded by subscriptions, donations and grants from public bodies, including support from the EU's Quality of Life programme. In 1997 it gave birth to Genova, a construction co-operative specialising in low-cost environmental housing with resident participation. Genova built two blocks in the new district, of 17 and 19 apartments respectively, with shared solar collector panels for water heating and various measures to make use of passive solar gain.

In the long term, when all development is complete, the Forum will become the residents' association, representing the interests of the new district's inhabitants.

As at Rieselfeld, Vauban is the subject of various on-going studies; as experience is gained, it can be put to good use in subsequent phases. The city news-sheet, *Stadt Nachrichten*, publishes regular updates of progress on the two sites, while potential land purchasers are given brochures containing clear and accurate information. The Vauban Forum also produces its own magazine, *Vauban Aktuell.*

Social tools

When the Vauban development was planned, the city authority aimed "to give everyone a chance". To ensure a good social mix, a model was developed, known as Blockprofil. The categories used in the model reflect the desired diversity of resident types:
- marital status
- number of children
- occupation
- age
- previous address
- location of workplace

- type of housing (low energy or passive)
- owner or tenant
- possible need for financial assistance.

Potential buyers are invited to attend a personal interview, at which these categories and criteria are defined. Requests to buy are then discussed by the Vauban working group. The final decision is taken by the city council.

An analysis of resident types in the first phase shows the effectiveness of this approach:
- 60 % own their homes, 40 % rent
- 25 % are labourers, lower-ranking employees or civil servants; 55 % are at management level, and 20 % are self-employed professionals
- 10 % of households are headed by single parents, 25 % are childless couples, and 65 % families with children
- 75 % of residents moved to Vauban from within Freiburg, and 25 % from outside the city.

Homeowner-developers

In Germany and Scandinavia, environmental and social aims in the context of sustainable development have often been achieved through a particular form of co-ownership, where groups of individuals or families together take on the role of property developer. The setting up of these homeowner-developer associations is encouraged by the city, and supported by the Vauban Forum. In the first phase of development, 100 homes, divided into 14 groups, were built in this way. This approach allows:
- relationships between future neighbours to be established early on
- co-operative planning of external treatment of the buildings
- significant cost reductions compared to more traditional approaches.

Building mix and density

Regeneration of former industrial and military sites is one aspect of sustainable urban development, increasing housing density is another. Terraced housing, where each home occupies only a small area of land, is within the reach of young families, helping to bring a young, dynamic and socially mixed population into the city centre. The first development phase, in the district's eastern section, included 450 new homes within apartment blocks plus some terraces. It also included schools, shops, and the renovation of around ten

buildings which were formerly the barracks' married quarters. These were converted into student lodgings, an asylum-seekers' centre, and the Vauban Forum offices. As an experiment, 143m^2 of solar panels were installed on the roof of one of the refurbished buildings, to provide hot water for 600 students.

The second phase covers an area of approximately 10 hectares, comprising 86 separate development plots ranging from 160m^2 to 620m^2 (see tables below). These will receive semi-detached and terraced houses and low-rise blocks, on up to four levels and with a maximum roof height of 13m. The land price was set at DM800/m^2 (€409/m^2), the current market rate within the city.

PLOTS FOR DEVELOPMENT BY PRIVATE INDIVIDUALS

Type	Terrace	Terrace	End-of-terrace
Width	6 m	7 m	7 m
Plot area	162 m^2	189 m^2	243 m^2
Number of floors	4 max.	4 max.	4 max.
Habitable area	227 m^2	265 m^2	340 m^2
Orientation	East-west	East-west	East-west

INDIVIDUAL BUILDING PLOTS FOR PASSIVE HOUSES

Type	Semi-detached	Terrace	Town house
Width	7 m	6 m	7 m
Plot area	275 m^2	180 m^2	210 m^2
Number of floors	3 max.	3 max.	4 max.
Habitable area	247 m^2	198 m^2	336 m^2
Orientation	North-south	North-south	North-south

PLOTS FOR DEVELOPMENT BY HOMEOWNER-DEVELOPER GROUPS

Type	Apartment block	Arcade block
Width	16 m	23 m
Plot area	432 m^2	621 m^2
Number of floors	4 max.	4 max.
Habitable area	734 m^2	1,056 m^2
Orientation	East-west	East-west

This housing project was built by homeowner-developer groups, reducing construction costs.

A naturally green area

The Vauban site had a natural advantage for which many developments must wait decades: mature trees.

The presence of around 70 planes, limes, poplars, maples and chestnuts creates leafy surroundings and a healthier atmosphere, bringing the cool of their shade and moisture to the dry summer air. To the south, the district borders on the protected "regenerated biotope" area beside the Sankt-Georgen stream. Buildings are separated by 30m wide "green strips"; where the buildings are oriented north-south, these lead to the open spaces at the foot of the Schönberg hill, allowing a flow of cool mountain air. A number of green spaces within the district provide areas for children's sport and play.

When development is complete, around half the surface area of the district will have been made impermeable by buildings or roads. To ensure that rainwater can soak into the soil and regenerate the natural water table, rain is channelled into 1m wide trenches on either side of the roads. Such trenches and channels are a traditional feature of the town, as seen also in the pedestrian areas of the city centre, where water circulates freely.

Rainwater is collected in roadside channels, even in the city centre.

A car-free zone

Vauban is designed to cut journey distances: housing, offices, services and public amenities are all close enough together to remove the need for car use. Public transport stops are designed to be a maximum of 500m from home or workplace, the same distance as the two car parks which are located at the edge of the "car-free zone". Aside from the main access road, cars have no place in the district, and the Vauban Forum encourages residents to use other forms of transport. Bicycles, car-sharing and low-fare public transport have convinced most households so far, and the majority have given up their cars.

There is already a city bus route through the district. In 1998 the authorities gave the go-ahead to the extension of an existing tram route, which will run the length of the main Vauban road. Work should be completed by 2006 at the latest, at a cost of DM1.3million (around €665,000), coinciding with completion of the Vauban development. Eventually, it is planned to connect the tram route with the regional rail network.

Streets and public space

The main through route, which runs from northwest to south-east across the district, links Vauban to the city centre and surrounding areas, and is the main transport artery leading to residential side-streets. A tree-lined avenue, most of its bordered on each side by a 6m wide footpath and cycle track, separates the roadway from the adjacent housing. To the south, the arcade blocks, which contain apartments above ground-floor business and retail units, are fronted by a 1.5m wide pavement and a parking area. There is a speed limit of 30km/h.

The side streets are designed as "communication spaces", or 'urban courtyards'. There is no parking, apart from for set-down and deliveries, and a speed limit of 10km/h. In an economical but also deliberate use of public space, all utility networks run beneath the 4m wide streets, which are bordered by rainwater ditches and a 1.5m green strip planted with trees. The northern section, still unbuilt, is planned to be still more pedestrian-friendly.

These streets are entirely residential, maintaining a quiet, undisturbed atmosphere. Along the southern half of the main avenue, however, close to the kindergarten and school, the ground floor arcades of the housing blocks are designed to house shops, workshops and services. Facing the Paula-Modersohn-Platz public square, the presence of these shops, offices, medical facilities and cafés will make for a lively, animated area.

Setting an example

The Vauban primary school and educational facilities are the result of an open architectural competition, the normal practice in Freiburg, and one which has contributed considerably to the quality of urban space. Setting an example, the city took an environmental approach to their design. The Karoline-Kaspar school has eight classrooms, three group activity rooms, a library, sports hall and a main hall which may be used by other groups outside school hours. The building layout was designed to preserve existing trees. Large areas of façade glazing, along with high-level glazed sections in the corridors, maximise natural lighting, making for both better internal conditions and reduced energy consumption. No PVC is used in the building; floors are in wood and linoleum, helping to create a warm, non-hazardous environment. The

An avenue in Vauban.
The public space benefits
from the presence of many
mature trees.

The primary school.

school conforms to Low Energy standards and uses natural ventilation. Its flat roof is planted with an extensive green roof system; rainwater is collected in a tank, and used for toilet flushing and irrigation of planted areas.

Similar measures were applied to the nearby primary school. With six south-facing classrooms and a hall, also available for use outside school hours, this is set in a quiet area surrounded by green, bordering the protected area beside the stream. The structure and internal fittings, in timber and timber derivatives, provide a rich sensory environment for the children's learning, a pointer for future generations.

A car-free zone on reclaimed industrial land

Location:
capital of the Netherlands,
in northern Holland.
Geographical context:
historical port town on the
Zuiderzee.
Total area:
220km^2 (48 % built-up area,
12 % green space).
Demographics:
population 722,000 in 1995,
731,293 in 2000; projected
population 792,000 in 2020;
the "greater Amsterdam" area
has 1.4 million inhabitants.
Economic context:
national capital, administrative
and cultural centre; university town;
industrial centre and the country's
second largest port.
**Sustainable development
measures:**
list of alternative environmental
materials incorporated into 1992
building regulations; restrictions on
city-centre car journeys and parking;
major infrastructure works to
improve public transport; extensive
cycle path network; regeneration
of former industrial land and
creation of new sustainable districts.

The Netherlands has seen numerous environmental projects, and the notion of sustainable development has been integrated into building and urban planning for more than a decade. The redevelopment of public spaces in the city, and the remodelling of several districts along socially and environmentally sustainable lines, have brought real improvements to quality of life. At GWL, the revitalisation of a former industrial zone provided the opportunity to create extensive green space within the district and to develop alternatives to car transport.

Context

Amsterdam's urban renovation programme, launched in the late 1980s, brought about a transformation of the city. The population rose, more businesses were attracted to the city, and the student population also grew, rising steadily from 1995.

A number of further, wide-ranging projects were then planned, to enhance the city's image at home and abroad:
- major public infrastructure works (the north-south metro line and IJ tram route)
- revitalisation of the Bijlmermeer district and the western suburbs
- refurbishment of housing and public buildings and generation of employment in the seafront areas
- landscaping and improvements to recreational and leisure areas in the inner suburbs.

2003 should see completion of the conversion of the Oostelijk Havengebied site, an industrial zone since the 19th century, into a residential district of 17,000 people.

This project includes shops and services as well as 8,000 homes of various types, from the characteristic Amsterdam terraces to large-scale housing blocks. To the east, the biggest development currently under way is at Ijburg, where six separate districts are being constructed on artificial islands. The first 700 homes were completed in 2001; when complete, Ijburg will house a population of 45,000 in 18,000 units.

GWL: sustainable development of former industrial land

The new district of GWL contains 600 housing units on a 6-hectare site formerly occupied by the city's water company. The site borders on the mediaeval town, close to the terminus of an existing tram route in the Westerpark and on the main route to Haarlem. The city developers wanted to combine high density with residents' stated desire for a "green", car-free area; accordingly the brief took account of environmental requirements, the available area and the wishes of future inhabitants. After consultation on this basis, Kees Christiaanse was engaged to draw up an overall plan. A landscape architect, West 8, was also engaged to design the public spaces between buildings, and the consultant Boom drew up an environmental building specification. At the same time, pre-tender studies identified more than 4,000 potential tenderers. Contracts were subsequently signed with five architects, and a management structure put in place to oversee the project and ensure the application of sustainable principles. This organisation includes representatives of the residents, the developers and the historic buildings department, assisted by a district manager.

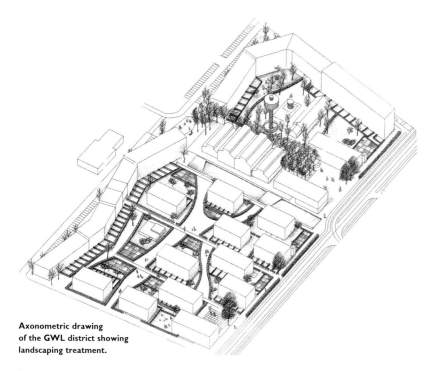

**Axonometric drawing
of the GWL district showing
landscaping treatment.**

Urban characteristics

The new district is very different from the city areas around it, although the urban context is taken into account in a number of ways. Some 60 % of the district's homes are provided by a single long, central block, between four and nine storeys high. To the west of the site, this main block acts as protection from the dominant winds and marks a clear separation between the residential areas and the adjacent industrial zone. To the north, it forms a barrier to the traffic noise from the main Haarlem road. Its high housing density allows the rest of the site to be planned as a more open area, with wide green spaces between the other, smaller buildings. The Van Hallstraat road, which runs between new and existing districts, has been remodelled, with widened pavements, cycle paths and frequent pedestrian crossing points, an expanded tram stop, a lowered speed limit and no parking spaces. The overall site plan has preserved the old water tower and industrial buildings, now converted to shops and services, bringing a strong local historical character to the area. One block has been transformed into guest accommodations which may be hired by residents.

Beside the former machine shed, which now houses a restaurant, café and TV studio, a canal divides the site into two. To the north of the canal, denser housing is set around an urban square fringed by shops; while to the south, emphasis is on the spatial relationships between houses and private and public gardens. There is also a nursery, accommodations suitable for dis-abled children and for the elderly, artists' studios, offices and a community centre.

The idea of a car-free zone was designed to help attract more comfortably-off families to what had been one of the poorest areas of the city, populated mainly by one- or two-person households. If there is a noticeable change in the social make-up of the area, the GWL district will have demonstrated that such developments can be highly attractive.

Landscaping and public space

The site's central area is designed as a park, with a rich and complex network of public spaces. Existing vegetation is integrated into the 120 private gardens, clearly defined by low, thick hedges, and around the villa blocks. Thus fluid circulation routes are created between public and private garden space, often linked directly with houses. Ground treatments are designed to maintain permeability while reducing the need for maintenance: brick paving on footpaths, granite in the public spaces between the former industrial buildings, and concrete blocks and slabs elsewhere. A network of gutters directs surface water to the canal, which functions as a rainwater retention basin. There are numerous bicycle storage racks. Composting units are available, and pre-sorted household waste is collected at the site perimeter so as to avoid the need for truck access.

A car-free zone

One of the key features of the new district, and one which gives it its distinctive "green" character,

Left, beside the canal which crosses the area, new buildings are in harmony with the converted industrial buildings on the site.

Above, individual gardens are directly outside the apartment blocks.

The many green spaces within the urban blocks also have a social function.

**Apartment block façade.
Architect: Kees Christiaanse.**

is the absence of cars. This is not a new idea in Amsterdam, part of whose extensive pedestrian area dates from 1945, but its application on this scale outside the city centre is so far unique. There are 135 parking spaces, of which 25 are reserved for visitors, at the western edge of the site. Since this is only enough for 20 % of households (the spaces being distributed by lottery), and residents are not permitted to park in the surrounding districts, a large proportion of households have dispensed with their cars. While stopping short of a complete ban on cars, this policy, combined with efficient public transport connections, has brought significant changes in behaviour,

GWL has four bicycles for every three inhabitants; 73 % of journeys are by non-motorised transport, and nearly half of them are limited to 2-6km within the Westerpark area. By contrast, the average distance travelled to work or school is 15.7km, and 17 % of journeys are more than 25km long. The central station, 2.5km away, is therefore a necessary connection to the wider network; 39 % of residents have public transport passes. There is also a car-sharing scheme. Around 10 % of households make use, at low cost, of the two vehicles owned by the transport co-operative; they have copy keys, and mileage is calculated by an in-car computer and charged to their accounts on a monthly basis. 57 % of households have no car, while the remainder use theirs relatively little, with ten journeys per passenger per week on average.

This level may change with the planned construction of a 400-space car park, which will serve a nearby cultural centre and provide space for service vehicles for GWL. Remaining spaces will be available to residents. However, the changed behaviour seen at GWL has demonstrated its effectiveness in maintaining levels of mobility.

Architectural quality and ecology

The architects selected were chosen for their innovative work, their attitudes to urban design and their lack of previous experience with "green" construction – the intention being to demonstrate that prior experience is not a requirement for the successful completion of sustainable projects. Relying on their innovative capacity, the constraints imposed by Christiaanse in the overall plan were simple: no high-level walkways, flexible layouts, plenty of incident sunlight, direct access to gardens. Brick, the dominant material of the existing buildings, is used as an identifying feature. The principal environmental features of the buildings in GWL are the use of non-hazardous materials, of solar gain, good insulation, and use of rainwater for toilet flushing. Heating is via a gas co-generator. Those apartments which do not give directly onto a garden have access to roof gardens. A wide variety of housing types was explored, including apartments leading off a central corridor, duplex flats and town houses. Apartments are often laid out over several floors so that as many as possible can have their own front door at ground level.

Sustainable development in Helsinki is being achieved through the commitment of the different parties involved, with the establishment of environmental priorities for the city as a whole, its different districts and individual buildings. Assessment tools have enabled projects to be evaluated with a view to reproducibility, particularly in the experimental district of Viikki.

Context

Helsinki lies on a peninsula on the Gulf of Finland. The city has grown up in sections, with separate, distinct built areas along five main circulation routes intersected by green belts. The most recent framework plan for development, in 1992, established the principle of increasing urban density in the large intermediate zones, together with more intense use of existing infrastructure. Achievement of these aims is made easier by the city's property policy: 81 % of building plots are publicly-owned (65 % by the city and 16 % by the state) on long-term leases of 50-100 years.

The city planning department aims to ensure, through studies and monitoring of projects, that districts contain an appropriate social mix and a balance between housing and business use.

Urbanism in Finland is characterised by the quality and human dimension of landscaping and public space. This is visible even in the large-scale developments of the 1950s, such as Tapiola, or the district of Ruoholahti, competed in the 1990s and featuring housing, offices, business units and amenities on each side of a canal.

A self-contained district centred on biotechnology

The new district of Viikki is 8km from the city centre and occupies more than 1,100 hectares. Designed according to sustainable principles, it is integrated into the existing development structure, as required by Helsinki's Agenda 21 programme.

The design concept for Viikki brought together the city authorities, the university, government bodies and private enterprise. The aim was to create an international centre for research and development in the areas of bio-sciences, biotechnology, agronomy and agriculture. Close co-operation was required in order to reconcile the three different sections of the project: a science and research park, a natural reserve, and residential areas.

Location:
Helsinki, capital of Finland.
Geographical context:
coastal town in the south of the country, on the northern part of the Gulf of Finland.
Area: 18,500 hectares (68,600 hectares including marine zones; area of the whole Helsinki region, 269,800 hectares); 7,700 hectares undeveloped land, 98km of coast, 315 islands; 100m² of green space/natural area per inhabitant.
Demographics:
city population 21,500 in 1850, 315,895 in 1941, 500,000 in 1970, 550,000 in 2000; regional population 1.2 million in 2000 (including 375,000 in the metropolitan zone which includes four municipal areas); population density for the region (twelve municipal areas in total) 39.5 inhabitants/km².
Economic context:
administrative capital (84 % of the working population is employed in the public sector); university city; economic centre at the heart of an expanding market encompassing northern Russia, the Baltic states and Scandinavia; major new-economy industries such as Nokia, and numerous technical centres of global reputation.
Sustainable development measures:
energy-saving programme for existing building stock; 91 % of housing and 95 % of offices heated by co-generation plant (fuelled 52 % by natural gas, 46 % coal, 1 % fuel oil); urban densification in progress; environmental protection and forest management programmes; 10m² of public gardens per inhabitant; well-developed public transport (70 % of rush-hour journeys); 850km of cycle track; new development zones built along sustainable lines.

General plan of the Viikki site.

An appropriate socio-economic balance was sought which would allow the district to be largely self-supporting in terms of employment – with 6,000 jobs, 6,000 student and research posts for 13,000 new residents – and services (to include schools and nurseries, university departments, shops, etc.). This automatically reduces the need for journeys outside the district. Within it, car traffic is kept low by the short distances between facilities (there are two separate urban centres), separation of pedestrian and car traffic, and efficient public transport, with good links to the wider network (bus and train, with land designated for a future rapid-transit tram line).

Protection of natural areas

Close to Viikki is a 250-hectare marshland reserve, important for bird life, with restricted public access. Particular care was necessary to protect this area when the new development was planned. The initial plan was modified to accommodate it, with built areas re-sited; a green corridor, running northward, was created to ensure the continuity of the natural ecosystem, while preserving the traditional agricultural landscape of open fields. The new buildings are in the district's northern sector, close to a slip-road, and take up a relatively small area compared to the undeveloped zones around. The university and service buildings screen the residential areas from

noise. The new district and its various innovative aspects are also the subject of studies by the university research institutes located on the site.

An experimental residential area

Viikki's main residential area is Latokartano. When completed, Latokartano will house 8,000–9,000 people in a wide variety of housing types (including rental and freehold) designed to create an appropriate urban mix.

In the southern part of this area, a pilot development to house 1,700 people was designated as part of the Eco-community programme. This is a joint venture between the Finnish Environment Ministry, the architects' association (SAFA) and Tekes, the national technology agency. The experience and data acquired will be applied to other, future projects. The application of the environmental building assessment system Pimwag (*see p. 82*) also aims to develop products, techniques and expertise in sustainable building.

The overall plan of the new development was decided by an open competition, based on a rigorous set of specifications. Petri Laaksonen's winning scheme reproduced the urban form seen elsewhere in Helsinki, with urban blocks separated by green corridors. As often in Scandinavia, the street space is secondary to the open courtyard spaces formed by the building layout, onto which the buildings give direct access.

Housing project by Helin & Siitonen.

Plan of the new environmental district. To the right, the stream runs around the edge of the site. Green corridors extend into the heart of the built-up areas.

The buildings are oriented to benefit as much as possible from sunlight, and spaced so as not to shade one another. Planting reduces exposure to prevailing winds, with building height kept lower than the trees around them. Biodiversity is conserved and strengthened by the creation of various biotope areas. The green spaces between buildings contain private gardens and public areas, designed to be pleasant places to walk, and allow rainwater infiltration into the underlying soil. Each urban block has facilities to produce compost for the gardens, and there are areas for recycling containers for household waste. There is a network of footpaths and cycle tracks, separate from the roads.

An urban watercourse and gardening centre

The stream which ran through the development site, the Viikkinoja, has been diverted to run around its edge, 50-100m from the residential areas. Falling by 400mm over a distance of 740m, its new course and banks were designed by a team of landscape designers, hydrologists, geotechnical engineers, botanists and horticulturalists. Rainwater is channelled from the housing blocks to three pools in the stream which form part of a natural purification system, with water flowing first down a waterfall, then through deep, densely-planted marsh areas. The whole has been designed to eliminate flood risk. The stream, which is crossed by several footbridges, is an essential element in the landscape of the district,

creating a specific environment which is home to particular plants and wildlife. It serves as an educational tool, and is the subject of various studies carried out by the university. The earth removed during diversion of the stream was used for landscaping and spread over existing topsoil in the centre of the site.

As well as individual gardens beside the houses, a gardening centre has been established at the edge of the neighbouring woodland. Occupying several fields, the centre is run by a private company in partnership with the city authorities, and provides advice to residents about gardening and smallholdings. There are garden plots of various sizes, greenhouses which residents can share, and space for animals. Joint projects are planned with schools and nurseries.

Public buildings show the way

Viikki's public buildings show how innovation, high-quality architecture and environmentalism can be successfully combined. The Korona university information centre, designed by the architects Ark-House (Erholtz, Kareoja, Herranen and Huttunen), has a triple-glazed envelope outside a concrete wall, the space between acting as a climatic buffer for preheating incoming fresh air. Three gardens – the Egyptian garden, the Roman garden and the Japanese garden – are situated within the glazed areas. The gigantic greenhouse building known as the Gardenia, designed by Artto, Palo, Rossi and Tikka, is run by the residents as a cooperative. It houses an environmental education

The stream, an integral feature of the new development.

The arrangement and scale of the courtyard spaces encourages social interaction.

Green corridors and gardens bring nature right up to the housing blocks.

Internal garden area at the information centre. Architects: Erholtz, Kareoja, Herranen and Huttunen.

centre for children, a gardening and information centre, lecture theatres and a café, as well as functioning as a public area and exhibition space. A nursery provides young children with year-round awareness of their natural surroundings.

Environmental housing developments

Viikki's 63,500m² of housing was the subject of an architectural competition in 1996, which resulted in commissions being given to eight groups of architects. Stringent specifications included conformity to Pimwag criteria. While most of the housing has been built by public or private developers (see pp. 160-165), one part of the site was set aside for residents' co-operatives to build small-scale projects. Consideration was given to the potential for neighbourhood gardens, home working, the installation of solar radiant floor heating, grey water treatment, and heat recovery via air intake/outlet heat exchangers.

Pimwag, the Finnish environmental building assessment method

In order to evaluate the effectiveness of the Viikki project in achieving its overall aims, and to bolster its credibility, the city authorities commissioned a group of experts to draw up a system of assessment criteria. Known as Pimwag from its authors' initials (Pennanen, Inkinen, Majurinen, Wartiainen, Aaltonen and Gabrielsson), the resulting method uses principles of "deep ecology", which emphasises the "interconnectedness" of all life and the understanding of man's role within it. Building projects can be assessed in five areas:
- pollution (CO₂ emissions, wastewater management, treatment/disposal of household and construction site waste, use of environmentally- certified products)
- natural resources (consumption of fossil fuels, purchased heating energy and electricity, primary energy, flexible use of building space)
- health (internal climate, moisture control, noise, exposure to wind and sunlight, variety of housing types)
- biodiversity (plants, habitat types, rainwater treatment)
- food production (planting, soil quality).

These criteria are applied to three levels of targets. Meeting the targets "scores" points; a project must gain a certain number of points in order to be awarded a building permit. A project whose CO_2 emissions do not exceed 3,200kg/m² over 50 years, a 20 % reduction on the average house in Finland, achieves the basic level of zero points. If emissions are reduced by 33 %, and the building demonstrates good use of passive solar energy, it scores one point. To reach the two-point level, emissions must be brought down by 45 %, with the introduction of buffer zones and an active solar energy system. Similarly, the different target levels correspond to heating energy consumption of between 105 and 65kWh/m²/year; drinking water consumption of between 125 and 85 litres per person per day; and site waste of between 18 and 10kg/m². The levels are set so that the basic level corresponds to additional construction costs of less than 5 %, to be recouped through saving in running costs.

The method does not impose any particular means by which these targets are to be achieved, and thus leaves considerable flexibility of approach while still ensuring that minimum criteria are met.

The Gardenia greenhouse, completed in 2000, has come to symbolise the district. Architects: Artto, Palo, Rossi & Tikka.

The methodical and "anticipatory" approach

Rennes has a long tradition of "anticipatory" planning; the authorities have preferred to take early or preventive action, in order to avoid the need for expensive and difficult remedial action in the future. In this spirit, the city council incorporated a number of sustainable development principles into their 1991 urban plan.

Context

Rennes' orderly arrangement dates from its first urban plan, drawn up in the 18th century. The city centre is organised around the two main squares, the place de la Mairie and the place du Parlement, sites of the town hall and administrative buildings, and the river Vilaine, which was canalised in the 19th century to protect the town from flooding. In the 1950s and 1960s, a far-sighted authority put in place a land purchase policy whose implementation has allowed today's city to achieve its urban planning aims.

Rennes and the surrounding areas

The development of the city itself has gone hand in hand with that of the surrounding area. The administrative district of Rennes was created in 1970 and included 27 separate local authorities (*communes*); in 1999 it was expanded to include 6 further authorities, and in 2000 became a metropolitan authority, with 36 communes. In 1994 the authorities approved a framework plan, entitled "*Rennes-District, vivre en intelligence*", which looked at development of the area from the point of view of four "indissociable elements": the urban quality of the city and surrounding region; social cohesion; a rational economy, and co-operation between those involved. These were expressed through a series of long-term objectives.

In terms of organisation of infrastructure and services, "greater Rennes" may be divided into three sections:
- the city itself, which wished to extend its influence at regional, national and international level;
- the six main "satellite" centres, which needed to retain a human scale, with sufficient amenities and services to allow them to remain socially cohesive communities in their own right;
- the other, smaller urban centres, which also needed a satisfactory level of local services and amenities.

The framework plan also listed five further areas:
- designation of land use
- natural areas
- urban areas
- journey management
- drinking water, drainage and sanitation and flood risk.

A far-sighted strategy

Rennes' rapid rise in population clearly called for measures able to cope with future changes, notably in housing and transport. The city estimated that the number of daily journeys made in greater Rennes would rise from 1.1 million in 1994 to 1.4-1.5 million in 2010. In anticipation of the traffic problems this would bring, the framework plan encouraged a diversification into different means of transport, particularly development of collective public transport solutions. As a result, significant investment led to a reorganisation of bus routes around an east-west axis and construction of a new light rail line.

In 1994, the Rennes district had a population of 320,000, a figure which was expected to rise to 400,000 by 2010. Such a rise would require the construction during this period of an estimated 20,000 new homes (1,250 per year) in the city itself, and 30,000 in the surrounding areas. In 1996, a local housing plan was drawn up with the aim of meeting these targets. This plan calls for:
- a remodelling and densification of the city-centre urban fabric;
- a shift in emphasis in the surrounding centres from a rural to an urban context, with denser development at the edge of towns and villages to prevent encroachment onto the countryside beyond;
- the preservation of a "green belt" of rural landscape around the city, to contain recreation and leisure areas and protected zones.

The urban plan

The city's urban plan is an expression of this overall strategy. It sets out a framework for development over a 25-year period, taking into account the need for progress and change as the city evolves. First drawn up in 1989, and ratified in 1991, the plan already incorporated a number of

---

Location:
Brittany, France.
Geographical context:
at the gateway to the Brittany peninsula, at the confluence of the Ille and Vilaine rivers.
Area:
the town itself takes up 5,022 hectares; "greater Rennes" is made up of 36 separate local authorities.
Demographics:
the town had a population of around 100,000 in 1950, 203, 500 in 1994, and 212,000 in 1999; the Rennes administrative district had a population of 295,300 in 1982, 320,000 in 1994, and 375,000 in 1999.
Economic context:
regional capital; university town (with 15,000 students in 1968, 55,000 in 1998); centre for public and private research bodies (employing 3,000 people); major industries car-making (Citroën has a Rennes plant) and relatively non-polluting, high-tech industries.
Sustainable development measures:
urban densification; mixed use and social mix; participatory approach; updated drainage system; urban heating and hot water plant fuelled by household waste; waste sorting and water conservation measures; improved public transport networks; measures to encourage journeys on foot or by bicycle; preservation of all green areas and their diversity; renovation of river banks.

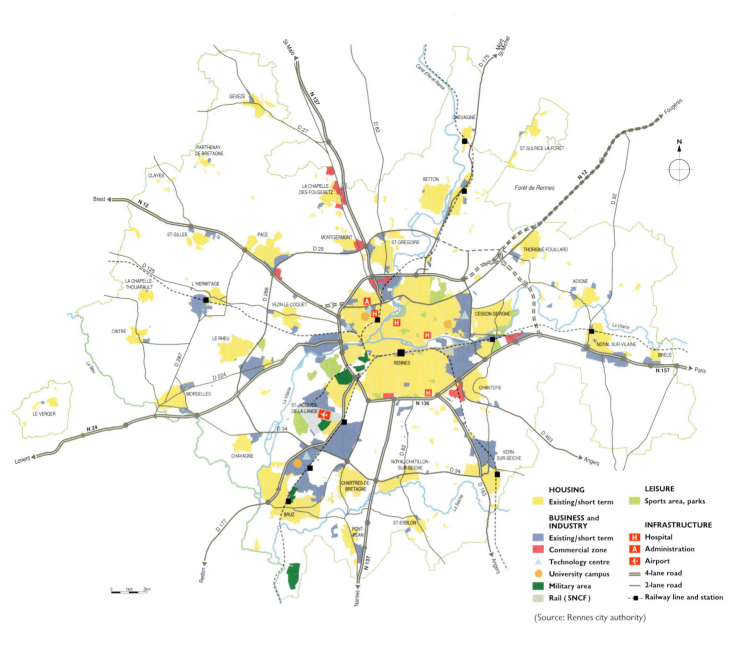

HOUSING
- ▨ Existing/short term

BUSINESS and INDUSTRY
- ▨ Existing/short term
- ▨ Commercial zone
- ▲ Technology centre
- ● University campus
- ▨ Military area
- ▨ Rail (SNCF)

LEISURE
- ▨ Sports area, parks

INFRASTRUCTURE
- H Hospital
- A Administration
- ✈ Airport
- ═══ 4-lane road
- ─── 2-lane road
- ·■· Railway line and station

(Source: Rennes city authority)

Above, plan of the Rennes conurbation.

Right, plan of the new development zones.

sustainable development principles. Far ahead of its time, it anticipated the provisions of the 2001 SRU law on solidarity and urban renewal, with an emphasis on social choices and a radical approach to the contemporary city.

The plan uses the results of studies carried out in various city districts, and is designed to establish interaction between all groups and sectors of the population concerned. In order to involve all such groups, giving them a stake in the project and enabling them to contribute to it, residents, professionals, the local elected authorities and technical services were brought together for discussions. This aimed to ensure an integrated result and to encourage development of sustainable initiatives. Rejecting a sector-by-sector approach, the plan is also a tool for ensuring development is appropriate to both the immediate surroundings and the broader urban context.

Seven years later, those in charge of implementing the plan found themselves regularly revising or refining their goals, looking at some areas in more detail and devising new methods in order to achieve them. These new approaches were bolstered by new theoretical and practical data, and by a number of studies carried out as part of the modification of the land use plan (POS) which was approved in 1998. In particular, they put emphasis on:

- making appropriate use of existing architectural assets, whether of local or national interest
- protecting green areas
- developing public transport
- measures to make walking and cycling more pleasant
- a more environmental approach to energy and water management
- creating new development zones (raising the

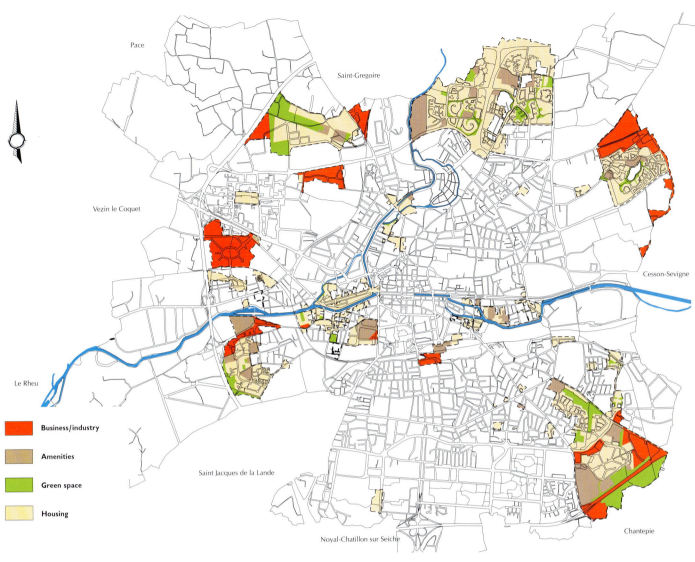

Pace

Saint-Gregoire

Vezin le Coquet

Cesson-Sevigne

Le Rheu

	Business/industry
	Amenities
	Green space
	Housing

Saint Jacques de la Lande

Chantepie

Noyal-Chatillon sur Seiche

(Source: Rennes city authority)

number to 27), including the Beauregard development (*see pp. 88-89*).

The revised version of the urban plan was published in 1999. Taking into account the experience gained, this document set out ten strategic areas, and three sets of goals, which were to become the basis of a consistent development policy.

Public property strategy

Property purchase planning has long been a feature of Rennes' urban policies, with an annual budget of FF20-30million. The strategy deals with the sale and purchase of land for public facilities (infrastructure and services, schools, cultural centres, etc.), the acquisition of land for strategic purposes, and the sale of serviced plots.

Although it requires considerable foresight, this planning strategy has worked in favour of a coherent urban composition:

RENNES URBAN PLAN

Ten strategic areas

1 Property strategy
2 Public control of planning strategy in partnership with local groups
3 Housing
4 Community life, and provision of the associated amenities
5 Education: schools, universities and research
6 Economic development
7 Urban journeys
8 Public space
9 The natural environment, within and around the city
10 Urban heritage today and tomorrow

Three sets of practical aims

1 To develop the city in its historical context:
   · the built and natural environment
   · architecture and modernity
   · distinct identity and landmarks
   · public amenities and services
2 To create a network of urban features enhancing the quality of city life:
   · public spaces
   · paths
   · parks and gardens
   · river banks
   · urban art
   · landscape
3 To organise urban transport to give a better and more dynamic service:
   · bus and light rail
   · car parks
   · pedestrianised areas
   · cycle use plan
   · key routes

- priorities can be clearly established

- mixed usage, high-quality public architecture and continuity in development of public space are easier to achieve

- housing development can be regulated to achieve an appropriate social mix (75 % of housing in Rennes is controlled by the city authorities)

- the city can influence the property market through modification of supply and demand.

Communication is facilitated through co-operation of developers, architects, solicitors, businesses and other interested parties.

Mixed use and social mixing

The city aims to maintain a social balance through careful monitoring of the balance of building types within individual districts: housing, offices, shops, workshops, services, leisure facilities and external public spaces. Various parties have signed an agreement designed to boost small local shops and limit supermarket developments.

Any development, whether in the city centre or towards the suburbs, must include at least 25 % social housing. This measure, aimed at creating and maintaining a social balance, is linked to significantly reduced rates of property taxes. Thus it is possible to build social rental housing in areas where it would otherwise be impractical due to high land prices.

In areas close to the city centre, these measures have required significant investment on the part of the city authorities. In 1999 city grants in these districts came to FF63,000 (around €9,600) per social housing unit built. This figure is increased by the fact that land is hard to come by and infrastructure works complex.

A permanent policy of co-operation between elected authorities, residents and local associations aims to maintain close links between interested parties, with emphasis on communication and exchange of information. Community councils provide information to residents and encourage individual responsibility, particularly with regard to environmental initiatives such as waste sorting and energy and water conservation measures.

Transport and parking

The city's transport policy aims to shift the emphasis away from private cars through a number of initiatives:

- ring roads to divert traffic round the city centre

- priority given to public transport, partly through the creation of large car parks at transport stops outside the city

- an expanded network of pedestrianised roads and city-centre shopping centres

- measures to encourage cycling.

Aerial view of western Rennes, showing the banks of the Vilaine.

Public transport is designed to bolster urban cohesion through more direct routes and reduced journey times. The network integrates the 8.6km light rail line, which runs from southeast to north-west via 15 stops, with the bus system, which incorporates numerous local routes branching off from a main, 4.8km east-west axis. Measures to make cycling a safer and more attractive option include the creation of a 132km cycle track network (separate cycle paths plus bus lanes); cyclists may use pedestrian areas at walking pace, and children under eight may ride on pavements.

In 1998, in partnership with the street furniture company Adshel, the city set up a computerised bicycle loan scheme. Holders of personalised smart cards, available free of charge, can access 200 bikes which are available between 6 a.m. and 2 a.m. in 25 docking stations distributed throughout the city.

Water conservation

Environmental water management calls for protection of water supply, control of distribution, and appropriate treatment of wastewater before discharging it into the environment. As the capital of a region suffering from high levels of water pollution, Rennes in 1997 opened one of the most advanced water treatment stations in Europe. The purified water is filtered through sand beds before discharge into the river. The resulting fall in pollution levels (organic matter 97 %, nitrogen 90 %, phosphates 95 %) should allow the natural balance of the river Vilaine to be restored.

Environmental protection is also assisted by smaller-scale measures and by economic initiatives. Following its signature with national government of the Environment Charter in 2000, Rennes launched a campaign to encourage households to purchase rainwater collection tanks. The city purchased 1,000 500-litre polyethylene tanks at a cost of FF150 (€22.87) each, and subsidised their re-sale to the public to the tune of FF110 (€16.77).

Waste management

In an attempt to reduce waste volumes, Rennes in 1999 initiated a waste sorting and recycling campaign. Calling on residents' sense of civic responsibility, the campaign encouraged the setting aside in housing blocks of areas for paper, card and glass recycling containers. Furthermore, 2,810 tonnes of "green" waste was collected in Rennes in 1999; in 2000, the city made available 1,000 compost bins for organic household and garden waste. While such measures have been standard for a decade in some European countries, they are still rare in France.

Nature within the city

The green belt, long enshrined in the city's framework plan, runs outside the ring roads which separate the city proper from the surrounding towns and villages. This natural buffer fulfils several roles. It forms a transition between city and countryside; it provides leisure and recreational areas easily accessible from the city (notably via footbridges over the ring roads); it protects nearby housing from noise. Tree-lined avenues and other traditional local features have been preserved or recreated. Detailed studies were carried out in order to draw up the regulatory and operational framework to ensure protection and best use of the natural environment. This regeneration of green space, begun at the same time as the establishment of the new development zones, is set to continue, notably via the creation of a new 17-hectare landscaped park in the Beauregard development zone.

The city authorities have also drawn up the *plan bleu*, a long-term regeneration plan for the banks and waterside areas along the Vilaine, the Ille and the Ille-et-Rance canal. This consists of an overall scheme to be put into practice gradually, in consultation with different project designers, through measures financed by developers.

Architectural and urban heritage

The principles of sustainable development encompass an appreciation of social and cultural roots, allowing development of the city to take place within a lasting and historical context. Studies of the different city districts that examine urban structure and existing building assets, have led to the renovation of buildings of interest, the protection of characteristic residential districts of individual houses and gardens, and a "soft" approach to redevelopment of the historical urban fabric.

Looking to the future, Rennes is creating new buildings which will enrich and extend its heritage. There is a strong architectural element to the

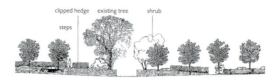

clipped hedge   existing tree   shrub

steps

Above, section showing landscaping details.

Right, landscaping details for part of the development. The site is criss-crossed by tree-lined avenues.

Below, aerial view of the Beauregard development site. As early as the 1980s, existing trees were protected and more planted in anticipation of the development.

Below right, a tree-lined lane.

city's urban policies, in the hope of inspiring private developers and project designers to produce creative, high-quality work.

The Environment Charter

Since the 1980s, the wide range of measures introduced in Rennes – modernised sanitation systems, urban heating plants, better waste and water management, developing public transport and bicycle use, preservation of green spaces – have formed an approach consistent with the principles of sustainable development.

Wishing to continue along this road, the city, in partnership with local community councils, public and state bodies, local organisations and environment specialists, drew up an Environment Charter. Signed in 2000 by the City of Rennes and the Environment and Land ministry, the charter is a commitment on the part of the city authorities to "effect lasting improvements to the environment and quality of life" of the region. It aims to strengthen the city's environmental advantages, and help improve areas in which it is lacking, over a period of five years. The document encourages private initiatives, partnership and collaborative work. This "charter for today and tomorrow" sets out four main themes – water, noise, waste, and living environment – and two basic goals:
- to raise environmental awareness among residents and corporate bodies, with the aim of influencing their behaviour;
- to make consideration of environmental issues standard practice, particularly in local authority departments.

The Beauregard development

The Beauregard development zone, to the northwest of the city, illustrates the city's far-sighted property strategy. During the 1980s a "preliminary greening" programme surveyed the hedgerows around then-cultivated areas, and ensured their protection and extension to form a network of tree-lined pedestrian avenues for the future development zone. Thus the new residential development has some continuity with the surrounding countryside, completed by the landscaping treatment within the new urban blocks.

The Salvatierra building (see pp. 166-171), part of the European Cepheus programme, sums up the aim of low-energy building and a healthy built environment. This approach is to be extended to phases 3 and 4 of the development, beside the new park, with three levels of architectural and environmental specifications compulsory for all buildings.

In 1995 the recommendations of a study entitled "Environmental and Energy Analysis of urban planning" put "green" considerations at the forefront of policy for the new area. Developers, architects and landscape designers worked together in shared offices to ensure smooth working and efficient communication. The stated goal was a unified whole, incorporating individual creativity – diversity tempered by dialogue.

Beauregard development environmental requirements

Priority aims
- A design concept which establishes a relationship between the buildings and the adjacent park
- Energy saving measures (reduction of household energy costs by around 30 %)
- Internal and external water conservation measures
- Comfortable levels of natural lighting in all living areas (including kitchens and bathrooms), stairwells and communal areas

Minimum requirements
- Noise:
  · sound insulation against external noise below 30dB
- Energy:
  · extra-thickness thermal insulation, high-performance windows
  · heating and hot water from the Villejean household waste plant
- Water:
  · bi-flow taps, pressure regulators, dual-flush toilets
- Lighting:
  · preference for class A low-energy household appliances
  · low-energy bulbs in communal areas
- Air:
  · avoidance of polluting products in construction; airtight building envelope
- Household waste:
  · space for five different waste containers for waste sorting
- Site:
  · cleaner site, with waste sorting
- Utility charges:
  · facility for individual and collective charging on the basis of consumption

Optional
- Solar panels for water heating
- Two-way ventilation with high-yield heat exchanger for heat recovery
- Rainwater recovery

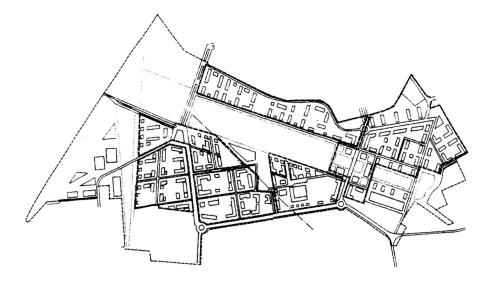

General plan of the development. A total of 2,350 housing units are planned.

ARCHITECTURE
AND ENVIRONMENTAL QUALITY

Environmental quality brings together human convenience and comfort, sustainable use of natural resources and control of waste. Applied to architecture, this concept requires the integration of fresh constraints into all stages of the construction process, along with a shift in attitudes on the part of both professionals and public.

The Riaux house, Montgermont, 1976. Designer: Jean-Yves Riaux.

THE ENVIRONMENTAL APPROACH

The environmental approach is an innovative approach to building issues, including the project brief, design, construction and building management. All parties are involved as a team; all have a common aim, that of environmental protection, and many use comparable methods to achieve it. Practice varies between countries and according to different building types, ranging from empirical approaches to performance specification methods.

Variety of approach

This chapter describes 23 projects, in nine European countries, which are representative of the variety of techniques employed. Most of them used empirical methods. Some made use of a more theoretical approach based on defined, sometimes quantified targets. For example, the house in the Perche used the French HQE system, and the Affoltern am Albis terraced housing used Energy 2000 concepts.

Several projects are experimental in nature: the Ölzbündt housing in Dornbirn; the home and workplace building in Freiburg im Breisgau; the Notley Green primary school in Essex; the Leonardo da Vinci secondary school in Calais.

A number of buildings were designed and funded under the EU's Thermie programme, and their performance is subject to continuing study. These include the housing block in Helsinki (designed under the Sunh programme), the Salvatierra building in Rennes (part of the Cepheus project) and the Avax headquarters in Athens (the EC 2000 project).

Interdisciplinary co-operation

If environmental issues are to be effectively taken into account in construction projects, consensus and co-operation is needed between all disciplines involved. A global, interdisciplinary approach, known generally as the integrated design process, allows a rationalisation of all aspects of the project through a combination of traditional and innova-

tive methods. User comfort, protection of the site, water and energy management and cost control are all taken into account. The conflicts between priorities which will inevitably arise can be resolved through pragmatic planning and co-ordinated action, when clients, architects and contractors work together from early on in the process.

Besides limiting environmental impact, this approach has a social dimension. Projects may involve users in both design and construction. Use of local materials and techniques boosts the regional economy. Design should also facilitate a sense of ownership of the space by its inhabitants, allowing for the changing nature of the family, the workplace and education.

RATIONAL USE OF ENERGY

A house built today uses half as much energy as one built at the beginning of the 1970s. However, heating and hot water still account for a quarter of energy consumed in Europe, and make a corresponding contribution to CO_2 emissions. Rational use of energy is one of the four priorities set out by the EU's 6th Environmental Action Plan for 2001-2010. Achievement of the targets set depends on a combination of active and passive energy conservation measures and increased use of renewable energy sources. In many case sophisticated, delicate and high-maintenance equipment can be replaced by simple and pragmatic solutions.

Bioclimatic principles

The bioclimatic approach, used traditionally throughout history, was rediscovered by the West at the time of the first oil shock. Applied principally to houses, this approach bases choice of building shape, site, orientation and spatial layout on the particular features of the site: climate, dominant wind direction, soil characteristics, topography, solar exposure and views.

Building volumes should be compact, limiting both internal circulation and façade area, and hence

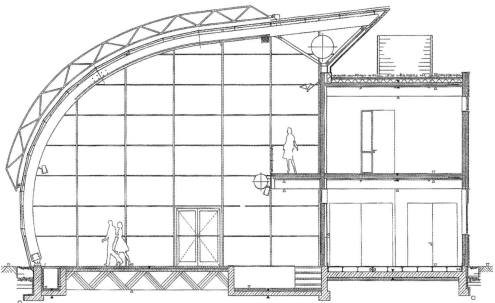

Forestry centre, Stuttgart-Degerloch, Germany, 1996. Architects: Jockers Architekten.

heat loss. Grouping rooms according to their functions can generate savings in heating and lighting. A bioclimatic building will generally have opaque northern façades, with access and service areas grouped on this side of the building, and large glazed areas to the south. A first generation of such houses, many of them timber-framed, appeared in France and other European countries in the 1970s and 1980s (*see illustration p. 92*).

Today, areas of high-performance glazing, of a size appropriate to the building volume and orientation, allows utilisation of solar gain. This should be combined with good insulation of the walls and roof. In Switzerland, Germany and Scandinavia, U-values of 0.2 W/m²K, with insulation thicknesses of 160-200mm, are increasingly common. Solid concrete or masonry elements work as thermal reservoirs: in winter, they absorb heat during the day and release it gradually at night; in summer, their high thermal mass helps prevent the space from becoming too hot.

At the forest and woodland centre near Stuttgart (*see above*), the large exhibition hall, supported on its north side by a compact service building, uses passive solar energy. In winter, solar radiation passes freely through the glazing and heats the space. In summer, the dense foliage of the adjacent trees shades the glazing, while a system of strips of opaque white cloth, sliding on rails fixed to the glued-laminated timber arch structure, screens the internal space from the sun's rays. The gap between this structure and the glazing creates a chimney effect, allowing warm air to be vented at the top. The presence of the wood-land on the building's south-west side thus contributes to its passive use of solar energy.

Optimising solar gain

Using passive solar gain for heating reduces a building's reliance on energy-consuming heating systems at no significant extra cost. Within compact apartment blocks, the smaller building envelope area per housing unit can allow a reduction in energy needs of around 40 % compared with detached houses.

Using Helios computer simulation software, studies carried out for the new developments at Rieselfeld in Freiburg im Breisgau (*see p. 70*) looked at optimum areas of glazing on the façades. They showed that for a five-storey housing block, optimal values of 55 % glazing on the south façades, and 11 % on the north façades, reduced energy consumption by 12 % compared to the "standard" design of 28 % glazing on each. Ideally, a building should be oriented with its long sides facing the sun and with a depth of 10-12m; however, strict application of this "rule" would clearly result in a formal resemblance between all low-energy buildings.

In winter, spring and autumn, best use can be made of solar gain as follows:
- incident solar energy is captured by suitably-sized areas of glazing: 40-60 % glazing on the south façade, 10-15 % to the north, and less than 20 % on the east and west;
- this energy is stored in high thermal inertia elements such as concrete, stone or earth floors or internal walls;

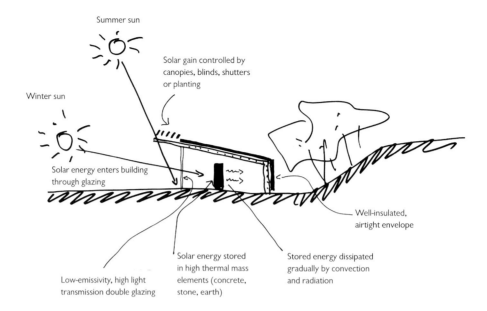

Summer sun

Winter sun

Solar gain controlled by
canopies, blinds, shutters
or planting

Solar energy enters building
through glazing

Well-insulated,
airtight envelope

Stored energy dissipated
gradually by convection
and radiation

Solar energy stored
in high thermal mass
elements (concrete,
stone, earth)

Low-emissivity, high light
transmission double glazing

Principles of bioclimatic design
(Drawing by Jean-Yves Barrier.)

**"Smart house", Chambray-
les-Tours, 1990.
Architect: Jean-Yves Barrier.**

- stored heat is then gradually released from these elements by convection and radiation;
- heat loss to the outside is limited by insulation, draught-proofing and minimising the area of the building envelope.

In summer, overheating caused by excessive solar gain can be avoided by:
- controlling the amount of direct incident sunlight by means of external sun-screens or slatted blinds, and use of glass with an appropriate solar factor; internal blinds, and screening by foliage from plants or trees, can also contribute;
- allowing excess heat to be dissipated through natural ventilation.

Comfort in summer

To allow comfortable temperatures in summer while maintaining sufficient levels of natural light, incident sunlight needs to be controlled by over-hanging roofs or other fixed or mobile external shading systems. Furthermore, openings can be positioned so as to encourage ventilation through natural convection. In the house at Autheuil (see pp. 126-131), and on a larger scale in the office building at Wageningen (see pp. 218-223), atrium or conservatory spaces are used to bring light into the centre of the building and aid ventilation. Water, as used traditionally in Arab palaces, can also help control the building environment in summer. Whether flowing over a solid wall as in the Datagroup offices in Pliezhausen (see p. 212), or evaporating from the gabion walls at the Terrasson cultural centre (see p. 208), water regulates air humidity and hence comfort.

Another way of regulating internal air temperature in summer is via earth cooling tubes, a natural ventilation system which uses the thermal mass of the underlying soil. Fresh air from some distance away enters a stainless steel inlet and is brought into the building via a (usually clay) underground pipe. A pipe length of 100m cools air by around 7°C in summer, and warms it by a similar amount in winter. This system was used at the Mäder secondary school (see p. 190), the Notley Green primary school (see p. 184), the experimental housing at Dornbirn (see p. 142), and the Datagroup offices (see p. 212).

Thermal bridges

Building insulation, whether in façades, roof or between basement and ground floor, can often have discontinuities or weak points arising either from the design detailing or from lack of precision in construction. These thermal bridges (or cold bridges) may occur at a point or along a line. In France, it is estimated that they account for more than 40% of building heat loss. The new RT 2000 regulations (see p. 98) address this point.
A thermal bridge can cause a local temperature drop on the internal surface, which can result in condensation, leading to damp and water damage. Typical locations are at lower building levels, in window frames, at the junctions between walls and floors or walls and roof, at eaves, balconies and similar perpendicular elements. They can be avoided by careful detailing.
At design stage, various measures can limit heat loss:

- compactness of the space to be heated
- separation of balcony and walkway secondary structures from the main building structure
- careful detailing of connections between walls, floors and roof
- external insulation of solid elements.

In timber frame construction, the U-value of a wall or roof can be improved significantly by replacing solid sections with timber I-beams. This was done, combined with double-thickness, overlapping insulation, in the home and workplace building in Freiburg im Breisgau (see p. 154). In a roof with rafters at 0.5m centres and 240mm of rockwool insulation, replacement of 80 × 240mm solid rafters with 241mm TJI beams reduces the U-value by 20 %.

Impermeability to air

To achieve significant reductions in energy consumption and a lasting brake on the greenhouse effect, application of bioclimatic principles on its own is not enough. Air infiltration through the building envelope results in draughts, which are not only uncomfortable but decrease energy efficiency. Conversely, low air permeability reduces consumption of heating energy and helps prevent damp, particularly in timber buildings. Ensuring continuity of the building envelope so as to prevent air entry requires careful design from an early stage, with particular attention given to connection detailing, window frames and penetrations such as flues, water pipes etc.

The German company Pro clima markets a range of products for this purpose, including vapour-proof membranes in natural recycled cellulose, airtight adhesive sealants in natural latex, and a range of adhesive strips (including double-sided, quick-setting and elastic strips). It also sells the Pro clima DB damp-proofing membrane whose permeability to water vapour varies with air humidity, so that permeability is lower in winter and higher in summer.

To check correct installation on site, various measures of air-tightness are available, such as the Minneapolis Blower Door test (see illustration, right). This creates a pressure drop of 50Pa across a wall and uses a door panel with integral fan to measure the resulting air flow. Results are given as a value of 1 (completely airtight) to 4 (insufficiently airtight) or more. This test is too expensive to use in every situation, but worth using on experimental or pilot projects; information from such tests can be put to good use by designers and contractors elsewhere. A simpler, more economical check is provided by air tests which assess air permeability without providing quantified measures. Pro clima's Wincon system, installed within a window-frame, enables assessment by non-specialists, over a period of one or two hours, of the airtightness of a detached house. In winter, thermographic devices enable critical areas and air entry points to be identified.

"Intelligent glazing"

Optimisation of building envelope performance requires careful choice of windows and glazing. In the mid-1990s, standard double glazing in France was 4-6-4mm or 4-12-4mm in thickness, with a U-value of around 3 W/m²K – while low-emissivity double glazing, used as standard in Germany and Scandinavia, was considered a top-of-the range product.

As early as 1990, in his "smart house", Jean-Yves Barrier (see illustration, left) used low-emissivity, high-transmission double glazing. In this building the living areas are oriented towards the southeast façade, which is designed to work like an integrated greenhouse on two levels. In winter, when the sun is low, curtain-wall double glazing traps solar radiation and retains the heat. In summer, the reflective layer limits the amount of energy passing through the glass. The roof forms a canopy, shading the façades and providing shelter to the balconies.

As requirements for high thermal performance have grown, this type of glazing has become standard, while industry is already producing still higher-performance products. "Intelligent glazing" combines high visible light transmittance, low U-value (which can be reduced to below 1.9W/m²K by means of a low-emissivity coating on the interior face of one pane) and a long-wavelength transmittance sufficiently low to limit solar gain as required. To achieve the Low Energy House rating (see p. 98) used in Germany, glazing units are made thicker and an inert gas is used in the air gap.

In 1999 the French glass manufacturer Saint-Gobain Vitrage launched its Climaplus 4S range. Its 4-15-4mm double glazing, with argon-filled insulation gap, has a U-value of 1.1 W/m²K and a solar factor of 42. This low-emissivity, high-trans-

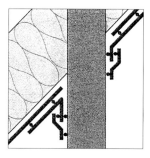
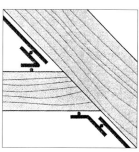

Reducing air permeability at connections and openings. Membrane in natural recycled cellulose, impermeable latex adhesive (products from Pro clima).

The Blower Door air permeability test.
(Source: Pro clima)

ENERGY PERFORMANCE VALUES

· U-value (W/m²K)

The U-value or heat transmission coefficient is the amount of heat which passes through unit area of a wall or partition for a unit temperature difference across it. Measured in W/m²K, this corresponds to the amount of heat passing through 1m² of wall for every degree Kelvin drop between its inside and outside surfaces. The lower the U-value, the less heat lost from the building. Formerly known as k in some documents, this coefficient is now known as U in the Swiss and German regulations, the new French regulations (the Th-U section of the RT 2000 standard) and the European standards, as well as in UK documents.

· Solar energy transmittance (g) or solar factor S

A measure of the solar protection provided by glazing, the solar transmittance is the proportion of incident solar radiation that is transferred through the glass. The French RT 2000 standard calculates the solar factor S using the Th-S rules, based on European standards.

· Energy consumption per unit of heated area (kWh/m²/year or MJ/m²/year)

This is a measure used in various standards and in the definition of the Minergie and Passive House labels. In Switzerland it is given in MJ/m²/year, and elsewhere generally in kWh/m²/year (1kWh = 3.6MJ). Energy consumption of 200MJ/m²/year is roughly equivalent to 5.5 litres of oil equivalent per square metre of heated habitable area.

mittance glass limits heat exchange between inside and outside and hence allows significant savings in energy consumption. Thermal performance is enhanced in winter, and greenhouse-type solar gain limited at other times of the year. The CSTB estimated in 2000 that the additional cost of such high-performance glazing products was offset over the long term by annual savings of around €7.60 per square metre of glazing for each 1W/m²K reduction in heat loss. With more widespread use of such products in France following the application of the RT 2000 regulations, their cost is likely to fall rapidly.

In Germany, U-values of 1.5 W/m²K for glazing are common. The Passive House label (see p. 100) requires a value of 1.0W/m²K or less. Vegla's Climatop Solar glazing has a U-value of 0.7W/m²K.

Double-skin façades

In several European countries, and particularly in the service sector, increasing use is being made of south-facing façades with a double skin which act as passive solar collectors. Depending on the height of the building and the system adopted, the air gap may run the full height or be divided at each floor. Solar gain is controlled by blinds between the façade skins, and stored heat dissipated by natural ventilation as the warmed air rises. Ventilated double skin systems provide effective thermal insulation and allow major savings to be made on heating and air-conditioning systems. They also contribute to user comfort in a number of ways:
- ensuring pleasant internal temperatures and humidity levels
- eliminating "cold wall" effects and window condensation
- protecting against summer overheating, reflection effects and draughts.

This chapter looks at a number of variants on the double-skin principle. At the Pliezhausen kindergarten (see p. 178), the south wall of the classrooms has a double-glazed inner skin and single-glazed outer skin, with the 300mm ventilated air gap between them functioning as a thermal buffer. The Mäder eco-school (see p. 190) is clad in single-glazed, non-jointed vertical panels in front of plywood panelling. The Avax headquarters in Athens (see p. 224) has a double skin of pivoting screen-printed glass panes. At the Bad

Elster spa pool (see p. 202), the principle of a glazed double skin has been applied to all four walls and the roof. This roof, with its ceiling layer in mobile printed glazing strips, was expensive, but fulfils several functions, including solar protection and natural ventilation.

In 2001 the French engineers OTH designed a "breathing" double-skin façade, with a blind in between the two layers of glazing. At €900/m², this system costs 45 % more than standard double glazing units with internal blinds. However, it allows significant savings on heating and air-conditioning systems, both in terms of specification and running costs.

Natural ventilation

Ventilation can account for between 20 % and 60 % of energy needs, particularly in the service sector. As buildings become better insulated, this proportion increases. To regulate temperatures in summer, air should be circulated from those areas (generally south-facing) heated by passive solar gain towards shaded (north-facing) zones. The warmer air then gradually rises, bringing in cool air at low level. The spatial organisation of the building can itself generate a natural thermal circulation between hot and cold zones, as in the Stuttgart-Degerloch house (see p. 132).

In offices and computer rooms temperature regulation in summer is particularly difficult, as electric lighting, computers and the presence of large numbers of people give off considerable heat. At the Wageningen research centre (see p. 218), users control the ventilation of their own offices, which give onto a glazed atrium, by opening the windows overnight. At the Datagroup offices in Pliezhausen (see p. 212), the architects and the Transsolar design team developed a combined natural ventilation system. Use of earth cooling tubes, together with a floor system with integral air circulation ducts, limits annual energy consumption by heating and air-conditioning to below 35kWh/m².

Industrial buildings can also use natural ventilation to control energy consumption. At the Strasbourg air cargo terminal (see illustration p. 97), cool air enters via low-level inlet grills in the north and south façades, which in winter allow it to be warmed on entry. Air then exits at a higher level via adjustable valves, situated along the four bands of roof-lights which allow natural lighting.

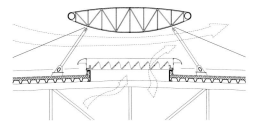

The Strasbourg air freight terminal, 2001. Architects: Jockers Architekten. View of the building, and detail showing natural ventilation system.

The air outlets are capped by aerodynamic wing elements, 5.75m by 7m, which increase air flow by creating a Venturi effect.

Natural lighting

Natural lighting is an essential part of environmental quality, both in terms of energy use and user comfort – particularly in the tertiary sector, where the dictates of profitability often result in deep plan buildings.

For the design of the iGuzzini administrative headquarters at Recanati, in Italy (see pp. 230-233), Mario Cucinella Architects worked with the Lausanne technical university to model light effects using a heliodon or "sun machine". This device simulates the earth's rotation, its motion relative to the sun and the seasonal variation in the angle of the sun's rays. A hemispherical "artificial sky", 5m in diameter and made up of 145 variable-intensity lighting discs, gives a wide range of potential configurations as well as good light distribution. The simulation uses a 1:50 scale model of the building, made of materials with similar reflectance to those used in the building design. Photometric devices, photos and videos then give information on the lighting levels at different points in the workspace, and are used to simulate natural lighting conditions to allow assessment of visual comfort.

THERMAL REGULATIONS AND EUROPEAN STANDARDS

In Europe, thermal insulation regulations were introduced in the wake of the first oil shock in 1973. Aimed mainly at housing, they helped bring about a noticeable reduction in energy consumption. The Scandinavian countries, used to combating the rigours of their climate, have long had stringent standards: in Sweden and Finland, wall insulation is typically more than 200mm thick. Other countries, notably Germany, France and Switzerland, have recently also introduced more stringent standards and ambitious rating schemes.

The development of the French thermal regulation

In France, the 1974 thermal regulations dealt only with insulation and ventilation of houses and apartments. Later, solar gain and the efficiency of heating and ventilation systems were taken into account. For the tertiary sector, the 1988 rules were concerned mainly with insulation, with no required performance standard for ventilation, heating, hot water or air-conditioning. The new RT 2000 regulations, which replace the 1988 document, are mandatory for all new buildings in the housing and tertiary sectors beginning on June 1, 2001 (with certain exceptions such as swimming pools, ice rinks and agricultural buildings). The new standards are likely to be further tightened on a regular basis.

RT 2000 is based on the 1996 energy use law. The issues involved are dealt with in the national strategy for combating climate change, ratified by the French prime minister on January 1, 2000 in response to the commitments made at Rio and Kyoto. It is estimated that buildings' energy consumption accounts for more than 25 % of greenhouse gas emissions, particularly CO_2. Application of the RT 2000 regulations should reduce energy consumption by new buildings by 20 % in housing and 40 % in the tertiary sector. The inclusion of calculation methods, and of product specifications defined according to European standards, should also allow RT 2000 to be adapted for use internationally.

However, the RT 2000 regards new buildings, which account for only 1 % of building stock. Estimates put average annual energy consumption of existing housing stock as high as $250kWh/m^2$ of useable space. It is therefore vital that these new measures are accompanied by a programme of improvements to existing buildings, through

LOW ENERGY HOUSE

• *Design principles*
Integration of energy concept from project outset
Compact shape
Increased insulation
Elimination of thermal bridges wherever possible
Impermeability to air
Efficient use of passive solar energy
Energy-efficient, easy-to-use technical systems
Low water use sanitaryware
Low-energy electrical appliances
Use of low embodied energy, recyclable construction materials

Comparison of heating energy consumption in Germany by different housing types, and variation of regulatory values (kWh/m²/year)

	Detached houses	Terraced houses	Apartment blocks
Pre-1982 building stock	260	190	160
1982 upper limit	150	110	90
1995 upper limit	100	75	65
Low Energy House	< 70	< 60	< 55

(Source: Pro clima 2000)

Average U-values for Low Energy rated building

External masonry wall	U < 0.25 W/m²K (120-180mm insulation)
External timber-framed wall	U < 0.20 W/m²K (200-250mm insulation)
Roof	U < 0.15 W/m²K (250-300mm insulation)
Internal wall between heated and unheated areas	U< 0.30 W/m²K (80-120mm insulation)
Glazing	U < 1.3 W/m²K (double glazing with inert gas)

better insulation and replacement of old, inefficient systems. Bringing such buildings up to RT 2000 standards would reduce energy use by around 22 % by the end of 2010.

The principles of RT 2000

The RT 2000 regulations are in effect a performance specification, setting out benchmark thermal properties but leaving specifiers the choice of materials and systems. They define limits on overall energy consumption for heating, hot water and ventilation systems in housing, plus lighting for tertiary sector buildings. They include requirements designed to improve user comfort in summer, and will be extended fully to cover air-conditioning systems in 2002. No technical solutions are imposed, leaving designers free to innovate.

Accompanying software, allowing energy consumption to be calculated as a function of temperature, will allow specialists to optimise designs. The document also allows a simplified approach, without calculations, based on technical criteria defined by the *Ministère de l'Equipement* and its advisors and checked by the CSTB. For different building types, this sets out the measures to be adopted to achieve the requirements, such as increased wall insulation, systematic use of insulated window-frames and low-emissivity glazing, elimination of thermal bridges, fitting of sunscreens, and use of low-energy heating and ventilation equipment.

The German Low Energy House rating

The 1982 German regulations put an upper limit on heating energy consumption in new buildings of 150kWh/m². In 1995 the regulations were revised, and this limit lowered further to an annual value of around 100kWh/m² for individual houses. Swedish regulations have integrated similar requirements since 1980.

The Low Energy House label *(see on the left)*, officially recognised in 1999 and now a necessary condition for obtaining certain grants, is linked to heating energy consumption below 65 kWh/m²/year. Another 25 kWh/m²/year is allowed for hot water and 30 kWh/m²/year for lighting, ventilation and household appliances. The Stuttgart-Degerloch house *(see pp. 132-135)* meets these requirements.

A Low Energy House consumes up to 80 % less energy than a building dating from the 1970s, and around 30 % less than a conventional new building. High insulation thicknesses and high-performance glazing have been standard in Germany for several years; Low Energy buildings are generally considered to be more economical than conventional housing as the additional capital outlay, usually between 1 % and 5 %, is recouped through reduced running costs. Since 1992 Freiburg im Breisgau (see p. 69) has required all buildings erected on publicly-owned land to conform to Low Energy standards.

The new German thermal performance regulations (*Energieeinsparverordnung*, EnEV), which came into force in February 2002, apply Low Energy House standards to new buildings. They also introduce the idea of an "energy passport", with the aim of increased transparency and encouraging improvements to existing building stock. Together, these measures should enable a reduction in CO_2 emissions of around 10 million tonnes by 2005.

The Swiss Minergie standard

The Minergie concept (see p. 23), established by the buildings department of the Zurich cantonal authorities, aims both to reduce energy consumption and to improve inhabitants' quality of life. Its ultimate goal is a reduction in greenhouse gas emissions through a lasting reduction in the use of non-renewable energy sources. The concept is applied to buildings via a rating, linked to fulfilment of precise requirements in terms of heating and electricity consumption, for both new and old buildings in the housing and service sectors (see on the right).

As with the RT 2000 regulations, Minergie is concerned with performance rather than methods, and specifiers may achieve the required standards by whatever means they choose. However, a compact building shape, good insulation, optimum-performance systems and appliances and an air-impermeable envelope will all be standard elements of a Minergie project. A certificate is obtained from the canton energy department on the basis of the project drawings; achievement of the required standards is then checked when construction is complete. By 2000 there were around 750 Minergie-rated projects.

Born out of the idealism of a few convinced environmentalists, Minergie has rapidly become a technical standard used widely by developers. For

THE MINERGIE STANDARD

Maximum values of heating and electricity consumption for the Minergie rating

Heating energy consumption	New buildings	Pre-1990 buildings
Housing	< 45 kWh/m²/year (160 MJ/m²year)	< 90 kWh/m²/year (320 MJ/m²/year)
Offices	< 40 kWh/m²/year (145 MJ/m²/year)	< 70 kWh/m²/year (250 MJ/m²/year)

Electricity consumption	New buildings	Pre-1990 buildings
Housing and offices	15 kWh/m²/year (53 MJ/m²/year)	15 kWh/m²/year (53 MJ/m²/year)

Average U-values for surfaces in Minergie buildings

	Compact building with increased insulation
Walls and roof	U = 0.2 W/m²K
Ground floor slab	U = 0.25 W/m²K
Windows and doors	U = 1.0 W/m²K

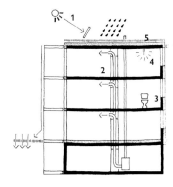

Sample Minergie housing block, schematic

1 Solar collectors for hot water heating (27m²)
2 Two-way ventilation with high-yield (65 %) heat exchanger
3 Low water use sanitaryware
4 Low-energy electrical and household appliances
5 Water-retaining turf roof

The values above are those for a block of twelve four-room apartments in Zurich. The additional cost of the energy and water conservation measures was 5 % of the total building budget; the reduction in running costs is equivalent to around 6 % of this additional cost each year. Various financial aid measures, such as low-interest loans, are available for Minergie buildings.
(Source: H.R. Preisig et al. *Ökologische Baukompetenz*, Zurich 1999)

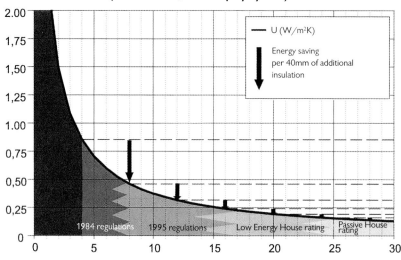

**Variation in the U-value
for walls as a function of insulation thickness
(mineral wool, cork or polystyrene)**

(Source: Cologne city authorities, Department of Employment, Social and Urban Development, Culture and Sport.)

the moment it is not compulsory, but it is an indicator of a clear trend in the Swiss building sector. Switzerland estimates that, thanks to improvements made to existing buildings, most buildings' heating consumption will soon be below 55 kWh/m^2. The generalised installation of better insulation (160-200mm thick) should result in a halving of CO_2 emissions, or an annual reduction of 10 million tonnes.

The European Passive House rating

The Passive House label was first introduced in the late 1980s in Hesse, one of the German Länder most active in environmental matters, by the director of the Passive House Institute, Wolfgang Feist. The basic requirement for this rating is heating energy consumption below 15 kWh/m^2/year. The first Passive Houses were built in 1991 in Darmstadt-Kranichstein (see illustration p. 101). A terrace of four houses with area of 156m^2, they combined bioclimatic principles with innovative elements: simple compact form; extra-thickness mineral-wool insulation (440mm thick in the roof, 260mm in the walls); triple-glazed windows with krypton between the panes; earth cooling tubes. Together with highly energy-efficient systems, such as two-way mechanical ventilation with a high-yield heat exchanger, and water heating via solar panels, these resulted in total energy consumption, including electricity, of less than 30kWh/m^2. The Hesse regional authorities provided 50 % funding for the energy conservation measures; data from this pilot project has allowed solutions to be refined for subsequent projects.

The Passive House concept soon spread beyond Germany. By 2001 several hundred detached houses, terraces and apartment blocks using these principles had been completed in Switzerland and Austria, besides around 1,000 in Germany. Several of these were associated with the Hanover Expo in 2000. A total of 250 passive housing units were built in five European countries as part of the Cepheus project, part of the EU's Thermie programme, between 1999 and 2001; among them is the sole French contribution to the project, the Salvatierra building in Rennes (see pp. 166-171).

Around 50 passive housing units are in use in Freiburg's environmental development zones, including 16 units in the experimental home and workplace building in Vauban (see pp. 154-159). The Ölzbündt development in Dornbirn (see pp. 142-147) is another Passive House project; while in Feuerbach, Stuttgart, 52 terraced passive houses were built in 2000. Europe's biggest passive housing development was competed in 2000 at Sonnenfeld in Ulm (see p. 50), with 104 houses and apartments designed by several architects, including Joachim Eble and Kottkamp & Schneider.

It is likely that the Passive House rating will eventually become standard in Germany, where some "zero energy" projects are already under way. Freiburg's Fraunhofer Institute, which works on solar and energy systems, has completed an "energy-independent" house which uses no more than 0.3 litres of oil equivalent per square metre of useable space, or one-third of the energy consumed by the Darmstadt houses.

RENEWABLE ENERGY

The use of renewable energy sources is linked to political strategy, depending on the political landscape and energy context of the country concerned (see pp. 26-29). Strategies rely on a combination of now-established and cost-efficient systems, such as heat pumps, solar hot water heaters and gas co-generation, and newer technologies, such as wind power and photovoltaic cells, whose current high cost will bring returns over a longer period.

Of heat energy sources, electricity from coal-fired power stations (principally in Germany) is by far the greatest generator of greenhouse gas emissions. Gas is considerably better in these terms, particularly with the use of power-vented (sealed-combustion) wall-mounted boilers. Emissions may be reduced by up to 60 % by use of an urban generating plant, particularly if it uses renewable fuels such as wood or biogas. Solar energy is the source which has the least environmental impact. (Source: *Bauen für eine lebenswerte Zukunft*, Freiburg im Breisgau 1996.)

Solar heating

Bioclimatic measures are often combined with the use of solar collector panels to heat hot water. Since they were first developed in the 1970s, these systems have see a number of improvements and have demonstrated their efficiency. The panels convert solar radiation into heat, which is transferred via a heat-carrying fluid (usually water) and a heat exchanger to a storage reservoir. They can be used all year round; even on cloudy days, there is enough sunlight to heat water above room temperature. In the temperate regions of Europe, correctly-sized and positioned solar panels can meet almost 100 % of domestic hot water requirements from April to September, and around 60 % of total annual needs, with corresponding reductions in CO_2 emissions. Following improvements to the technology over the years, panels are now relatively cheap and their installation is one of the most cost-efficient ways of using renewable energy sources. In 2000, they generated a return on investment after around ten years.

As prices fall, the use of solar panels should become widespread in Europe. In several countries grants or subsidies are available for their installation. Germany, Austria, Belgium and the Netherlands all have large-scale programmes to promote solar heating for domestic hot water.

Solar collectors are particularly efficient for apartment blocks, as used on the south-facing roofs of the Ölzbündt housing block in Dornbirn (see pp. 142-147), the Salvatierra building in Rennes (see pp. 166-171) and the home and workplace project in Freiburg im Breisgau (see pp. 154-159). The various school and college projects described in this chapter use solar heating for both environmental and educational reasons: the kindergarten in Pliezhausen (see p. 178-183) and Stuttgart-Heumaden (see pp. 172-177), the Calais secondary school (see pp. 196-201) and the secondary school at Mäder (see pp. 190-195).

The main problem with solar heat is the difficulty of storing it. In response to this, the German company UFE Solar, together with the Fraunhofer solar energy institute, has developed a technique whereby heat can be stored within a small volume for several months by means of silica gel. In summer, heat produced by the solar collectors heats the silica gel.

The heat dries the gel, producing water which is removed and stored, leaving the energy embodied in the dried gel. In winter, the water is restored to the gel, liberating the heat. Solar collectors equipped with this system would be able to meet domestic heating and hot water requirements all year round. The company hopes to begin marketing such products in 2003.

Photovoltaic conversion

Photovoltaic (PV) modules convert solar energy directly into electricity by means of silicon semiconductor cells which react with light to generate direct current. They are used in many applications, including parking meters, roadside telephones and signage. Positioned on the façades or roof of a building, PV panels can generate electricity either

Principles of Minergie housing. Passive Houses; prototype at Darmstadt-Kranichstein, Germany, 1991. Architects: Bott, Ridder, Westermeyer; engineer: Wolfgang Feist.

Training centre, Herne-Sodingen,
Germany, 1999. Architects:
Françoise-Hélène Jourda and Gilles
Perraudin with HHS Architects.

THERMODYNAMIC
HEATING IN HOUSING

· **Air to air system**
- heat energy taken from the outside air
- the building is heated by warm air,
  with fresh air being added as necessary
- air-conditioning possible in summer
  if required
- average energy consumption
  32-35 kWh/m²/year

· **Air to water system**
- heat energy taken from the outside air
- the building is heated by hot water,
  via under-floor radiant heating or
  convector heaters
- system takes up little space; under-
  floor heating gives complete flexibility
  of heated areas
- average energy consumption
  28-32 kWh/m²/year

· **Ground to water system**
- heat energy taken from the soil,
  via an evaporator below ground level
- the building is heated by hot water,
  via under-floor radiant heating or
  convector heaters
- system takes up little space;
  underfloor heating gives complete
  flexibility of heated areas
- average energy consumption
  22-25 kWh/m²/year

for internal use or for distribution to an external
network. They may become elements of the
architectural design, or double as sun-screens, as
on the Total Energie offices (see pp. 234-239). At
the German interior ministry training centre at
Herne-Sodingen in the Ruhr (see *illustration
above*), built as part of the Emscher Park IBA, a
huge 16m high glazed space contains the library,
conference hall, canteen and living quarters, a
total floor area of 12,000m². The 20,000m² of
glazing in the walls and roof incorporates
10,000m² of Pilkington Solar PV modules, which
generate enough electricity to heat the whole
space. A Mediterranean climate is thus recreated
without the need for conventional heating or air-
conditioning systems.

PV modules are still very expensive, but there are
significant financial incentive schemes to encourage their use in Germany, where a number of
large-scale production plants have recently come
on stream (see pp. 27). In the future they could
have very significant applications in some developing countries, which have few other energy
sources but plentiful sunshine.

Thermodynamic heating

Thermodynamic heating dates from the 19th century, and is widely used in the US, Japan and Scandinavia. Heat pumps are robust, and their
efficiency has improved by more than 25 % over
the past decade. The system is based on the
transfer of heat via a fluid. It uses no burner, and
there is hence no combustion, which is a significant source of localised pollution.

A heat pump takes heat from the ground and air,
which have been warmed by the sun, and transfers it to a heat exchanger. The efficiency of the
system is measured by the ratio between the
heat energy delivered to the condenser to provide heating, and the energy consumed by the
compressor and its attachments. For domestic
heating, this varies between 2.5 and 5. Thus when
the system is working in optimum conditions, up
to 80 % of useable heat can be supplied free of
charge from the surrounding environment.

Different thermodynamic systems use different
natural heat sources (air, water or soil) and different ways of dissipating the recovered heat
within the building (in air or water). In Switzerland, around a third of heat pumps use underground heat extraction systems, as the constant
temperature of the ground gives a better energy
yield than air-water or air-ground pumps. Recovery of stored heat from the water table is also fea-
sible. In the terraced houses at Affoltern am Albis
(see pp. 136-141), the heat pumps used by each
four-house terrace take heat from salt water at
20°C, 180m underground. In the Ölzbündt housing block in Dornbirn (see pp. 142-147), each of
the 13 housing units has its own heat pump.

Energy from wood

In several European countries the timber energy
sector is growing, drawing on under-exploited
forestry resources (see p. 24) and thus contributing to a reduction in carbon dioxide emissions.
Wood-fuelled heating effectively contributes nil to
the overall quantity of atmospheric CO_2, as the

amount emitted on combustion is equal to that absorbed by the trees from the atmosphere during their lifetime.

A wood-fuelled stove is often enough to heat a home during spring and autumn, shortening the period during which conventional heating systems are needed. Some are built in stone, inspired by the traditional ceramic *Kachelöfen*. Scandinavian-type cast iron stoves are more efficient. Still better are the wood pellet fuelled stoves whose use is beginning to spread to Europe from the US. These commonly have a fuel hopper of 20-30kg capacity and can burn untended, with thermostatic regulation, for between 24 and 72 hours. Efficiency can reach 75 %, much higher than standard stoves.

In the mid-1990s, the urban-industrial sector was revolutionised by the advent of automatic combustion systems. These may be fuelled by sawdust, woodchips, bark, roundwood or other sawmill residue, at between 5 % and 60 % water content. Smokestack systems have a refractory combustion chamber with fixed or mobile grate; fuel enters via a continuous feed auger or a hydraulically-controlled push system. Smoke is treated by a multivortex dust collector or an induced draught fan. The French manufacturer Compte markets lower-capacity combustors (200-900kW) and standard models (1,200-1,500kW) for industry and local authorities.

In 2000 there were around 1,500 wood-fuelled industrial or public heating plants in France. The 3 Suisses building in Hem, for example, has a 2MW heating plant fed by wood shreds from sawmill residue and hedge trimmings, with a maximum capacity of ten days' worth of fuel. The development of the wood energy sector in France is being assisted by the French energy agency ADEME.

Biogas

Biogas is a product of fermented household waste, sewage sludge and agricultural and industrial effluent. The gas is then burnt to produce heat or electricity. In France, it is estimated that around 10 % of natural gas consumed could be replaced by biogas. As with wood biomass energy, several European countries offer financial aid for biogas use (see p. 29). In southern Germany, it is used increasingly by farmers to produce energy for their own use.

In the home and workplace building in Freiburg im Breisgau (see pp. 154-159), garden waste, compostable kitchen waste and sewage from the vacuum toilets are collected in a single container. Their fermentation produces biogas, which is used for cooking in place of the mains natural gas supply. As cookers account for a significant proportion of household energy consumption, the resulting savings are considerable. The remaining compost is spread on the fields as fertiliser by local farmers, thus completing the natural cycle (see schematical drawing below).

Wind energy

Wind turbines convert the kinetic energy of the wind to mechanical energy. This may either be used directly, e.g. to power water pumps, or be converted to electricity, for use on site or distribution to a network.

Wind can be an unpredictable, inconsistent energy source. To function, wind turbines generally need a minimum wind speed of 5m/s. However a number of European countries have the potential for economically viable wind energy generation, and this is being exploited to an increasing degree, notably in Germany, Denmark, the Netherlands and Spain.

Wind turbine supplying power to a service station, Denmark.

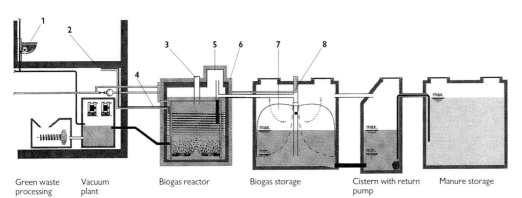

| Green waste processing | Vacuum plant | Biogas reactor | Biogas storage | Cistern with return pump | Manure storage |

Home and workplace building, Freiburg im Breisgau, Germany, 2000. Architects: Common & Gies. Schematic diagram of the biogas facility. (Drawing by Jörg Lange.)
1 vacuum-operated toilets
2 heating circuit
3 inspection opening
4 heating
5 access opening
6 insulation
7 biogas "pockets"
8 biogas outlet

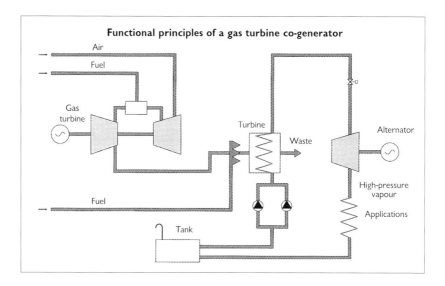

Functional principles of a gas turbine co-generator

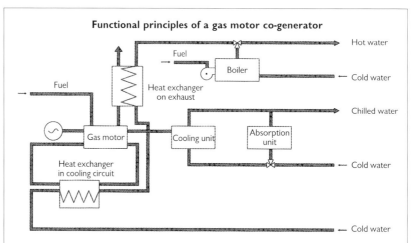

Functional principles of a gas motor co-generator

Smaller turbines, with capacity of 30kW or less, provide power for single households. Larger turbines can power housing estate or district, public amenities or industrial areas.

The Perwez turbine in Belgium has a 600kW capacity and provides electricity for 450 homes; that at the Baie de Somme service area in France (see pp. 240-245) has a capacity of 250kW, and provides 500,000kWh per year. The electricity supply to the Calais secondary school (see pp. 196-201) comes in part from a 135kW Seewind turbine. In both these cases, as the energy produced cannot be stored, energy surplus to immediate requirements is sold to the national electricity distributor.

Co-generation

While co-generation does not use renewable energy, it is highly efficient, as lost heat is recovered and used. A single generator produces both heat and mechanical energy, which drives alternators to produce electric current. Co-generators

work off natural gas, which produces fewer undesirable combustion products than oil. Turbine co-generators are used in high-capacity plants, while motors are suitable for more moderate power requirements.

At the Calais secondary school (see pp. 196-201), a 165kW gas motor co-generator supplies electricity needs not already covered by wind power. The advent of fuel cells, which are extremely efficient, is likely to make smaller co-generation facilities, of 100-250kW, more viable.

Fuel cells

A fuel cell generates electricity and heat from a chemical reaction between a fuel and an oxidant, such as oxygen from the air. It is highly efficient and very "clean", involving minimal carbon dioxide and sulphur emissions

There are currently around 200 functioning fuel cell systems in the world, but the technology is very expensive and effectively still at prototype stage. However, research and development is

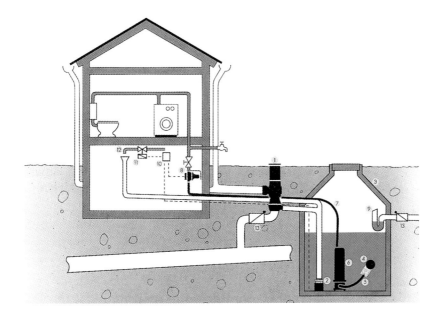

Rainwater recovery system with underground cistern and Multigo immersed pump.
(Source: Wisy)
1 self-cleaning filter
2 filter
3 cistern
4 floating inlet filter
5 inlet pipe
6 Multigo pump
7 pressurised tube
8 automatic valve
9 overflow
10 control panel
11 magnetic valve
12 drinking water feed
13 non-return valve

gathering pace as the big energy producers and manufacturers become more interested.

A stand-alone, non-polluting system, fuel cells will allow in situ energy production for industry, hospitals, schools and housing. In France, the energy agency ADEME and the national energy suppliers EDF and GDF have together funded a pilot project in Chelles, where 200 families use electricity from phosphoric acid fuel cells with a capacity of 200kW. A French-German consortium is leading a far-reaching project to bring into service a 1MW fuel cell plant in 2002 which will supply enough power for a town of 2,000 people.

CONTROLLING THE WATER CYCLE

Water is an increasingly precious resource, which is used wastefully in industrial countries. In the US, average daily water use is 1,000 litres per head. By contrast, in areas of South America, Africa and Asia few have access to more than 40 litres a day. In the building sector, particularly in housing, a number of measures can be taken to improve management of the water cycle:
- reducing consumption, through use of water-saving appliances and responsible behaviour
- rainwater collection
- roof greening
- natural filtering of grey water
- creation of biotope zones.

Water can become an architectural element, helping to regulate the humidity levels of internal air, as in the internal atria at the Datagroup offices in Pliezhausen *(see pp. 212-217)* or the Wageningen research centre *(see pp. 218-223)*. In the latter, where the site had been heavily polluted by intensive agriculture, the water cycle is regulated using turf roofs and use of recovered rainwater for toilet flushing and to feed the atrium pools.

Rainwater recovery systems

In Europe, average daily consumption of drinking water is between 110 and 200 litres per head. This would be reduced by around 30 % if we were to use drinking water only for food, drink and personal hygiene, and rainwater for other requirements. A series of studies over several years, notably in Germany by Otto Wack, have shown that when purified by a well-designed and correctly-installed system, rainwater has comparable quality and characteristics to distilled water.

In the most reliable and effective systems, rainwater falling on the building roof is recovered and filtered through a self-cleaning system before being collected in a cistern. A two stage purification process, with no maintenance requirements, is carried out within the cistern, and the resulting water is stored in a cool, dark place. This recycled water is then distributed using low-energy pumps, the whole network being clearly labelled "not drinking water".

The development in the 1990s of efficient self-cleaning filter systems, such as those marketed by Wisy, have contributed to a rapid rise in rainwater recovery systems in Germany. As turnover in the sector has grown, creating significant numbers of manufacturing and skilled jobs, export of these products has spread to other European countries, in particular Denmark and the Netherlands.

Rainwater is suitable for irrigation, toilet flushing and cleaning. Its use in washing machines has further environmental advantages, as its low hardness prolongs the machine's life and allows

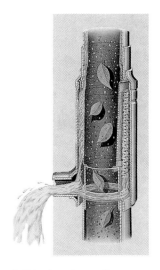

Self-cleaning rainwater filter
(Source: Wisy)

ZinCo extensive greenroof
systems.
a Edge detail for flat roof
with projecting eaves.
b Edge detail for sloping roof with
gutter outlet.
1 vegetation (sedum mat)
2 layer of "Zincobum" organic
material (15 l/m²)
3 anti-erosion sheet in open-mesh
jute, for roof slopes above 15°
or very windy sites
4 "Zincolit" substrate (60 l/m²)
5 profiled drainage elements
6 moisture retention/protection mat
7 root-resistant waterproofing
8 water outlet
Overall thickness 100mm approx.;
wet weight, including plants,
70kg/m²; water retention capacity
19 l/m² approx.
(Source: ZinCo)

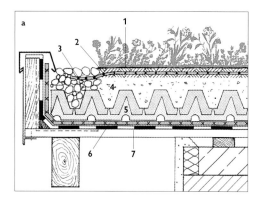

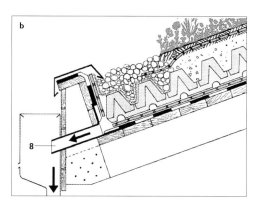

use of smaller quantities of detergent and fabric conditioner.

In Germany, use of rainwater recovery systems is becoming increasingly widespread, particularly in schools, sports and cultural centres and administrative buildings. They are regularly proposed by both builders and developers for all types of developments, both small and large scale. A properly-installed system generally produces a return on investment in three to ten years, depending on its size and the use to which the recycled water is put. In France, where health regulations are very limiting – special authorisation must be obtained from the regional health ministry department (Ddass), which oversees health and hygiene in buildings – rainwater recycling is still almost non-existent. The HQE school buildings in Caudry, Limoges and Calais (*see pp. 196-201*) are among the few projects to use rainwater recovery systems.

Industrial use of rainwater

Rainwater can also be used in industrial production processes, where motives are both environmental and economic. As part of the Quality of Life European research programme, Renault in 1999 brought on stream a rainwater recovery system at its Maubeuge plant. Around 320,000 m³ of water is collected over the 39-hectare site, and provides 35-40 % of the water required. The cost of this purified rainwater comes to around FF2 (€0.3) per cubic metre, before depreciation costs, compared with around FF4.5 (€0.7) for mains drinking water. While the system cost FF17m (€2.6m), this investment will be recouped in three to four years. This project allowed extensive methodological studies to be undertaken and resulted in completion of the Sirrus software, designed to help other companies come up with

comparable systems. Renault intends to extend the experiment to its Douai and Flins factories. At the Volkswagen plant in Wolfsburg, rainwater is used in place of the demineralised water normally used in car manufacturing processes. In Hamburg, rainwater collected from the roofs of Lufthansa aircraft hangars is used both for toilet flushing and cleaning aircraft, with a resulting saving of 15,000m³ of water each year.

Green roofs

In several countries, as the environmental results of the loss of soil permeability make themselves felt, greening of flat or slightly sloping roofs is becoming more common. Stuttgart incorporated the concept into its city development plan over 15 years ago, and several other German towns have since followed its example (*see p. 53*). The principle is simple: to provide at roof level the area of grass or planting that was removed by the building at ground level. A green roof increases thermal and acoustic insulation, and extends the life of the roof by regulating temperature changes at the roof membrane. The vegetation helps reduce atmospheric dust and maintain air humidity in built-up areas; while in periods of heavy rainfall, green roofs act as temporary 'sponges', retaining 70-90 % of rainwater and thus reducing pressure on drainage systems.

Extensive (shallower soil profile) green roofs are relatively light (50-100kg/m²) and need only minimal maintenance. They are planted with self-seeding mosses or sedums, which require less than 10cm of soil depth. There are several proprietary systems on the market; the German enterprise ZinCo distributes the Floradrain system, which can be constructed with different soil depths, depending on the roof slope and the type of planting required. It is designed on an environmental basis using recycled materials. A flat roof may also be converted wholly or partly to an intensive green roof, or roof garden, with larger plants or trees. Intensive greenroofs are necessarily thicker and heavier, and need more maintenance.

Wastewater management

Various projects in Europe have looked at alternatives to conventional wastewater treatment systems. One of these is constructed wetlands, or reed bed filtering. In the Järna hospital complex near Stockholm (see illustration, right), constructed according to the "anthroposophic" principles of the Austrian educationalist and philosopher Rudolf Steiner, the landscaping integrates a water treatment system comprising seven ponds and cascading pools. The Traiselect system, developed at Mons-Hainaut university in Belgium, is based on selective treatment of sewage effluent and grey water. Grey water is treated in an anaerobic tank, followed by aeration in a separate container, after which it is suitable for cleaning and garden use. For sewage, the researchers propose dry composting "biocontrolled" toilets, or a reed bed type system as used in various other countries (including Germany and Scandinavia).

In Germany, an example of a truly innovative system is that used at the home and workplace building in Freiburg im Breisgau (see pp. 154-159). This aims to be a complete, stand-alone water management system. Grey water from kitchens and bathrooms is used for garden irrigation and toilet flushing. The toilets operate with water-saving vacuum systems, as used on aeroplanes, which use less than one litre per flush. Sewage is transferred to a small biogas plant, which provides fuel for cooking (see p. 103). Rainwater is channelled into a perimeter trench.

In France, health regulations make innovation in this area difficult. In 2001, however, the construction company GTM, in its PLA housing development in Annecy, set up an experimental grey water recycling scheme using a bioreactor membrane system, which should provide useful data for future projects. In the house at Autheuil (see p. 126-131), rainwater, de-greased grey water and sewage are filtered by a four-basin system planted with reeds, rushes and irises.

Biotopes

In Germany, a common practice is diversion of rainwater to areas which thus become wetlands, encouraging local flora and fauna through establishment of a natural ecosystem. The presence of water allows plants to flourish, which then attract insects, hence insect-eating birds, who spread seeds, which grow into more plants, and so on.

In the Affoltern am Albis development (see pp. 136-141), a proportion of rainwater is temporarily retained by the extensive green roofs; this then flows slowly through three biotope pools before reaching a stream. At the Stuttgart-Heumaden kindergarten (see pp. 172-177), the water from the rainwater tank overflow runs into a biotope area, which serves both ecological and educational purposes.

Water treatment can also be integrated into landscaped areas around buildings. At the Baie de Somme service area (see pp. 240-245), the run-off from the motorway carriageways and car parks, after passing through hydrocarbon separators, is filtered by reed-bed systems in planted canals which ring the service buildings.

THE IMPACT OF MATERIALS ON THE ENVIRONMENT

Choice of materials has effects on the natural environment, the internal environment of the building and the health of its occupants. Evaluation of environmental impact must take into account the environmental damage which may occur at each stage of the material life cycle: fabrication, construction, service and maintenance, demolition and disposal. Application of this idea to construction is complicated by the interactions, and indeed contradictions, between different aims.

Air quality

Air quality inside buildings is a sensitive subject, made so by public fears about links between cancers, asthma and other allergies and the dust, fibre particles and volatile organic compounds (VOCs) which are present in some construction materials.

Natural materials may not always be healthy, as the example of asbestos shows. Some people may react badly to the presence of chemicals contained in various building products such as glues and paints. The use of a number of others, such as

Pond system at the Järna hospital complex, Stockholm.

Biotope area in a private garden.

ENVIRONMENTAL
IMPACT OF MATERIALS

Environmental assessment of building products and materials takes into account the quantity of raw material, energy and water used at each stage of the product's life cycle:

- raw materials extraction and transport
- fabrication
- transport to site
- construction
- maintenance, repairs and replacement during the building's life
- demolition
- disposal

mineral wool, is strongly opposed in some quarters. However, we must distinguish between the risks to those involved in manufacture, handling and installation of these products and those which affect the building's occupants.

Realistically, we can draw a line between products which are directly in contact with the air and those which are not. In areas where people spend long periods, such as housing and offices, as well as schools, sports centres and other areas intended for children's use, it is particularly important to err on the side of caution and ensure the use of only those materials carrying no risk of toxicity.

Life cycle assessment

As set out by the ISO 14040 standards, Life Cycle Assessment (LCA) is a method of evaluating the environmental impact of a material or product over its whole life. In the Netherlands, the government and the building industry have worked together to produce an environmental performance standard, the *Dubo-eisen* (requirements for sustainable construction), to apply to all new housing. The method is based on LCA and considers the whole life cycle of the different components, but sets an environmental performance standard for the building as a whole, allowing significant flexibility in choice of materials and processes. The resulting Material Based Environmental Profile for Buildings, or MEPB, is applied alongside other environmental requirements such as the energy performance coefficient defined in the Netherlands building code.

Factors influencing product choice

Assessment of a product's impact on the environment and health is very complex. In a global context, products and materials can be classified according to a number of criteria. They should have no associated health risks, come from renewable sources, and be recyclable. Preferably, they should also have low embodied energy and be sourced or manufactured locally, boosting regional economies and limiting transport requirements. Rail or water transport is preferable to road transport. Specifiers should also favour products requiring little or no maintenance.

To meet all these requirements, especially on a tight budget, is a near-impossible task. In the absence of regulatory requirements or guidance, specifiers must make pragmatic choices, taking

into account cost, availability, procurement processes and available expertise. Environmental quality also involves optimising the quantity of material used, and use of a mix of materials, making best use of the qualities of each.

Environmental certification
of materials

Clear labelling of products, with transparency regarding their composition and fabrication processes, is vital for the long-term establishment of the environmental approach. Unfortunately this is rarely achieved; companies with ISO 14001 certification and eco-labelling systems are few and far between. The German company Auro is a pioneer in this regard: since 1983 it has manufactured organic paints and adhesives made from natural, renewable organic materials, produced locally wherever possible. The Swiss particleboard manufacturer Kronospan began looking at this area in 1991, with publication of an environmental impact report. Kronospan belongs to the WWF Wood Group, and is ISO 14001 certified. Its products use FSC certified timber (see p. 24) and water-soluble resins.

The lack of available information on building materials and products makes decisions difficult. To make up for this, for the design of the Wageningen research centre (see pp. 218-223) the architects Behnisch, Behnisch & Partner built up their own reference base, researching the origins and embodied energies of various materials. The resulting information served as the basis for the Netherlands' new MEPB environmental performance standard.

Other countries have already published guidance. In Switzerland, a catalogue of building components includes a list of environmentally friendly materials and products. In France, the standards organisation AFNOR has awarded environmental certification (*NF environnement*) to a number of products, particularly paints and finishes. The CSTB analyses products using its Equity life cycle software, designed specifically for the building sector, and publishes environmental impact information sheets summarising the results.

Towards a European materials
standard

The European Community published a directive on building products in 1989, which was incorporated into French law in 1992. Since then, publication of the necessary standards, Eurocodes and technical certification systems has enabled these principles to be put into practice, with free movement of EU-certified products throughout Europe. The process has been slow; a number of standards, for example concerning traditional processes such as timber framing, sawn and glued-laminated timber, have still to integrate harmonised provisions for CE marking.

The basis for future European environmental certification of building components is subject to approval by member states. In 2001 AFNOR published an experimental standard in France, XP P 01-010-1, entitled "Information on environmental characteristics of construction products; methodology and model environmental statement". This defines the type of data required, its origin and presentation.

A European classification would encourage more widespread use of some "green" products which are already accepted in a few EU countries. In France, first use of such products requires authorisation through an Atex (*Appréciation technique expérimentale*), a long and arduous process which can eventually lead to regulatory approval. Even products which are fully approved in neighbouring countries are often rejected by developers, consultants and checking authorities as too risky when they do not have the equivalent stamp of approval from the domestic authority.

Such barriers to innovation must be lifted. Widespread environmental quality will only be achieved when products and materials with Europe-wide environmental certification become cheaply and easily available.

Secondary materials

As the market for such products grows, more manufacturers are marketing "green" alternatives: wood board products using polyurethane glue to avoid formaldehyde emission; paints without chemical solvents; insulation made from cellulose, hemp or flax. Local authorities, private developers and designers are increasingly making choices either on principle or so as to increase their green credentials.

In Spain, Barcelona and around 50 other towns have banned the use of PVC. Bergen, Norway's second city, resolved in 1991 to remove all PVC from public buildings. The Swiss agency Metron

(*see pp. 136-141*) also avoids its use. There are many alternatives to PVC, depending on the required use:
- wood in window frames
- polyethylene or polypropylene in pipes
- wood or linoleum in flooring
- polyethylene, polyamide or silicon products in cable trunking.

Various natural finishes are available, including paints and protective finishes with natural oil, resin and wax bases, vegetable solvents and natural earth and mineral pigments. These are still little-known in France, but widely used in Germany, and are often significantly more expensive than their synthetic counterparts.

Cheaper alternatives are also beginning to come onto the market. The Stuttgart-Heumaden kindergarten (*see p. 172-177*) used Auro wood treatments containing flax oil and mineral pigments, with an orange oil solvent. In the terraced houses at Affoltern am Albis (*see pp. 136-141*), the natural ingrain wallpaper was overpainted with a casein-based paint.

Structural materials

Few contemporary structural materials can be termed truly green. The best approach is to determine the most appropriate material for each part of the building, given the properties required and budgetary constraints. The most commonly-used structural materials – steel, concrete, timber and earth – do however differ widely in their environmental impact. Sustainable development calls for the limited use of such materials as concrete and steel, which result from heavy industrial processes using large quantities of energy and non-renewable resources.

In 1950, annual sand and gravel extraction for the French construction industry was 17 million tonnes. In 2000 it was over 400 million tonnes, resulting in significant environmental damage. The use of concrete in building construction is unavoidable in many situations; however, its use can be limited and alternatives sought wherever possible.

Earth is a construction material containing no toxic fibres, volatile organic compounds or heavy metals, and with beneficial thermal and humidity-regulating properties. However, hardening earth by baking it uses large amounts of energy. One way around this is to use unbaked earth, such as the traditional clay mortar used in the Salvatierra building (*see pp. 166-171*). Timber, an abundant raw material requiring little energy for conversion to building products, is a highly attractive environmental alternative provided certain conditions are fulfilled.

TIMBER CONSTRUCTION AND ENVIRONMENTAL QUALITY

Construction is the timber industry's biggest market: in France, 65 % of all timber, and 80 % of softwood, is used in the building industry. This fact provides a strategically valuable example in terms of public opinion. The use of wood is a pertinent response to the desire to improve quality of life in the home or workplace: its associations include unpolluted air, with natural humidity regulation, surfaces pleasant and warm to the touch, and a comfortable temperature.

A natural, recyclable material

Timber is a renewable resource. It is in abundant supply in Europe, and requires little energy for transformation into useable products, installation or transport. Air, soil and water pollution resulting from timber production processes is very low. It has uses in structure, internal fittings and external cladding. Its low density means that timber structures can be erected without heavy lifting equipment, reducing the noise and dust associated with construction sites. Standard elements can be prefabricated in the factory, making con-

struction quicker, easier and cheaper. Timber frame systems allow high insulation thicknesses within relatively thin walls. By-products can be recycled, burnt to produce energy or biologically treated to produce methane for combustion.

At the Hanover Expo in 2000 the Swiss pavilion, inspired by storage areas in timber yards, was constructed of walls of stacked timber, larch in the east-west direction and Douglas fir running north-south, forming a network of 9m high box-like enclosures. The resulting maze-like structure used a total of 37,000 100 × 200mm sections cut from 2,800m^3 of green timber. To help them dry, there were spacers between the beams, held in place via a system of tension rods and stressed springs. At the end of Expo 2000, the structure was dismantled and the timber sections removed for re-use; a perfect illustration of the principles of sustainable development.

Eco-certification schemes

Timber from sustainable managed forests is now increasingly available. Eco-certification schemes include the Forest Stewardship Council (FSC) label for European, North American and Asian timber, and the Pan European Forest Certification Council (PEFC) rating for European products (*see pp. 24-25*).

Similar schemes exist for tropical hardwoods, and the corresponding labels should be required by designers who continue to specify such woods for their appearance or natural durability. For the

**The Swiss pavilion at the Hanover Expo, 2000.
Architect: Peter Zumthor;
engineers: Conzett, Bronzini, Gartmann.**

Sports hall at Künzelsau-Gaisbach,
Germany, 1994.
Architects: D'Inka + Scheible.

external decking at her house in the Perche (see pp. 126-131), Sonia Cortesse used padouk from a sustainable managed forest. At the Baie de Somme service area (see pp. 240-245), the plywood panels used in the ceiling are veneered with okoumé from managed plantations. These panels, manufactured by Isoroy, carry the Eurokoumé label.

Although environmentally approved tropical hardwoods are available, it remains preferable to use native timbers where possible in order to reduce transport energy consumption. In Germany, Austria and Switzerland, the use of tropical hardwoods has all but disappeared over the last 15 years.

Solid timber

The recent surge in the popularity of solid sawn timber in Europe corresponds to a resurgence of public interest in natural products. Boosted by the social consciences of some developers and designers, the use of native species and local raw materials constitutes a noticeable trend towards environmental quality.

In France specifiers are increasingly turning to local native timbers, despite the sudden fashion for ipe and iroko following their use in a few high-profile projects. This may take the form of the use of smaller-section, lower-quality wood in the form of glued-laminated or nailed-laminated products. The kindergarten at Stuttgart-Heumaden (see pp. 172-177) uses panels of medium-grade local spruce planks for the floors, walls and roof.

In a number of European countries, where forests are generally under-exploited, Douglas fir has been the most common forestry plantation species over the past half-century. Currently widely available, it provides a local alternative to imported north American red cedar, suitable for general external use (biological hazard class 3, according to the European standard EN 335). In Germany, Douglas fir is used increasingly for cladding, usually with a plain sawn finish and no surface treatment. The external wall of the Heilbronn car park (see pp. 246-249), 400m long and 15.2m high, is composed of 40×60mm chevron sections in Douglas fir. At the house in Degerloch, Stuttgart (see pp. 132-135), it is used for the sliding shutters as well as cladding.

Douglas fir is also suitable for structural use. The Essertines house (see pp. 122-125), by Atelier de l'Entre, has closely-spaced structural joists in 40×100mm Douglas fir sections.

Engineered timber products

The European architecture of the 1990s was marked by the advent of high-performance composite materials. Laminated veneer lumber is a layered composite of wood veneers and adhesive which can be used as flat panels, rectangular beams or, for example, I-beam webs. In Europe it is mainly found as Kerto, manufactured by the Finnish company Finnforest. Its fine-grained appearance, along with a policy of materials optimisation, led to the use of this product through-

Summary of the different biological hazard classes for timber
(defined by BS EN 335-1)

Class	Situation (type of element)	Timber humidity	Risk of exposure to wetting	Insect attack	Fungal attack	Vulnerable region
1	Internal, under cover (flooring, ceilings, internal window-frames)	<18 % at all times	None	Larvae, termites		0-3mm
2	Internal, under cover (structural frames, ground floor joists)	May rise above 20 % on occasions	Occasional	Larvae, termites	Superficial, low damage potential	0-3mm
3A	External, no contact with ground (cladding, external window-frames)	Frequently above 20 %	Frequent; **no** water retention	Larvae, termites	Superficial, low damage potential	0-3mm (no water retention in vertical elements)
3B	External, no contact with ground (cladding, external window-frames)	Frequently above 20 %	Frequent; **with** water retention	Larvae, termites	More significant, moderate to high damage potential	laterally 6mm and more, up to 30-50mm in vertical and connection elements
4	In contact with ground or fresh water (column bases, fence-posts or similar)	>20 % at all times	Permanent, with water retention	Larvae, termites	Deep and highly damaging; "soft rot"	Whole thickness (in at least part of element)
5	In contact with salt water (marine piling, piers and jetties)		Permanent	Marine boring insects	Deep and highly damaging; "soft rot"	Whole thickness

(Source: *Construire avec le bois*, Editions du Moniteur 1999)

out the structural system at the Künzelsau-Gaisbach (see *illustration p. 111*) sports hall.

Another product, known as oriented strand board or OSB, is frequently used in structural panels for timber frame buildings. Composed of wood strands bonded with adhesives to form a mat, this can also be used as internal decorative panelling. In France, Triply, manufactured by Isoroy, has been commercially available since the mid-1980s; while KronoFrance, a French subsidiary of the Swiss company Kronospan, has been producing its Kronoply OSB product at its Sully-sur-Loire plant since 2000. The US company Trus Joist uses yellow pine and other abundant softwoods to make a parallel strand lumber (PSL), Parallam. Made from parallel-grain laminated veneers, this is a structural product which is up to 25 % stronger than glulam in some applications. These engineered wood products make use of industrial processes to obtain enhanced properties through homogenisation. They have better structural properties than sawn timber and are more resistant to rot, allowing section sizes to be considerably reduced. They have transformed the image of timber in construction, allowing it to be seen as an industrial material able to provide a real alternative to steel or concrete. Engineered lumber retains the appearance and warmth of wood, in a more stable form and with more consistent, reliable characteristics. Available in large sections and long spans, it increases the competitiveness of timber structures and has opened up new perspectives to designers.

Adhesives

Most of these engineered products use adhesives containing volatile organic compounds (VOCs), in particular formaldehyde, which carry health risks. In 1980, most particleboards contained around 60mg of formaldehyde per 100g. By 1995, this had been reduced to less than 2.5mg/100g.

To aid specifiers, the European standard EN 120 defines a class E1 board which has minimal risk of VOC emissions. Similarly, EN 1084 defines plywood class A, such as Navyrex, used by Sonia Cortesse in her house in the Perche (see *pp. 126-131*). Glulam timber, such as 3-ply or 5-ply Multi-

**Simplified table showing suitability of species
for use untreated in different hazard classes**

Species	Class 1	Class 2	Class 3	Class 4
TEMPERATE HARDWOODS				
Chestnut	yes	yes	yes	yes[1]
Oak	yes	yes	yes	no
Maple	yes[3]	no	no	no
Beech	yes[3]	no	no	no
Poplar	yes[3]	yes[3]	no	no
Robinia	yes	yes	yes	yes
TROPICAL HARDWOODS (excl. sapwood)				
Doussie	yes	yes	yesi	yes
Ipe	yes	yes	yes	yes
Iroko	yes	yes	yes	sometimes
Dark red meranti[2]	yes	yes	yes	no
Sipo	yes	yes	yes	no
Teak	yes	yes	yes	sometimes
SOFTWOODS				
Douglas fir	yes	yes	yes	no
Spruce	yes[3]	yes[3]	no	no
Larch	yes	yes	yes	no
Norway pine	yes	yes	yes	no
Red cedar	yes	yes	yes	no
Fir	yes	yes[3]	no	no

1. In some moderate-risk situations, when design life is around ten years.

2. Where density > 670kg/m³.

3. Conditional on acceptance of a small risk of insect attack, which may be reduced by application of an insecticide coating.

(Source: *Construire avec le bois*, Editions du Moniteur 1999)

plan from the Austrian manufacturer Kaufmann, OSB and similar products contain only around 3 % adhesive, reducing the risk of emissions to a negligible level. Designers can also specify the use of polyurethane glue, which contains no formaldehyde, although this carries its own, allergy-related, risks to those involved in the production process. In many countries in Europe, industry has begun to explore the economic viability of environmental alternatives, with considerable success. Adhesive-free composite panels, manufactured by high-pressure polymerisation of the lignin contained in wood fibres, have been produced by, among others, Schlingmann (with its Natura panels). In France, the CTBA is working on starch- and rape-seed-based adhesives, while Antonio Pizzi at Enstib has developed adhesives based on tannins.

Preservative treatments

The use of timber in construction is only "green" if it is used without the addition of toxic treatment products. Many of these carry health risks for users and for building occupants, and treated wood is hazardous to remove and dispose of. Timber treated with products containing copper, chromium and arsenic salts (chromated copper arsenate, or CCA) is classed as hazardous waste (see p. 117) and the cost of disposal is correspondingly high. Such products have been banned in Germany since the late 1980s, being replaced by copper and boron-based products, though they are still used in France.

Protective treatments should therefore be kept to a minimum, depending on the biological hazard class of the species in question, with species chosen as appropriate (see tables above). For external use, many species have natural durability corresponding to biological hazard class 3 (such as oak, chestnut, larch and Douglas fir) or class 4 (including doussie, ipe and robinia). After removal of the sapwood, these are suitable for use without preservative treatment and are often used without any surface finish. The Pont de Merle in Corrèze, France, is a 56m long road bridge built

**Hall at Empfingen, Germany, 2000.
Architects: D'Inka + Scheible.**

of Douglas fir. Opened in 1999 and designed by the architect Hervé David and the engineers Jean-Louis Michotey and Christian Poumeau, it uses 320m^3 of untreated glulam timber, in a system of multiple T-section struts supporting the road deck across a gorge.

As another alternative to chemical treatments, various high-temperature processes can increase durability and dimensional stability of timber. There are a number of patented procedures and products, such as Rétifié treated timber, which was developed at the Ecole des Mines university in Saint-Etienne and is manufactured by the French company Now. Rétifié is currently used in window frames and cladding; its structural properties are being researched and an environmental impact assessment drawn up.

Constructive preservation measures

The ideal solution for a healthy environment is constructive preservation, or designed-in protection. In Germany, Switzerland and Austria this approach has been adopted for around ten years; structural elements which are left clearly visible, and can be regularly checked, do not require preservative treatments. In 1998 Austria published its B3804 standard, entitled "Protection of timber used in construction; prefabricated timber elements in housing; constructive and chemical timber preservative measures". Intended for use in housing which uses storey-height prefabricated timber panels, this allows the number

of elements requiring chemical treatment to be reduced to a minimum.

Constructive protection can be an efficient solution, but requires designer and contractor to have adequate knowledge of the materials concerned. Provision of effective protection against fungal and other biological decay requires:
- choice of suitable species
- timber to be installed at less than 18 % moisture
- a well-ventilated building
- careful detailing to avoid water retention points
- regular checks of structural elements.

Wall and roof panels must be able to "breathe", allowing passage of water vapour between inside and outside. To prevent condensation within the walls, a high-permeability micro-porous membrane, such as Delta-Vent, should be incorporated into the design.

In regions where termites are present, specific protection measures are necessary to protect all parts of the structure. Solutions include chemical treatments, such as injection of termicides into the walls and surrounding ground; barrier products such as Termifilm, from the French company Cecil; or installation of physical barriers such as stainless steel mesh or granite particles.

OPTIMISING CONSTRUCTION

Green construction is not in itself achieved simply through energy-saving measures and the use of non-hazardous materials. The environmental quality of sustainable buildings also depends on good use of materials: a mix of materials, with optimum use of their different capacities and the minimum necessary quantity of each of each.

Mixing materials

The use of concrete, steel and glass in conjunction with timber is a response to technical requirements, and makes use of the qualities of each material. Used as a thermal sink, acoustic or fire barrier, concrete offers a massivity which is otherwise lacking in timber buildings. The use of steel enhances the mechanical properties of timber products: cast and fabricated steel fixings and connection elements provide elegant and efficient timber detailing solutions. In long-span structures, light, efficient structural systems are provided by tensioned steel cables and rods used with timber compression elements.

Such materials mixing has created new, contemporary uses for timber in construction in Germany, Switzerland and Austria. European architects are now able to build not *in* wood, but *with* wood, achieving optimum technical and economic solutions while also creating new aesthetic qualities.

In Vorarlberg, co-operation from initial design stage between architects, engineers and builders has allowed innovative solutions to be developed to meet specific project requirements. Thus the roof of the public hall in Empfingen (*see illustration, left*) is supported by a lightweight steel structure, with circular-section struts and beams carrying a wooden ceiling, and an independent façade structure in glulam timber.

Prefabrication

In many European countries, there is now a noticeable trend towards economic and environmental optimisation through the use of standard and prefabricated elements. Standard elements are well suited to minimalist architecture, and to the simple, compact forms of low-energy housing, while designs using simple, repeated details go hand in hand with optimisation of material quantity. Standardisation also generally has benefits for both quality and cost. With the use of standard elements comes the possibility of prefabrication in the factory; elements are produced under controlled conditions, and disposal of debris and waste can be more efficiently dealt with. Less time is spent on site, with a corresponding reduc-

tion in noise, dust, site traffic and other environmental nuisances (*see next page*).

A number of the projects described in this chapter have prefabricated timber structures: the Ölzbündt housing development at Dornbirn (*see p. 142*), the house in Degerloch, Stuttgart (*see p. 132*), and the terraced housing at Affoltern am Albis (*see p. 136*). The staircases, walkways and glazing for the offices at Wageningen (*see p. 218*), and the structure and cladding of the Total Energie building (*see p. 234*), used standard catalogue parts. The use of such mass-produced elements has an environmental as well as economic aspect, as the quantity of material and the industrial processes used in their production have been optimised to reduce costs to a minimum.

Electronic transfer of data

The advent of electronic data transfer and computer-aided manufacturing have made industrial production significantly more efficient. Data transfer allows automatic fabrication of structural elements directly from the design engineer's drawings. This in turn allows shorter lead times and better quality control. To be successful, use of such tools requires a well-structured, well-motivated team of architects, engineers and fabricators who are prepared to work together. Some technically innovative, or exceptionally logistically demanding, projects have only been possible with the aid of this technology.

Electronic data transfer is used widely in the timber industry in Germany, Austria and Switzerland. In France, it has been largely the preserve of the big glulam manufacturers, but is now beginning to be used by smaller, more traditional timber fabricators. Computer-aided fabrication permits the routine and highly accurate production of complex shapes, which in the past would have been very costly, from quality-controlled and correctly-dried timber. Timber's low self-weight allows large sections of structural frames to be prefabricated; while the accuracy possible with automated fabrication means that connections and details can be optimised, to reduce or eliminate thermal and acoustic bridges and increase air impermeability and insulation (with U values of 0.2 - 0.3 W/m²K). In Germany, increasing numbers of houses are being built in this way; an example is the house in Degerloch, Stuttgart (*see pp. 132-135*).

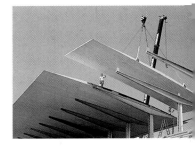

Grandstand roofs, Bregenz stadium, Austria, 1994. Architects: J. Kaufmann and B. Spiegel; engineers: Merz Kaufmann Partner. Erection of prefabricated timber elements.

Prefabricated timber frame module for the Schindler offices, Ebikon, Switzerland, 1998. Architects: Kündig-Bickel; engineers: Merz Kaufmann Partner.

SITE MANAGEMENT

Sustainable construction requires architects to take on new roles. One of these is to convince developers and contractors of the need to reduce the negative environmental impact which construction on site often has for both workers and nearby residents. Improving working conditions on site can only benefit quality of work, and hence of the finished product.

Cleaner sites

A "cleaner site" demonstrates the commitment of those concerned to reduce nuisance and annoyance for workmen and residents of the surrounding area. However, it depends on careful selection of the main contractor, with the lowest bidder not necessarily being the best choice.

In France, the ADEME has attempted to instil this attitude through its funding of "green sites" such as that of the Calais secondary school (see pp. 196-201). On these sites pollution and other nuisances are kept to a minimum, and waste is sorted on site to facilitate recycling and processing. New working practices demand modified working methods, and knowledge of both regulations and technical solutions by those involved. The experience of the Rex HQE projects (see p. 31) shows that the volume of construction site waste can be reduced by around 20 % through proper planning of the installation sequence for components such as partitions, boarding and floor coverings, and taking account of their manufactured dimensions in the design.

Limiting disruption

While protection of building workers has improved dramatically over recent years, the presence of a construction site still brings with it many inconveniences for those living and working nearby:
- traffic and parking problems
- noise, dirt, dust and pollution
- less than pleasing views.
Several countries have introduced new working practices in response to this. Effective, efficient and reproducible solutions have been found to problems affecting the site itself, its immediate surroundings, the natural or urban environment and local residents.

Some measures are designed to limit noise, meeting regulatory requirements on maximum noise levels and hours:

- use of prefabricated elements to reduce time on site
- use of soundproofed elements
- closing down concrete batching plants during certain hours
- connection of steel elements with keys so as to avoid the use of hammers.

The French construction company GTM has developed software tools which estimate the likely noise level on a given site, allowing concerted management of this potential nuisance as necessary. The Cornac programme calculates noise levels from the equipment and materials used, while Ressac uses a database of materials characteristics to allow levels to be brought down to permissible figures.

To reduce the hazards from site traffic, suitable protection should be installed and deliveries grouped together whenever possible. Wheel-washing facilities as trucks leave site limits mud, which makes roads slippery. Sensibly-positioned, well-maintained and sometimes decorative hoardings help give a positive image to the site.

Limiting pollution

Spillages of solvents, hydrocarbons and other noxious substances on construction sites pollute the soil, groundwater and drainage systems. In France, prevention of pollution by hydrocarbons is becoming standard, with impermeable membranes in the ground beneath site vehicle parking areas, oil removal systems and pre-treatment of water in decantation basins. Pollution from formwork mould oils is reduced by using them only when necessary, using suitable equipment and educating site personnel accordingly. Specifiers may also insist on biodegradable vegetable-based oils, which have the further advantage of being less unpleasant to work with.

Controlling waste

In France, the building industry generates over 31 million tonnes of waste each year, more than the total from household waste. The nature of construction site waste varies widely; composition and element or particle size depends on the type of building and the region. More than half is demolition rubble; 30 % comes from refurbishment projects, and 10 % from new building sites. Management of this waste must form part of the overall environmental approach, being directly

linked to the life cycle of the materials and products used. The costs of waste management are reduced by use of environmentally-friendly materials, but even more so by producing less waste. All parties can contribute:
- developers, by including a waste management strategy in the project brief;
- designers, by specifying non-polluting, recyclable products and materials;
- manufacturers, through use of renewable or recycled materials;
- suppliers, by not using unnecessary packaging;
- contractors, by sorting waste.
On "cleaner sites", waste is sorted into between six and ten categories. Metal, card and untreated wood can be recycled; inert waste goes to landfill sites; hazardous waste is sent to an appropriate processing plant; and "everyday" rubbish is treated as household waste. The logistics of sorting and collection depends on the space available; the number of separate containers and their labelling, their position relative to work areas, the frequency of collection and replacement. Instructions must be simple enough to be properly understood and carried out by those working on the site; and precautions must also be taken to ensure health and safety and limit pollution and disruption.

Construction site waste

The average construction site produces:
- 65 % inert waste: excavated earth and rocks, plaster, clay, ceramics, glass, mineral wool and separate types of demolition debris,
- 29 % household-type waste, consisting of packaging, untreated wood, plastic, and mixed demolition debris,
- 6 % hazardous waste, mainly industrial products such as paints, wood treated with compounds containing heavy metals, asbestos and hydrocarbons.
Waste disposal sites fall into three classes, depending on the permeability of the underlying soil and the method of treatment of waste:
- class 1 sites for hazardous waste
- class 2 sites for household waste and similar
- class 3 sites for inert waste.
From 2002, there will no longer be traditional tips, and the centres which will replace them will take only "final" waste products. Direct disposal of primary waste as landfill, or incineration without making use of the energy produced, will no longer be accepted.

Disposal of construction site waste

To reduce volumes of construction waste, both economy of materials and sorting of recyclable waste are necessary. In France, the FFB estimates that waste disposal accounts for between 1 % and 8 % of total project budgets. Sorting and separate collection incurs labour costs, plus those associated with siting the different waste containers; however, the FFB believes that this will save around 40 % of total disposal costs, which are currently rising sharply. Processing of construction site waste is only worthwhile if there is a suitable processing plant nearby, but this should become more likely as the number of plants rises to keep pace with changing laws. Waste sorting is likely to become compulsory from 2002, when only tertiary waste, rendered inert and reduced to minimum volumes, will be accepted at disposal sites.
Although in southern Europe recycling is only gradually entering the public consciousness, in Germany a third of total waste is already treated in this way. A number of companies entered the market early; the German enterprise ZinCo, for example, which produces green roofs, makes systems with recycled polyethylene supports and a granular substrate composed of inert construction site waste (mainly crushed ceramics).

Disposal of demolition rubble

Rubble from demolition and refurbishment works in France amounts to 28 million tonnes each year. The systematic use of bulldozers or similar heavy equipment makes sorting of rubble difficult. In 1999, the ADEME launched a programme to explore possible alternative demolition methods, and evaluate their costs, on nine different construction sites. Methods depend on the construction materials; a timber building is much easier to dismantle or remodel than a concrete frame, and the resulting waste simpler and cheaper to dispose of. Some elements are easily removed and may even be directly re-used; others are reusable as lower-grade material after appropriate processing (a process known as downcycling). Timber, when no longer reusable in construction, can become an energy source; only elements treated with CCA compounds or creosote (whose use has been banned in the building sector for some years) are classed as special industrial waste.
The new Swiss Federal Statistical Office at Neuchâtel provides a good example, particularly with

respect to its construction. Before demolishing the existing buildings on the site, the developer invited the public and industry to salvage any components. After this, a specialist demolition firm dismantled the remainder in a manner which allowed 40 % of materials (bricks, structural beams, etc.) to be recycled.

ENVIRONMENTAL MANAGEMENT OF BUILDINGS

Design along bioclimatic principles and good use of materials are necessary but not sufficient conditions for a truly sustainable building. For a building to continue to remain both economically and environmentally viable, proper management is essential. Once again, all parties must work together to achieve this.

Changing behaviour

The primary aim of the environmental approach is to improve quality of life. In former times, comfort in the home was a function of traditional culture and the features of the site and the geographical region – topography, climate, available materials. By the early 20th century, new technologies and the industrialisation of production had led to the beginning of internationalisation and uniformity of building methods, along with the development of more advanced sanitation.

Today, our requirements for comfort have increased, but the capacity of inhabitants to maintain their home environments seems rather to be in decline. Our rising expectations need to be matched by responsibility, and a sufficient familiarity with the technology (the ability to unblock a fan vent, or operate a thermostatic valve) through which we expect them to be fulfilled.

As set out by the French system of HQE criteria (see p. 22), a satisfactory internal environment has acceptable levels of air humidity, sounds, sights and smells as well as the obvious temperature criterion. In practice, this will seldom be the case unless users themselves adjust the instruments available to them. In France the annual energy bill in the collective housing sector is between FF2,000 and FF5,000 for a living space of 65m². Better management requires clear, precise information, enabling environmental measures to be properly understood and applied.

Ecoconsumerism

A number of European countries have public "energy management" bodies to provide free advice and information to individuals concerning environmental measures and the various financial aid schemes available for them. A rising interest in ecoconsumerism is generated by publications, exhibitions, product comparisons, courses and public information campaigns. Little things need to become automatic to us: recycling our household waste, buying energy-efficient appliances and non-hazardous products. Reducing our consumption of water and electricity is one aim which can be achieved quickly through very moderate investment.

A good example of the spread of information is provided by the workings of the construction cooperative for the Salvatierra building (see pp. 166-171). The developers and future residents worked together from the beginning of the project, enabling future neighbours to meet and become acquainted; among other things, groups of residents then came together to purchase low-energy household appliances.

Reducing energy consumption

The reduced energy consumption of low-energy buildings is often made possible by the use of computer-controlled equipment: smart appliances in the home, or building management systems (BMS) in offices and public buildings, which work automatically according to varying building occupation. However these systems, which use advanced and sometimes innovative technology, can require substantial investment.

Heating energy consumption (and hence greenhouse gas emissions) may also be reduced by less environmentally correct, but cheaper and easier, means such as wall-mounted power-vented (or sealed-combustion) boilers. Suitable for use in both new and older buildings, these are very compact, being fixed directly to an outside wall, and use little energy. Air inlet and exhaust is via two concentric flues passing through the wall. This system is used in the house at Degerloch, Stuttgart (see pp. 132-135).

Reducing electricity consumption

In France, lighting, air conditioning and electrical appliances account for around 10 % of annual energy consumption. This could soon be reduced by around 30 %, or up to 50 % for lighting, with no loss of quality by the introduction of a number of simple, low-cost measures. In the passive house at Kranichstein, Darmstadt (see p. 101), electricity requirements were cut by 70 % through the installation of highly energy-efficient appliances (washing machine and dishwasher) and a solar water heating system.

The French RT 2000 standard encourages use of movement detectors linked to light-switches and timer interrupter systems to cut unnecessary use of lights in tertiary sector buildings. Designers should also limit the need for artificial lighting and mechanical ventilation, by adapting spatial arrangements to bring as much natural light and ventilation into the building as is practicable. Specifiers can list energy-efficient equipment and appliances, suitable lighting systems and low-energy bulbs.

While most household appliances today consume around half the energy of their 1970s equivalents, some still use up to 80 % more than others. The European labelling system classes them as A (lowest energy consumption) to G (highest energy consumption).

Reducing water use

Drinking water is an increasingly precious commodity; water conservation measures are becoming more and more important. The quantities consumed in the industrialised world are remarkable. In Switzerland the average person uses 180 litres per day, half of which is used in baths, showers and toilet flushing. This could be reduced by around 40 % through the use of dual-flush toilets, taps fitted with flow limiters, low-volume shower heads and more economical washing machines. Such measures require minimal investment, offset by savings within one or two years; for a family of four, they could save around 100,000 litres of drinking water each year. In collective housing blocks, the installation of individual water meters encourages individuals to save water.

FUNDING ENVIRONMENTAL QUALITY

In most European countries financial incentives of some sort, whether at national, regional or local level, are available for renewable energy projects and energy or water conservation measures. Grants or other incentives are frequently avail-

able for solar water heating systems, photovoltaic panels, heat pumps or wood-fuelled heating systems, and green roofs.

European experiments

In France, where "green" construction most often involves specialist professionals using the 14 HQE targets, the additional cost of environmental measures is generally estimated to 8-10 % of the budget. This figure should soon begin to fall as accumulated experience and expertise increase.

In Germany, where an environmental approach to buildings has existed for longer, the additional costs of environmental quality are estimated at 2-5 %. These costs come mostly from the use of non-hazardous materials, high-performance windows and better insulation, more energy-efficient lighting and domestic appliances, and solar water heating. They are partly offset by savings in other areas, such as simpler building plans and compact volumes, optimised structural systems, prefabrication and use of standard elements. Depending on the choices made, and the more or less effective participation of building users, the resulting decrease in running costs compensates for the additional investment over between ten and 20 years.

Figures for a privately-funded project

The Salvatierra apartment block, in Rennes (see pp. 166-171) was built as part of the European Cepheus programme, and aimed to combine energy efficiency with the use of "green" materials. It received funding from various sources, including the European Commission, the ADEME and the Brittany regional council. A financial analysis shows that such an experiment could be reproduced elsewhere.

For the 40 Passive House apartments which came into service in 2001, total building costs were 13.5 % higher than the sale price of FF9,200/m^2 (€1,403/m^2) including taxes (the local market price for housing of equivalent standard). This excess was covered by the different grants received. Of the excess, 1 % of cost was attributable to modifications at the developer's request, and a greater proportion (5.4 % of cost) was due to the experimental nature of the project – research, instrumentation and analysis of results, communications and publications. The actual cost of the environmental measures put in

**Price-performance ratios (PPR) for the home
and workplace building, Freiburg im Breisgau**

		Years' use (y)	Additional cost DM	Energy saving kWh/year	PPR, DM/kWh
Insulation	External walls 360mm	30	58,394	41,178	0.05
	Roof 430mm	30	28,413	7,809	0.12
	Ground floor membrane 200mm	30	19,553	10,430	0.06
Glazing	Triple glazing, U = 0.6, g = 0.42	25	30,760	7,023	0.18
	Triple glazing, U = 0.7, g = 0.6	25	69,210	12,448	0.22
	Insulated window frames	25	208,890	8,207	1.02
Technical systems	Gas co-generator	20	31,200	38,997	0.04
	Heat recovery from co-generator exhaust	20	3,000	7,295	0.02
	Pipework and duct insulation	25	1,900	1,731	0.04
	Ventilation system with heat exchanger	20	117,561	28,900	0.02
	Ventilation with heat pump from used air	20	49,938	21,690	0.11
	Earth cooling tube	30	15,800	500	1.05
Hot water	Solar collector panels	25	42,800	20,625	0.08
	Pipework insulation	25	2,223	2,132	0.04
	Expansion chamber insulation	25	200	400	0.02
Electrics	Energy-efficient household appliances	15	8,150	9,960	0.05
	Photovoltaic panels	25	15,000	2,850	0.21

(Source: *Sonnenenergie und Wärmetechnik*)

place was 7.1 % of construction costs, or around FF58,000 (€8,842) for a 77m^2 four-room apartment, including taxes. This should be offset by reductions in running costs. Annual energy consumption by heating, which for an average gas-heated four-room apartment comes to FF7,000 (€1,067), will be only around FF2,000 (€305). If a purchaser takes out a 15-year loan, at current rates these savings would allow him or her to repay additional borrowings of FF50,000 (€7,622). Thus clearly such projects can be economically viable, even without subsidies.

Return on investment

Of the additional costs specifically attributable to green measures, some can be priced accurately, such as extra insulation or solar panelling. Others, such as those linked to the aims of visual and olfactory comfort, are harder to evaluate.

The table (see above) gives values for the home and workplace building in Vauban, Freiburg im Breisgau (see pp. 154-159) of price-performance ratio (PPR) of the different environmental measures put in place. The ratio is calculated as :

$$PPR = \frac{additional\ cost}{annual\ energy\ saving \times years'\ use}$$

The limiting value for the measures to be a worthwhile investment is €0.026/kWh ; where the price-performance ratio is higher, at current energy prices the investment is not worthwhile. This is not to say that it will not become so in the future, nor that such measures should be abandoned, as clearly they carry environmental benefits, such as reduction in greenhouse gas emissions.

TOWARDS SUSTAINABILITY AS A WAY OF LIFE

If environmental quality of buildings is to become taken for granted as an integral part of building construction in Europe, the building and architectural professions must inform and educate the general public. The message must be put across more widely and efficiently, taking health and user comfort as the starting themes.

A duty to inform

If we are to preserve our natural environment, it is vital:
- that public authorities provide education in "ecocitizenship";
- that designers alert building users to the benefits of environmental quality;
- that social housing developers assist residents in initiating and continuing co-operative management and maintenance.

If building users are not adequately informed about the changes in behaviour expected of them, for example in a bioclimatically-designed building, energy consumption in practice may be disappointing compared with values obtained from advance modelling of the project.

In public buildings, particularly in the education sector, architecture itself can play an educational role. At the kindergartens in Pliezhausen *(see pp. 178-183)* and Stuttgart-Heumaden *(see pp. 172-177)*, overflow from the rainwater tanks feeds biotope areas which are used as educational tools. At the secondary school in Mäder *(see pp. 190-195)*, the use of solar collector panels for water heating and photovoltaic modules to supply electricity fulfils a similar function.

Encouraging prospects for the future

Faced with the need to protect our natural surroundings, the combination of stricter regulations and financial incentives is beginning to bear fruit. It has been underpinned by the actions of a relatively small number of developers, designers and construction companies who have long since committed themselves to sustainable development. Now, public opinion must be brought on board, and the rest of the building sector convinced of the importance and urgency of integrating sustainability into our daily lives.

In Germany, Austria, Switzerland, Scandinavia and the Netherlands, building environmental quality has made the transition from the experimental phase and is already integrated into day-to-day life to a large extent, via architecture which respects both people and their environment. A similar approach is emerging in France and the UK. If these issues are addressed in a concerted and pragmatic fashion, sustainable building could quickly become standard practice throughout Europe. Contributing to a rise in quality of life without damaging natural resources is a challenge which should inspire all parties to work together.

Sustainable building has its constraints. The projects described here show that it also has the potential to generate remarkable creativity.

HOUSE AT ESSERTINES-EN-CHÂTELNEUF, FRANCE

Atelier de l'Entre

ENVIRONMENTAL FEATURES

■ *Bioclimatic features*
Integration into the site; south-facing glazing, opaque north wall; use of local and naturally durable timbers; natural air humidity control via internal water feature; use of natural materials without finishes.

■ *Materials and construction*
Combination of timber and concrete structure; in-situ fair-faced concrete walls, structural timber floors in Douglas fir; glazing in Douglas fir frames; roof clad in larch decking over multi-layer waterproofing system; cladding and external fittings in larch; waxed anhydrite screed floor in living area, larch flooring in bedrooms.

■ *Technical features*
Wood-burning stoves in some rooms; gas boiler for heating and hot water; warm water pipes cast into ground floor.

■ *U-values*
- Walls 0.34W/m²K;
- south-facing glazing 1.1W/m²K (façade 60% glazed); east and west glazing 1.6W/m²K (façades 40% glazed);
- roof 0.20W/m²K.

Built on a modest budget, this bioclimatically designed house uses minimal finishes and no special equipment. The emphasis was on the human dimension, with the creation of spaces which bring a naturally harmonious relationship between man and his environment.

CONTEXT AND SITE
Built on a rise overlooking the Montbrison plain, this solid concrete and timber house is topped by a gently curving roof, echoing the contours of the surrounding land. Partly hidden by pine trees, it gradually becomes visible to visitors approaching along the lane. The orientation, shape and materials of the building were determined with reference to the site and the existing planting, linked to the application of bioclimatic principles.

FUNCTION AND FORM
The house is never visible in its entirety. Capped by a wide, wave-like roof, the larger of the two volumes is set along an east-west axis. This contains the main living space: sitting-room area around a fireplace beneath a mezzanine, kitchen, and dining area, which opens onto a terrace constructed in larch decking supported on blocks of local granite. This spacious living area is separated from the main bedroom by an entrance hall featuring a pool, whose evaporation regulates air humidity. Above the bedroom, the lower part of the main roof is an accessible roof terrace with decking in larch. A covered gallery links this first volume to the concrete cube containing the office and children's areas, with a smaller living area and three bedrooms, looking out onto the Forez plain.

STRUCTURAL PRINCIPLES
The structure combines 200mm concrete walls, cast in situ using steel formwork, with timber floors, constructed of closely-spaced joists carrying floorboards in Douglas fir. Timber sections are 40 × 100mm in the bedrooms and 40 × 130mm in the living area (where spans are longer), with pairs of joists supported at the façades by timber columns of the same section. This system creates an attractive soffit without the need for a ceiling, and allows the structure to be made of small-section timber. Its aspect is refined further by the continuation of the structural system into the vertical walls behind the kitchen and mezzanine glazing. The profiled surface gives good acoustic absorption, in a space otherwise dominated by flat, reflective surfaces of concrete and glass.

MATERIALS AND FINISHES
Concrete and timber, often seen as the antithesis of each other, are here combined to good effect. The stark, grey, unyielding concrete walls seem to rise from the rock, while the curve of the overhanging roof is punctuated by the rhythm of the timber structure. In the living area, light from the south façade, filtered by the glazing and coloured by the warm tones of the timber, falls on the self-levelling anhydrite screed floor, polished and waxed but otherwise unadorned. The floor and façade structure is in Douglas fir, with external cladding and window-frames in larch – both local species, whose natural durability makes them suitable for external use to biological hazard class 3 without chemical treatment. No finish is applied to any timber. During their lifetimes, the 20m³ of Douglas fir and 10m³ of larch used in the building stored around 30 t of CO_2.

The house is set amongst
pine trees.

ENERGY AND CLIMATE CONTROL

The design is based on bioclimatic principles, making best use of solar gain and limiting heat loss from the building to ensure comfortable temperatures in both summer and winter. The house is situated to reduce exposure to westerly rains, and allow plenty of incident sunlight in the south-facing living spaces. The north wall of the living area is in concrete, forming an opaque shield against the weather. This wall is externally insulated by 100mm of mineral wool, continuous with the roof insulation, protected by a waterproof membrane. Vertical larch planks form a ventilated skin.

The house benefits from sunlight at all times of day, including when the sun is directly over the pool. Internal and external views, some made possible by changes in level within the building, were the subject of consultations with the future residents. The bedrooms, with their panoramic view over the plain below, get the early-morning sun. In the main living area, windows around the fireplace give a view to the west, while the dining area looks out onto a stand of pines. From the kitchen and mezzanine, the glazed bands punctuated by timber columns filter the incoming light, modifying its quality and giving rhythm to the view.

In the Forez region, winters are cold but summers can be very dry. Rainwater falling on the roof is channelled onto the surrounding ground via projecting water spouts.

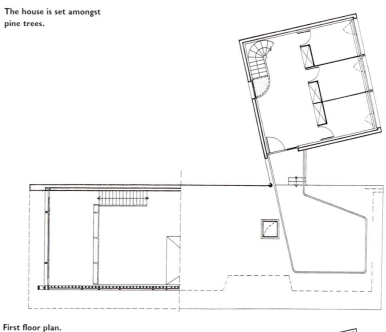

First floor plan.

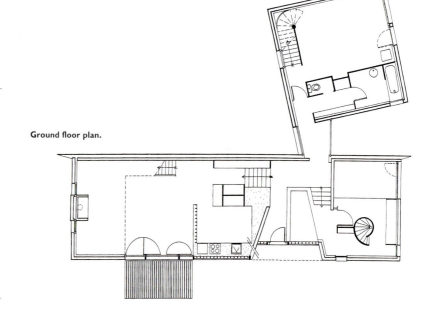

Ground floor plan.

Address: 42600 Essertines-en-Châtelneuf, France.
Project brief: private house for a family with three children.
Client: private client.
Architect: Atelier de l'Entre (Marie-Renée Desages, Aline Duverger, Yves Perret), Saint-Etienne.
Timetable: design 1996; construction February-November 1997.
Area: living areas 200m^2, cellar 40m^2; ground floor, 1st floor, mezzanine in living area, part basement.
Contractors: concrete and civils work: Bâti-Rénove; timber structure: Bezacier; external fittings: Chambon.
Cost: FF1.2m (€182,940) including mains services connections, excluding fees.

The structure combines timber with the high thermal mass of concrete.

The timber structure is made up of closely-spaced joists in local Douglas fir.

HOUSE IN THE PERCHE, NORMANDY, FRANCE

Sonia Cortesse

Sonia Cortesse is a consultant to the French institute of environmental medicine. In this house she has successfully combined style, comfort and economy. The environmental options added around 5 % to the building cost; this additional expense will pay off in the long term not only through reduced energy consumption, but also via the less easily quantified benefits of a healthy living environment.

ENVIRONMENTAL FEATURES

▮ Bioclimatic features
Integration of the building into its surroundings; passive use of solar energy; added insulation, double glazing; conservatory; use of recyclable materials, non-hazardous finishes and naturally durable timbers; waste-water filtration by macrophytic beds.

▮ Materials and construction
Wall framing in solid fir; reinforced concrete floors; roof structure of curved glulam beams in Douglas fir; interior fittings in beech, Douglas fir and Navyrex plywood; ceilings in red cedar; window frames in stained Bieber glulam pine; external cladding in red cedar and Navyrex plywood; shutters of red cedar louvres in galvanised steel frames, with Naco aluminium fixing elements; roof cladding in Vieille Montagne patinated zinc; floor finishes in Portuguese slate, Junckers oiled beech parquet, and rice tatami matting; verandah decking in padouk.

▮ Finishes
Holzweg organic paints and protective finishes.

▮ Technical features
- Humidity-controlled unidirectional ventilation; high-yield gas boiler; Ciat twin-tube finned radiators.

▮ U-values
- Timber-framed walls 0.31W/m²K;
- glazing 1.6 to 2.4W/m²K;
- concrete walls with internal insulation 0.25W/m²K;
- ground level floor plate 0.25W/m²K.

▮ Site
Minimal environmental disruption due to timber structure.

CONTEXT AND SITE
The house looks out over the slopes of a valley, on the outskirts of a hamlet in the Perche region of Normandy. Long and narrow and with a dominating Zen aesthetic, it was designed for a pianist and martial arts enthusiast. Its position, set back from the access road, allows it to be set in its own space amid the surrounding planting. The house is set at right-angles to the steep slope; at the north-west end, it is partly built into the hillside, while the rest of the building is on two levels. Organised along an east-west axis, the house faces south, towards the wooded countryside.

FUNCTION AND FORM
Before any decision was taken, discussions were held with the client about his lifestyle, tastes and expectations. This enabled a detailed specification to be drawn up, including performance specifications for services.

The house is designed to fit the family's changing needs. On the lower level there is separate access to the bedroom, office, bathroom and sauna via the conservatory. On the ground floor, the living spaces – music room, dojo and dining area – are set around a large living area which opens onto the terrace. Sliding partitions separate the different areas, allowing flexible use of the space.

STRUCTURAL PRINCIPLES
The gentle curve of the matt, grey zinc roof echoes the shapes of the surrounding hills. It is visually separated by a band of glazing from the main body of the building, which forms a rectangular box clad in red cedar. Structural elements are slender, thanks to cleverly designed load paths, the use of both timber and steel and a careful optimisation of section sizes. The main rafters are 12m long glulam beams, supported at their north ends by a timber-framed wall, and on the south side by steel elements supported by a row of timber columns. These columns, in Douglas fir glulam, are set outside the façade line and thus free the façade itself from vertical load-bearing elements. The façade glazing is supported by a horizontal beam which is suspended via cables from the roof structure and braced back to the columns by steel compression elements. Elegant connection pieces, with no water retention points, ensure the durability of the timber.

MATERIALS AND FINISHES
Timber is used for the structure, interior fittings and cladding. The different timbers were chosen to avoid the need for preservative treatments; the structural Douglas fir and the red cedar cladding are naturally durable for external use (biological hazard class 3 to EN 335). The padouk tropical hardwood used for the veranda is from a sustainably managed forest, with only 0.5-3 out of 250-400 trees/ hectare felled each year. The beech parquet is oiled, while the interior wood fittings received a natural, oil-based treatment. Navyrex plywood, used in cladding and internal fittings, is low in

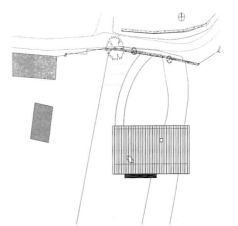

formaldehyde. The roof is insulated between the rafters by 200mm of glass wool, and the walls by 120mm of rockwool between Navyrex panels. Cost prevented the use of linen or hemp insulation, as well as that of clay pipework (which was replaced by PVC).

ENERGY AND CLIMATE CONTROL

Energy design is based on bioclimatic principles. The ancillary areas, grouped behind the low north façade, act as a thermal buffer. To the south, the roof is high enough to allow increased solar gain to the glazed façade of the living areas in winter, while the 2.5m overhang provides shade in summer. The conservatory is at the centre of the house, maximising benefit from greenhouse warming and from the thermal mass of the solid elements. At night and on cloudy days, stored heat from the masonry walls, concrete floors and slate paving passes into the different living spaces via the pivoting, adjustable internal doorways. Openings in the north and south façades are positioned to allow natural ventilation. Sliding and folding shutters with swivelling louvres help maintain a comfortable temperature in summer, adjusting the area of openings in the façade and "sculpting" the natural light which is allowed to enter. The sunlight is softened by linen blinds, while a screen of deciduous shrubs will eventually shade the main glazed façade in summer.

WASTE-WATER TREATMENT

The poetry of the site is accentuated by two garden areas: the Japanese-style conservatory, and the "transformation garden". The latter is used to filter rainwater, grey water (with fats and grease removed) and sewage by means of macrophytic beds planted with rushes, reeds and irises. The water flows along a gentle gradient through four lined basins, 5m² in area, and a trench, around 50m from the house. Cheap and easy to install and maintain, the system uses no energy or chemicals. The water is purified by filtering through layers of sands, gravel and pebbles; the plants eliminate organic contaminants, help reduce bacteria levels and ease sedimentation of suspended particles.

The building's main façade faces south.

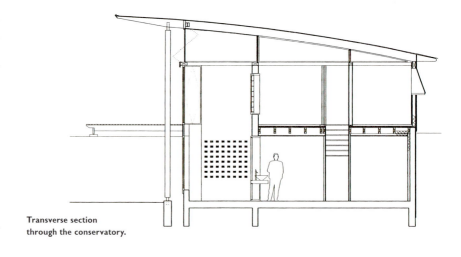

Transverse section through the conservatory.

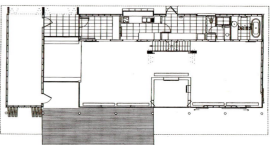

Plan of the lower, garden level (left) and the ground floor (right).

0 1 2 3 4 m

The structure is in Douglas fir glulam, cladding in red cedar.

The Japanese-style conservatory adds to the house's dominant Zen aesthetic.

As in Japanese houses, sliding partitions can be rearranged to modify the internal space.

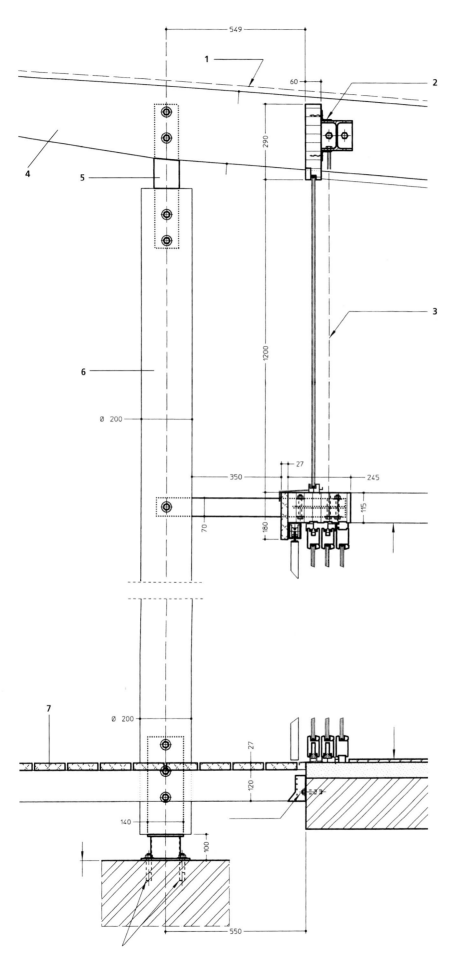

**Vertical section
through the south façade.**
1 22mm tongue-and-groove facing
2 40 × 40 × 4mm angle section, connecting
  steel H section to upper timber panel
3 10mm cable supporting glazing beam
4 Curved roof beam in Douglas fir glulam
5 Steel section
6 200mm diameter column in Douglas
  fir glulam
7 padouk decking

Address: La Basse Duquerie, Autheuil,
61190 Tourouvre, France.
Project brief: private house with dojo
(martial arts studio), music room,
sauna and conservatory.
Client: private client.
Architect: Sonia Cortesse, Paris.
Engineers: timber structure: Batut;
thermal engineering: Sophie Brindel-Beth;
acoustics: Delage & Delage.
Timetable: design May 1996 - May 1997;
construction July 1997 - November 1998.
Area: total area 326m², habitable area
285m²; ground floor and garden level.
Contractors: masonry and external civil
works: Guillet; timber structure, roofing
and external fittings, partitions and sauna:
Le Toit; interior fittings and timber
flooring: Les Enfants de Crosnier;
heating, plumbing and ventilation: Gomez;
electricity: Le Vilain; paintwork: Kervaon;
decorative paintwork: Bodnar.
Cost: FF2.43m (€370,450) incl. tax.

HOUSE IN STUTTGART, GERMANY

Schlude + Ströhle

ENVIRONMENTAL FEATURES

■ *Bioclimatic features*
Compact shape; passive use of solar energy; additional insulation; natural ventilation; use of non-hazardous materials; use of local and naturally durable timbers; rainwater recovery system.

■ *Materials and construction*
Timber structure using standard elements; walls in large-dimension prefabricated panels with solid spruce frames and mineral wool insulation; prefabricated floor elements with glulam beams and Kerto laminated veneer lumber (LVL) panels; window-frames in larch; ventilated cladding in Douglas fir; shutters in Douglas fir on galvanised steel frames; pergola and balconies in galvanised steel; roof in aluminium panels.

■ *Technical features*
Sealed-combustion gas boiler.

■ *U-values*
- Walls 0.27W/m²K;
- roof 0.21W/m²K;
- glazing 1.1W/m²K;
- ground level floor plate 0.24W/m²K.

■ *Energy consumption*
Heating energy 62kWh/m²/year.

■ *Site*
Rapid, low-impact construction due to standardised, prefabricated timber structure.

This small town house is notable for the simplicity of its floor plan and structural system and the clear design of the façades. The contractor, a manufacturer of prefabricated buildings, now includes this design in its standard catalogue.

CONTEXT AND SITE
Located within an existing city district in southern Stuttgart, the house retains the traditional form and the 45° roof slope of the buildings around it, but is given a contemporary aspect by its timber façades. It is oriented east-west, parallel to the road and slightly set back from it to allow an area of planting between house and street.

FUNCTION AND FORM
The main door is in the north gable, where a cloakroom, lavatory and store-room are grouped together to form a thermal buffer. The rest of the ground floor is taken up by a single open-plan, multi-functional space, with the kitchen and dining areas visually separated by a central, open steel stairway. The first floor is divided into four rooms, each of 14m², with sliding partitions to allow creation of either smaller, private spaces or a more open arrangement. The façades are composed of alternately opaque and glazed panels. Their aspect varies with the position of the external slatted shutters, which slide to provide privacy or screening against the sun. By night, light filtering from between the slats makes the house appear to glow.

STRUCTURAL PRINCIPLES
The structure, made up of standardised, prefabricated timber-framed elements, was erected in three days on top of the reinforced concrete basement. The walls are closed storey-height panels, with 180mm of mineral wool between vertical elements plus 40mm thick softwood fibreboard on the outer face. Inside, the structural panels are faced with cellulose plasterboard, an environmentally friendly product which has good fire resistance, good acoustic performance and provides some membrane stiffness. The floor elements, which span 6.2m between the east and west walls, are also prefabricated, consisting of 29mm Kerto LVL panelling fixed to groups of three 300 × 60mm glulam beams. These slender beams are spaced at 400mm centres, giving a regular pattern to the internal space.

MATERIALS AND FINISHES
Materials are used without applied finishes to maintain their natural textures. They require little maintenance; the balcony and pergola steelwork is galvanised, and the timber is uncoated and untreated. The species selected – larch for window frames, Douglas fir for cladding and shutters – are naturally durable to biological

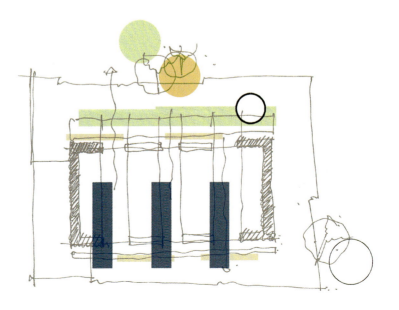

hazard class 3 for external use. The ventilated cladding is made up of storey-height elements, prefabricated and then fixed on site to the structural walls. Cladding panels are constructed of horizontal planed Douglas fir sections, fixed on their internal faces to a timber frame. The shutter slats are mounted on galvanised steel frames in a similar way. As well as having aesthetic advantages, this fixing method avoids screw holes on the exposed external faces, reducing the risk of timber deterioration.

ENERGY AND CLIMATE CONTROL

With annual energy consumption below 65kWh/m², 25 % below the German regulatory maximum of 1995, the house conforms to Low Energy Housing standards *(see p. 98)*. To meet this standard, only passive measures are used: a simple, compact volume; additional thermal insulation, with 220mm of rockwool-insulation in the walls and 200mm in the roof; insulating double glazing. The highly efficient sealed-combustion boiler, located in the (useable) roof space, eliminates the need for a separate flue. To ensure comfortable temperatures in summer, the tall windows in the east and west walls are set opposite each other, allowing efficient natural ventilation in all areas of the house. In front of the west façade, a pergola supports climbing plants, which both bring shade and help regulate air humidity in hot weather. Rainwater is collected in a concrete tank and used for watering the garden.

The timber-clad house fits in beside its neighbours.

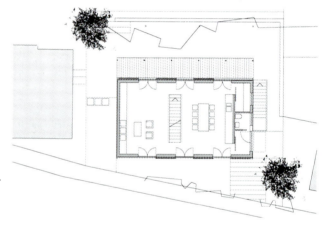

Ground floor plan.

A timber staircase, surrounded by an open-work steel structure, separates the kitchen from the dining area.

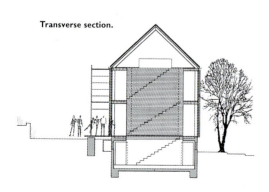

Transverse section.

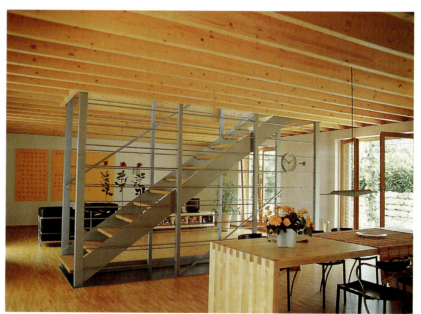

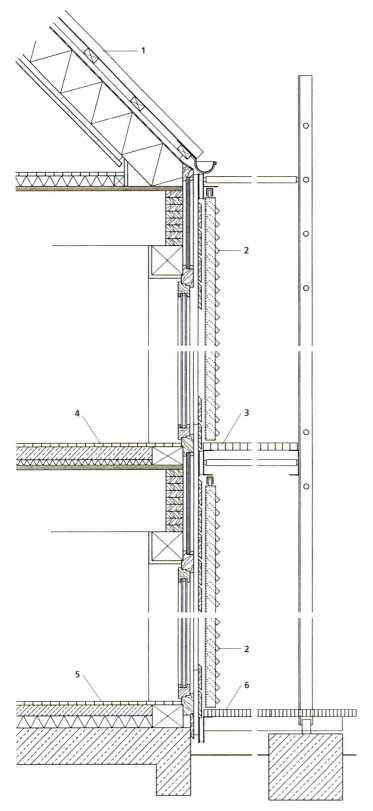

A galvanised steel pergola
protects the west façade
from direct sunlight.

Vertical section on the west façade.

1 roof
- aluminium cladding panels
- 30/40mm counter-battens
- 40/60mm battens
- waterproof membrane
- 220 80mm rafters
- 200mm mineral wool
- 30/80mm battens
- 12.5mm plasterboard

2 sliding shutters
- Douglas fir slats on galvanised steel frame

3 galvanised steel grille

4 level 1 floor plate
- 18mm wood flooring
- 65mm cement screed
- 29/25mm acoustic insulation
- 29mm Kerto laminated veneer lumber
- 300 60mm glulam beams

5 level 0 floor plate
- 18mm wood flooring
- 60mm cement screed
- 29/25mm acoustic insulation
- 70mm mineral wool
- 200mm concrete slab

6 timber decking

Address: Kleine Falterstrasse 22, Stuttgart-Degerloch, Germany.
Project brief: private house.
Client: the Schlude family.
Architect: Schlude + Ströhle, Stuttgart (project architect Martina Schlude).
Structural engineers: Friedmann + Partner, Saulgau.
Timetable: design begun 1996; construction on site April-December 1997.
Area: habitable area 130m²; basement, ground floor and first floor, plus useable attic space.
Contractor: Carl Platz GmbH & Co., Saulgau
Cost: DM480,000 (€245,420), including DM100,000 for the basement.

TERRACED HOUSES AT AFFOLTERN AM ALBIS, SWITZERLAND

Metron Architekturbüro

ENVIRONMENTAL FEATURES

■ *Bioclimatic features*
Compact volumes; active and passive use of solar energy; use of local timber, with external elements in naturally durable timbers; use of non-hazardous materials and finishes; green roof
with rainwater retention.

■ *Materials and construction*
Concrete basement; walls in large-dimension prefabricated panels with solid spruce frame and cellulose insulation; structural beams and columns in glulam spruce; balcony structure in Douglas fir; window-frames in spruce, cladding and shutters in sawn Douglas fir; railings in galvanised steel; green flat roofs.

■ *Technical features*
Water-to-water heat pump for each group of four houses; optional solar collector panels for hot water heating.

■ *U-values*
- Walls 0.28W/m²K;
- roof 0.22W/m²K;
- windows 1.4W/m²K;
- ground level floor plate 0.38W/m²K.

■ *Energy consumption*
Heating 51kWh/m²/year.

■ *Sound insulation*
Party walls between living areas, airborne noise, 63dB (measured);
living room floors, impact noise, below 30dB (measured).

■ *Site*
Rapid, low-impact construction due to choice of standardised, prefabricated timber structure.

The Looren development embodies the aims of the Swiss Metron practice: low-cost, high-density housing with optimum environmental and economic characteristics and a high level of user comfort. Structure, façades and building services are standardised; the layout of internal space is adapted to the needs of each family, making use of the particular features of the site.

CONTEXT AND SITE
Located in a quiet, sunny area to the south of the village of Affoltern, the development consists of ten terraces of four houses. Two parallel access roads divide the area into three sections, corresponding to three different house types. In the centre, a community hall opens onto an open area, functioning as a meeting place and public space. The upper part of the development slopes up towards the south-west, with type B and C terraces set parallel to the slope. The lower, flatter area beside the stream contains type A terraces running south-east, at right-angles to the others. This layout allowed excavated material to be re-used within the development site.

FUNCTION AND FORM
While the building layout is deliberately dense, the internal spaces are generous. All houses are set out on a 6m grid and are based on the same plan, but with varying areas and numbers of floors. Type A houses are on two levels, plus a basement giving onto an external area.
The other terraces have three habitable levels: type B houses make use of the sloping site to gain an extra floor, along with garages beneath the ground floor deck, while type C houses have an attic level with a second bathroom, private terrace areas and large basements, accessed via the garages.
Front doors and lavatories are all on half-landings with respect to the rest of the house, giving varying natural light levels within the buildings and generating interesting height differences

between rooms. Inside, glazed partitions provide transparency between entrance hall and kitchen. Glazing above the bathroom looks onto the surrounding landscape. On each floor, balconies running the length of the south façade act as extensions of the internal space and shade the living areas and bedrooms from direct sunlight.

STRUCTURAL PRINCIPLES
The prefabricated wall panels were erected on top of the concrete basement structures. Accurate design and efficient co-ordination meant that each four-house terrace took no more than a week to construct. Party walls between houses are composed of two timber-framed wall panels, separated by 30mm of rockwool. Each panel is made up of 13mm thick Fermacell, 60mm rockwool, a 60mm air gap and a further 3 × 13mm layer of Fermacell. This construction gives good acoustic insulation and allows the wall to form an effective fire barrier.

MATERIALS AND FINISHES
The wall panel frames and the prefabricated floor elements are in local spruce. The walls are insulated by 140mm of sprayed cellulose (with density 60kg/m³) between uprights, and 20mm softwood fibreboard on the external face. The structure is clad internally with Fermacell cellulose plasterboard, which provides shear stiffness for lateral stability. Roof insulation is by two 80mm layers of rockwool. The walls are permeable to water vapour, helping to maintain a pleasant and healthy internal

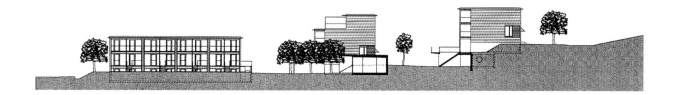

atmosphere. Floor elements are made up of exposed beams and triple-layer boards, with an in situ cement screed to improve sound absorption. Balcony structures and ventilated cladding are in Douglas fir, a native species suitable for external use to biological hazard class 3 without finishes or preservative treatment. Above the waterproof membrane, the flat roofs have a 70mm extensive green roof complex. During heavy rain, this retains a proportion of the rainwater, which then runs off gradually, via three retention basins, into the stream.

ENERGY AND CLIMATE CONTROL

The development is part of the EC 2000 sustainable construction programme. Each four-house terrace has a water-to-water heat pump, which takes heat from salt groundwater at 20°C via 180m deep, 100mm diameter boreholes. This system requires no fuel transport. Heating is via radiators, with separate thermostats and meters for each house. All houses are equipped with pipework for the installation of solar panels for hot water heating. Particular attention was paid to ensuring the use of non-hazardous materials throughout, containing no PVC: the Fermacell partitions are lined with ingrain wallpaper and painted with a casein paint; floors are in wood, linoleum or ceramic tiles.

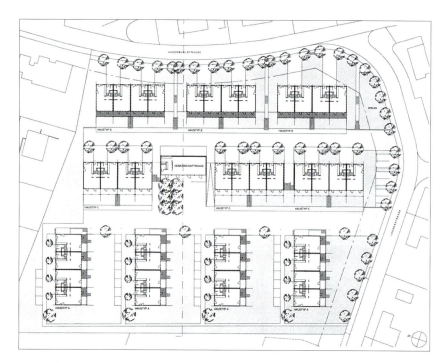

General plan.

Treatment of the outside areas creates private space within this very dense development.

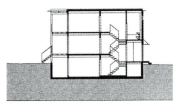

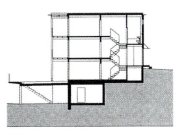

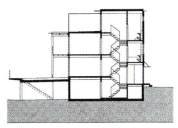

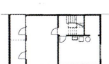

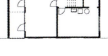

The three house types
make use of the
varying topography
of the site.
Transverse sections
and plans.

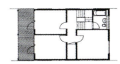

The structure is
of large-dimension,
timber-framed panels
above a reinforced
concrete basement.

External cladding
and sliding shutters are
in local Douglas fir.

Inside, the spruce
floor beams are left
exposed.

Sections through the walls, showing sound insulation and fire barrier measures.

Connection between party wall and green roof

1 2 × 80mm mineral wool (120kg/m³)
2 30mm mineral wool (50kg/m³)
3 15mm Fermacell board
4 2 × 60mm mineral wool (18kg/m³)
5 13mm Fermacell boards

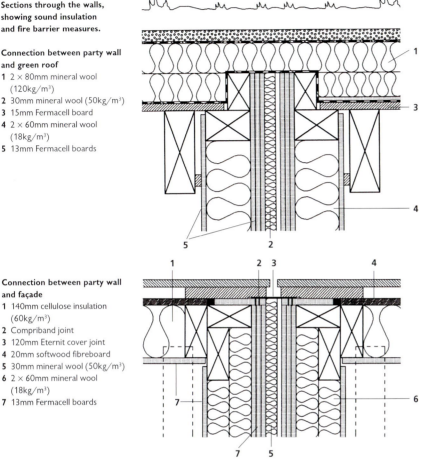

Connection between party wall and façade

1 140mm cellulose insulation (60kg/m³)
2 Compriband joint
3 120mm Eternit cover joint
4 20mm softwood fibreboard
5 30mm mineral wool (50kg/m³)
6 2 × 60mm mineral wool (18kg/m³)
7 13mm Fermacell boards

Connection between party wall and floor

1 30mm mineral wool (50kg/m³)
2 60mm mineral wool (18kg/m³)
3 13mm Fermacell boards

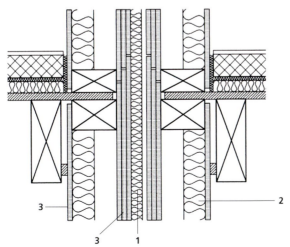

Railings, gratings and shutter supports are in galvanised steel.

Address: Loorenstrasse, Affoltern am Albis, Switzerland.
Project brief: ten terraces of four houses, community hall and car garaging.
Client: Kurt Schneebeli, Affoltern am Albis.
Architect: Metron Architekturbüro AG, Brugg (project architect: Urs Deppeler).
Engineers: structural concrete: Steinmann; timber structure: Rupli Holzbautechnik.
Timetable: design begun February 1997; construction on site November 1997-November 1999.
Area: net habitable area 10,596m²; type A houses, basement plus two floors; type B and C houses, basement plus three floors.
Contractors: timber construction: Rupli Holzbautechnik.
Cost: SF16,124,321 (€10,909,554). Cost of a five-room house SF300,000 (€190,000 approx.) at April 1997.

HOUSING BLOCK IN DORNBIRN, AUSTRIA
Hermann Kaufmann

The Ölzbündt development is a good example of the contemporary interpretation of the traditional, local timber building techniques of the Vorarlberg region. Simple without being ordinary, the design combines technical efficiency with an environmental approach.

ENVIRONMENTAL FEATURES

■ *Bioclimatic features*
Compact shape; active and passive use of solar energy; additional insulation; airtight envelope; insulating triple glazing.

■ *Materials and construction*
Spruce structure made up of standard elements; glulam columns; prefabricated box-beam floor elements constructed of triple-layer board on timber frame; walls in prefabricated timber-framed panels with mineral wool insulation; external stair tower with Intrallam central wall and Reglit façades; galvanised steel balconies and walkways; cladding in larch.

■ *Technical features*
Earth cooling tubes; heat pumps; two-way ventilation with heat recovery via heat exchanger; solar panels for hot water heating.

■ *U-values*
- Walls 0.11W/m²K;
- roof 0.10W/m²K;
- glazing 0.7W/m²K;
- ground level floor plate 0.12W/m²K.

■ *Energy consumption*
Heating 8kWh/m²/year.

■ *Sound insulation*
Walls, airborne noise, 60-75dB (measured); impact, 48dB (measured).

■ *Site*
Very rapid, low-impact construction due to choice of prefabricated timber structure.

CONTEXT AND SITE
At the western tip of Austria, Vorarlberg is a densely populated region where villages and urban areas are crowded together. As many other developments in the area, the success of the Ölzbündt project, in a residential suburb of Bregenz, lies in close and effective co-operation between developer, designers and contractor.

FUNCTION AND FORM
Environmental and economic concerns are brought together in this building to achieve a durable result. With its innovative structural system and energy concept, the 13-apartment block represents a concrete step towards the development of a mass-produced housing system combining innovation with high quality. Features include deliberately simple shapes, a building envelope designed to minimise heat loss, and use of a new prefabrication technique which reduced time on site to 4 months.

STRUCTURAL PRINCIPLES
The structure is based on the K-Multibox system, developed by the architect and structural engineers with the timber contractor. The building is on three levels, above a concrete basement, with a frame set out on a 2.4m × 4.8m grid. Glulam columns and floor box beams, which slot together via specially-made steel connection pieces, take vertical loads. The prefabricated floor and roof elements stabilise the primary structure through in-plane action. Walls are made up from prefabricated panels of six standard types: solid panel, corner panel, door panel, window panel and two French window panels. Each apartment can thus be indi-

vidually designed from this standard kit of parts. Bathrooms and kitchens for the upper floors are also pre-assembled in the factory. A comparison between these and the ground floor bathrooms and kitchens, built on site, showed no significant cost difference, but pre-assembly brought significant time benefits. On the east façade, the external stair tower, leading to the steel walkways, is clad in Reglit profiled glass, with an internal wall in Intrallam LSL (laminated strand lumber), a high-performance timber composite made from yellow pine by-products. The stair structure and walkways, along with the galvanised steel balconies on the west façade, are supported vertically on the basement concrete.

MATERIALS AND FINISHES
The timber cladding, in naturally durable larch, is carefully detailed for a long design life. To reduce shrinkage and deformation effects at the mitred corners, cladding joints are positioned at around 300mm from the corners of the building, on the column line. The sides of the window bays are timber, but the more exposed horizontal elements are in galvanised steel.

ENERGY AND CLIMATE CONTROL
Ölzbündt was one of the first Passive Housing projects (see p. 100). With their compact shape, very thick thermal insulation (350mm of rockwool), airtight window-frames and triple glazing, the apartments have no need for traditional heating. With such an airtight building envelope, user comfort in both winter and summer requires an efficient ventilation system. To ensure that the target energy consumption

figure of 8kWh/m^2/year, an extremely low value, is achieved, fresh air is brought into the building in stages. Outside air enters through a stainless steel inlet in the garden. It flows through an earth cooling tube, which warms it by around 8°C in winter and cools it by a similar amount in summer, before passing through a heat exchanger incorporated in the ventilation system. When necessary, it is heated further by individual heat pumps before distribution to the apartments. Used air is taken out via the kitchen, bathroom and lavatories; fresh air is blown into bedroom and living areas.

On the roof, an assembly of 33m^2 of solar collector panels, with a 2,650l reservoir, provides around two-thirds of the building's hot water. Despite the use of innovative technology, construction costs for these modern, elegant houses were only around 5 % above those for a comparable conventional project. This extra investment will be recouped over the long term, as the figure of 8kWh/m^2 (including heat pumps) is only around 10 % of typical energy consumption in conventional housing.

Schematic section showing heating and ventilation principles.

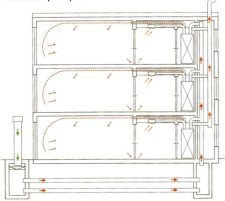

Cladding is in naturally durable larch.

Solar panels provide over
60 % of hot water needs.

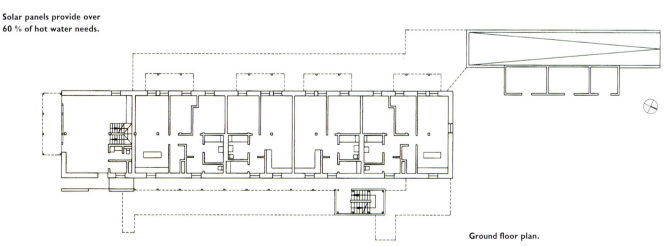

Ground floor plan.

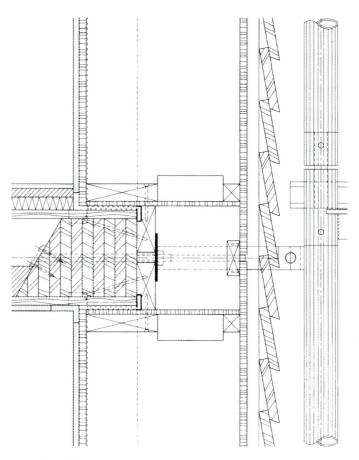

Connection detail
between galvanised floor
and balcony structure.

The galvanised balconies
and walkway elements are largely
separated from the main structure.

The prefabricated
wall panels take no vertical
loads.

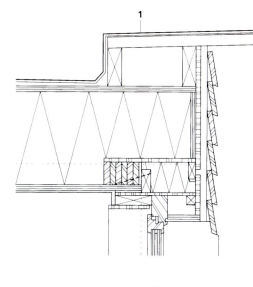

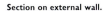

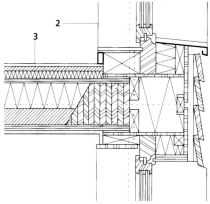

Section on external wall.

1 roof
- waterproofing
- 16mm particleboard
- 460mm glulam beams
- 400-480mm mineral wool
- damp-proof membrane
- 16mm particleboard
- 12.5mm plasterboard facing.

2 façade (solid panel)
- 12.5mm plasterboard
- 16mm particleboard
- damp-proof membrane
- 350mm mineral wool
- 12mm particleboard
- 30mm counter-battens
- larch cladding

3 typical floor
- 10mm glued wood flooring
- 25mm particleboard
- 35mm sound insulation
- 20mm triple-layer board
  (K1 Multiplan)
- 180mm glulam beams
- 110mm mineral wool
- 70mm granular fill
- 20mm triple-layer board
  (K1 Multiplan)
- plasterboard facing

The structural system combines columns with prefabricated structural floor and wall elements.

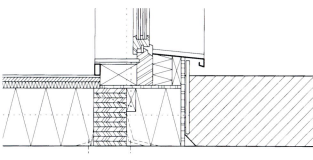

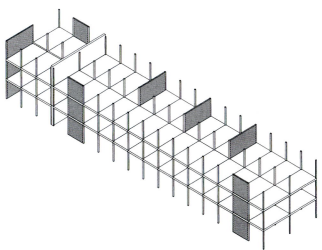

Schematic diagram of the structure, showing the solid elements which provide lateral stability.

Address: Hamerlingstrasse 12, 6850 Dornbirn, Austria.
Project brief: twelve passive housing units plus an artist's studio.
Client: Anton Kaufmann, Reuthe.
Architect: Hermann Kaufmann, Schwarzach.
Structural engineers: Merz Kaufmann Partner, Dornbirn.
Timetable: design begun July 1996; construction on site January - May 1997.
Area: habitable area 940m^2; basement, ground floor and two further habitable levels; roof space not useable.
Contractors: timber: Kaufmann Holz AG, Reuthe.
Cost: ATS19 million (€1.4 million approx).

STUDENT HOUSING IN CONSTANCE, GERMANY
Schaudt Architekten

Schaudt Architekten aim to achieve environmental quality through respect for the site and an optimisation of form, structure and materials to give users the quality of life they expect and aspire to. Here, economy of means results in a minimalism which highlights architectural quality.

ENVIRONMENTAL FEATURES

▪ *Bioclimatic features*
Compact volumes; use of local timber; additional insulation; insulating double glazing; rainwater recovery via biotope area.

▪ *Materials and construction*
Standard structural elements; beams and columns in solid spruce on concrete footings; solid spruce framing; rockwool insulation plus softwood fibreboard with bituminous coating; internal partitions in particleboard on timber framing; internal stairs in galvanised steel hollow sections with beech treads; timber window-frames; floor coverings in synthetic rubber; cladding in unplaned sawn larch; walkway railings in steel mesh; roof in profiled aluminium sheeting; Desovag Consulan transparent coating to timber structure and cladding.

▪ *Technical features*
Sealed-combustion gas boilers for heating and hot water, located in the roof space of each house.

▪ *Sound insulation*
Party walls, airborne noise, 65dB.

▪ *Site*
Rapid, low-impact construction due to use of standard timber structural elements.

CONTEXT AND SITE
Designed to house 102 students, the buildings are on a hillside site above the town of Constance, close to the university. These 17 bright, welcoming houses provide a friendlier, more relaxed atmosphere than traditional halls of residence, whose long corridors do little to encourage social contact. The buildings are elevated above ground level, with a view to preserving plant and animal life in the damp ground environment. Rainwater is collected in a concrete trench, from where it flows through a biotope area where the water is naturally purified by aquatic plants.

FUNCTION AND FORM
The houses are grouped into five terraces of two, four or five houses each, laid out on an orthogonal plan so as to create courtyards and semi-public spaces between them. The elevated houses are on three floors, including an attic floor; each house has its own ground-floor entrance at level 1, accessed via a walkway. Each floor comprises two study-bedrooms and some shared areas: dining room, kitchen and store-room at level 1, bathroom and lavatories at level 2, and a laundry room at level 3. The stairway, constructed of steel stringers supporting beech treads and with tubular steel hand-rails, acts as a visual screen between the dining room and the kitchen and entrance areas.

STRUCTURAL PRINCIPLES
The desire to preserve the natural characteristics of the site, along with a number of technical constraints such as low load-bearing capacity of the ground and flood risk, led to the choice of a lightweight timber structure, supported on concrete footings. The structural frame is set out on a 6m grid, a suitable span for solid timber elements. The structural system is simple, repetitive and economical, with only a small number of section sizes: 120×120mm for the columns, 120×220mm for the beams, and 120×180mm for the rafters. The floors are acoustic barriers, acting as a mass-spring-mass system: floor finish in synthetic rubber, 40mm cement screed, 25mm mineral insulation against impact and 30mm of sand, with a ceiling of 25mm tongue-and-groove timber supported on exposed beams. The roofs are pitched at 32°, with the two pitches offset at the ridge to allow a band of glazed roof-lights. The clarity of the architecture is further increased by the use of only a small number of materials, principally

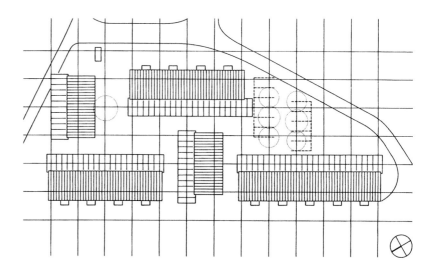

timber and steel. The use of low-cost, mass-produced components for secondary elements such as handrails, stairway and walkway structures left more resources available for improving environmental quality.

MATERIALS AND FINISHES

The building envelope is insulated by 120mm of rockwool between frame uprights and rafters, plus two 13mm softwood fibreboard panels behind the ventilated timber cladding. A bituminous coating to these panels provides a waterproof membrane. External walls are faced internally with plasterboard; partitions are two thicknesses of 19mm particleboard fixed to 100 × 48mm uprights, with 80mm mineral wool infill to provide sound insulation. The buildings are carefully proportioned, with interest added by the juxtaposition of plain and lap-jointed cladding panels, finished in pastel colours – pale blue or green for vertical elements, white for structural and horizontal elements. The wooden frames of the double-glazed windows are painted white. The aluminium roofing projects over the eaves and gables, giving the impression of flat plates placed on top of the building volumes below. The buildings were competed in 1992; thanks to the careful detailing and accuracy of construction, they have so far aged very well.

ENERGY AND CLIMATE CONTROL

Besides passive energy conservation measures and the use of non-hazardous materials, environmental quality is also achieved in this project through a user-friendly architectural style, well-thought-out and well-executed. There is plenty of natural light, entering through windows of different shapes and sizes: in the lower-level bedrooms, full-height glazing and a small, square window in front of desks; in the upper rooms, dormer windows and bands of glazing at eaves and ridge. The internal fittings are similarly simple and well-designed; furniture is neutral and practical, with beds and wardrobes on castors allowing students to rearrange their rooms as they wish.

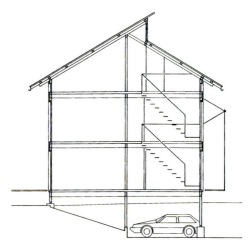

Transverse section.

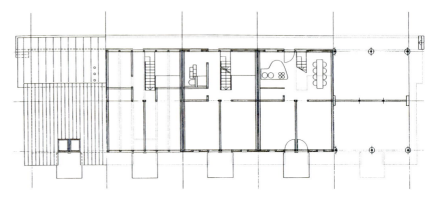

Plan on the different levels.

The architects designed moveable furniture for the study bedrooms.

Right
To reduce costs, standard catalogue components were used where possible.

The cladding, in pastel colours, juxtaposes horizontal and vertical panels.

The space beneath the buildings is used as a bicycle and car parking area.

Vertical section through the façade.

1 roof
  - aluminium sheet
  - 120mm mineral wool
  - damp-proof membrane
    (0.4mm polyethylene)
  - ceiling in 25mm tongue-
    and-groove
  - 180 × 120mm rafters
2 typical floor
  - 3.2mm synthetic rubber floor
    covering
  - 40mm cement screed
  - damp-proof membrane
    (0.2mm polyethylene)
  - 25mm acoustic insulation
  - 30mm particleboard
  - 30mm granular fill
    (beneath living areas)
  - ceiling in 25mm tongue-
    and-groove
3 double-glazed window in spruce
  frame
4 façade
  - exposed beam-column
    structure in spruce
  - 12mm plasterboard on
    40 × 107mm timber supports
  - damp-proof membrane
  - 120mm mineral wool
  - 2 × 13mm woodwool boards
    with bituminous coating
  - cladding in 24mm unplaned
    sawn larch
  - 40 × 60mm battens
5 level 1 floor
  - as typical floor, plus
  - additional thermal insulation
  - 40mm fire protection skin
6 galvanised steel grille

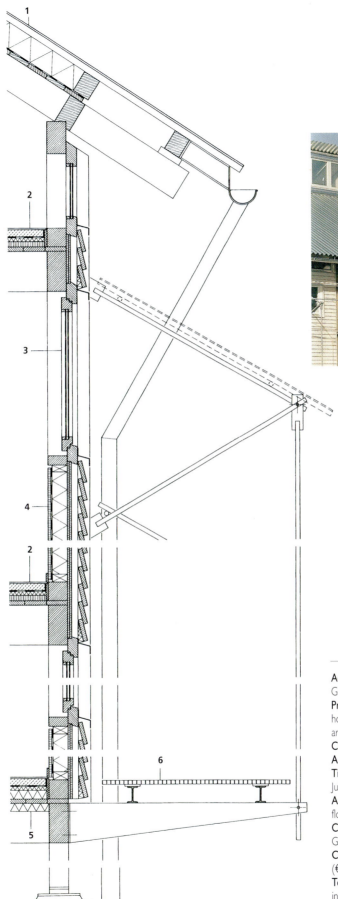

The façades are
enlivened by the stainless
steel walkway supports.

Address: Jungerhalde, 78404 Constance, Germany.
Project brief: 17 semi-detached and terraced houses, each with six study-bedrooms plus shared areas.
Client: Studentenwerk, Constance.
Architect: Schaudt Architekten, Constance.
Timetable: competition 1991; construction on site July 1991-September 1992.
Area: habitable area 1,774m²; elevated ground floor, first floor, attic.
Contractors: Structure: Kaspar, Gutach/Schwarzwald.
Construction costs: DM5.7 million (€2.914 million).
Total project costs: DM7 million (€3.579 million) including fees, landscaping, furniture and fittings.

HOME AND WORKPLACE BUILDING IN FREIBURG IM BREISGAU, GERMANY

Common & Gies

ENVIRONMENTAL FEATURES

■ Bioclimatic features
Compact shape; external stairs and walkways separate from structure; passive and active use of solar energy; airtight envelope; triple glazing with insulated frames; use of natural and recycled materials; green roof.

■ Materials and construction
Concrete, brick and timber superstructure, concrete basement. Gable and partition walls in calcium silicate brick; reinforced concrete slabs cast on permanent concrete formwork; north and south façades in timber-framed panels with Kaufmann I-beam uprights; mineral wool and cellulose insulation; Vega Climatop Solar glazing; window-frames in spruce; cladding in Douglas fir; steel balconies; extensive green roof.

■ Technical features
Gas co-generator; two-way ventilation with heat recovery via heat exchanger; solar collector panels for hot water heating; solar photovoltaic panels; Roediger vacuum toilets; production of biogas for cooker fuel from sewage and organic waste.

■ U-values
- Timber-framed walls 0.12W/m²K;
- masonry walls 0.15W/m²K;
- roof 0.1W/m²K;
- triple glazing 0.6W/m²K (DIN figure);
- ground level floor plate 0.16W/m²K.

■ Energy consumption
Heating 13.2kWh/m²/year; total consumption 36.2kWh/m²/year.

This building was built by 16 families who wished to bring together their homes and workplaces to increase social contact, with the emphasis on comfort and sustainability. Exemplary in a number of ways, it meets Passive Housing standards. The highly ambitious environmental concept includes economical use of water and recycling of organic waste to produce biogas, making the building virtually independent in terms of energy needs.

CONTEXT AND SITE
The site forms part of the first phase of the Vauban environmental development *(see pp. 71-75)*, on former military land near the centre of Freiburg. The co-developers met via the community development association, the Vauban Forum. Their varying needs led to a highly individual building design: the block contains four offices, 16 apartments, ranging from one-room flats to family apartments on two levels, communal areas and an artist's studio.
Several members of the development group are science and ecology professionals; their involvement encouraged the development of optimum technical solutions and ensured continuing technical input, important in an experimental project such as this. The architect, specialist engineers and future residents worked closely together to ensure the project's success.

FUNCTION AND FORM
To make best use of solar gain, the building is a long, narrow box running east-west. Windows are freely distributed along the façade, a result of residents' active participation in the design process, lending animation to the otherwise very simple building form. The four floors are

accessed on the north side by stairs and walkways. Optimum solar gain is obtained via 50 % glazing on the south façade, and 20 % only on the gables and north façade. The south side is shaded by balconies running the length of the block, structurally separate from the main building structure, and by mature trees along the avenue bordering the site.

STRUCTURAL PRINCIPLES
The building structure consists of transverse load-bearing walls in calcium silicate brick, and concrete slabs cast on precast concrete units which function as permanent formwork. This system is economical, provides good sound insulation and has a high thermal mass for natural temperature regulation. The building is 10m wide, with ceiling heights of 2.65m, and grids of 4m, 5m or 6m between transverse walls, allowing a wide range of different apartment plans. The north and south façades are constructed on non-structural timber framing; the low thermal conductivity of timber limits heat loss, which is decreased further by use of I-beam uprights to reduce thermal bridge effects. The compact form, simple primary structure and use of prefabrication reduced construction costs considerably.

MATERIALS AND FINISHES
Priority was given to use of simple and natural materials: brick for the walls, spruce for structure and window-frames, Douglas fir for

cladding. The prefabricated, timber-framed façade panels have 240mm of mineral wool insulation. A second, internal insulation layer is either mineral wool or cellulose, according to residents' preference, while further insulation on the external face is provided by Agepan fibreboard. There is almost no PVC in the building. The flat roof is planted with an extensive green roof system.

ENERGY AND CLIMATE CONTROL

Various active and passive measures have brought annual heating energy requirements down to a figure of 13.2kWh/m². Solar gain through the south-facing glazing, use of the structure's thermal mass, the additional insulation to the building envelope, and a mechanical ventilation system with an 85 % efficient heat exchanger all reduce heating needs. A 12kW gas co-generator, and 50m² of solar collector panels with a 3,400-litre hot water reservoir, meet remaining requirements. The solar collector panels contribute to heating in winter and produce 100 % of hot water requirements from April to September. The co-generator, and a 3.2kW array of photovoltaic modules positioned above the highest walkway, together provide around 80 % of electricity. Computer simulations were used to achieve optimum use of sunlight. These measures combine to make the building virtually independent in energy terms, and reduce greenhouse gas emissions by around 80 % compared to a conventional new housing block.

Water and waste management (see p. 103) are also designed to meet ambitious environmental aims. Grey water from kitchens and bathrooms is cleaned by an on-site ventilated sand filtration system and then used for flushing the vacuum toilets, which themselves use only 20 % of the water needed for a typical conventional toilet. Sewage and organic waste are collected in a tank; the biogas produced from their decomposition is used to fuel cookers, and the residue used as fertiliser. Rainwater, and any overflow from the filtered grey water, flows into a trench which runs along the avenue at the south edge of the site.

This building was built as an environmental research project, with funding obtained specifically for researching the solutions adopted and monitoring the results.

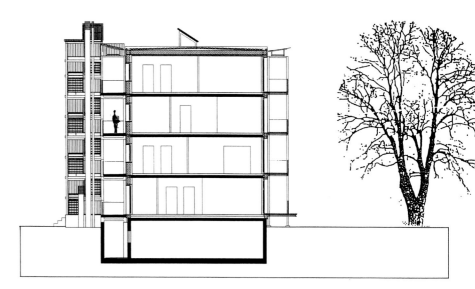

Transverse section.

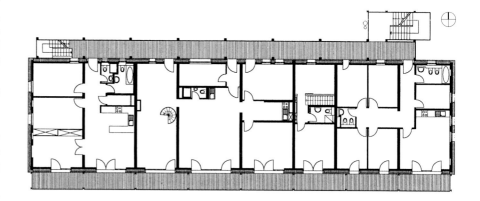

Plans of two typical floors. The structural system, with varying distances between transverse walls, allows numerous different arrangements of apartments and offices.

To avoid thermal bridges, the walkways and balconies on the north and south façades are structurally separate from the building.

The mix of housing and offices leads to a friendly, social atmosphere.

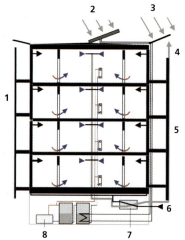

Principles of the building's energy concept.
1 Balconies
2 Solar collector panels for hot water
3 Photovoltaic modules
4 Used air
5 Walkways
6 Fresh air
7 Heat exchanger
8 Gas co-generator

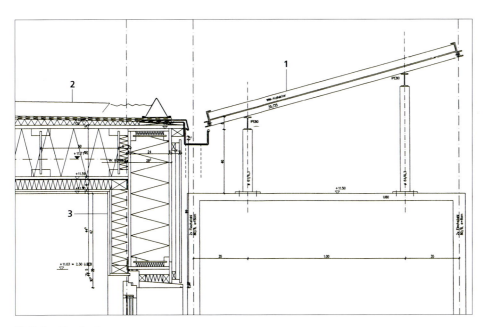

**Vertical section showing
the connection between the
north façade and the roof.**

**The structure is in brick and
concrete, with non-structural
timber-framed façades.**

1 PV panel, inclined at 15°
2 roof
  - extensive greenroof
    system, 100mm
  - waterproofing
  - insulation laid to falls,
    minimum thickness
    20mm
  - 22mm OSB panel
  - 300mm timber I-beam
    (Kaufmann D13-300)
  - 300mm mineral wool 040

  - 16mm OSB panel
  - damp-proof membrane
    in 0.4mm polyethylene
    with sealed joints and
    edges
  - 40/60mm battens
  - 60mm mineral wool 040
  - 2 × 12.5mm plasterboard
    panels
3 façade
  - 2 × 12.5mm plasterboard
    panels

  - timber frame, 50 × 100mm
    sections at 625mm centres
  - 100mm mineral wool 040
    or cellulose
  - 16mm OSB panel with
    sealed joints and edges
  - 240mm timber I-beam
    (Kaufmann W240)
  - 240mm mineral wool 040
  - 16mm Agepan fibreboard
  - 24/48mm battens
  - 24/48mm counter-battens

  - 12mm woodwool board
    cladding
4 brick wall
5 balcony support structure
    in 120mm galvanised steel
    H-sections.

**Horizontal section
through the south façade.**

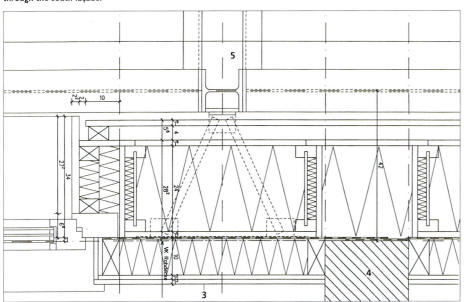

Address: Walter Gropius Strasse 22,
79100 Freiburg im Breisgau, Germany.
Project brief: 16 apartments, from 36m²
to 170m², and four offices.
Client: co-developers' group
(Bauherrengemeinschaft Wohnen
und Arbeiten).
Architect: Common & Gies, Freiburg.
Engineers: structure: Wolfgang Feth,
Freiburg; building physics: Fraunhofer
Institute for Solar Energy with Solares Bauen
GmbH, Freiburg; fluids: Krebser & Freyler,
Teningen; waste management concept:
Jörg Lange, Freiburg.
Timetable: design begun 1996;
construction on site June 1998-July 1999.
Area: habitable area 1,553m²
(housing 1,360m², offices 193m²); four floors,
communal space and basement technical
services area.
Cost: DM2,400/m² (€1,227/m²) including
taxes; cost of Passive Housing measures,
around 7 % of total.

HOUSING IN VIIKKI, HELSINKI, FINLAND
Arrak Architects

ENVIRONMENTAL FEATURES

■ *Bioclimatic features*
Whole life cycle assessment of materials; active and passive use of solar energy; glazed balcony conservatories; additional insulation.

■ *Materials and construction*
Structure and floors in precast concrete; façades in prefabricated timber framed elements.

■ *Technical features*
Low-temperature floor-based heating using return water from urban heating plant; individual mechanical ventilation with heat exchanger and seasonal adjustment capability; solar panels for hot water heating.

■ *U-values*
- Walls 0.21W/m²K;
- ground floor 0.18W/m²K;
- roof 0.13W/m²K;
- glazing 1.0W/m²K.

■ *Energy consumption*
67kWh/m²/year.

■ *Solar gain*
12.25kWh/m²/year (estimated).

■ *Sound insulation*
Walls, impact, 35dB.

■ *Site*
Use of prefabricated structural and façade elements.

As part of a European experimental programme, this project involved extensive study of the thermal aspects of the building. It combines the use of prefabricated elements, a high thermal inertia with additional insulation, an innovative ventilation system and the use of solar energy.

CONTEXT AND SITE
The building is located in a residential area in the environmental district of Viikki, 7km from central Helsinki (*see pp. 79-82*). The site is bordered to the north by a road, and to the south by an urban park. The city's rental social housing programme includes a grant scheme, aimed at ensuring a social mix; before acceptance, applicants for housing must complete a questionnaire on their attitudes to environmental issues.

The project is part of the EU's Sunh programme, which aims to produce innovative and reproducible solutions for energy conservation and the use of solar energy in sustainable building. It is the subject of a two-year study of the results, carried out by the Finnish research centre VTT. The city authorities also have stringent specifications for developments in Viikki. The prefabricated timber façades incorporate a number of technical innovations, development of which was funded by the technology agency Tekes.

FUNCTION AND FORM
The buildings are set out in typical Finnish fashion, to form an open courtyard space between them. The courtyard is screened from the dominant southerly wind by a two-storey terrace looking onto the park, and to the north by a four-storey block A small building housing the shared laundry and building services areas forms the east side. The four-storey block consists of superposed two-level apartments, with access either at ground floor or from walkways at level 2. These link the building to a smaller block housing the stairways, the shared saunas and the smallest apartments. The south façades incorporate glazed conservatories, with terraces at the top floor. The terraced houses also have south-facing conservatories, extending into individual gardens enclosed with thick hedges and fruit trees to encourage ecosystem development. The courtyard features a children's play area, shared with the neighbouring buildings. This arrangement, with semi-public space and shared amenities, favours social contact and the development of a community atmosphere.

STRUCTURAL PRINCIPLES
The building is set on piled foundations and ground beams, with a readily accessible void space, well-ventilated to dissipate any radon emanating from the granite below. The main load-bearing and lateral stability structures are in precast concrete, with prefabricated elements integrating insulation and finishes, on a 6m grid. Floors are 265mm hollow-core slabs, without further sound absorption measures. The timber-framed façades and roof have additional insulation, conceived by the architects as a "protective woollen jersey". The roof is insulated by 450mm of cellulose between the steel roof covering and the plywood soffit, sprayed between the solid structural timber beams. Façades are composed of prefabricated timber-framed elements complete with insulation, external and internal cladding. The balcony and walkway structures, in glulam timber with 45mm waterproofed Kerto laminated veneer lumber panels, support decking in autoclaved pine, with fire protection by an external sprinkler system. The use of prefabricated elements, widespread in Finland, allows high-quality finishes and high performance to be achieved with economy of materials and little site waste.

MATERIALS AND FINISHES
The relatively traditional materials used were selected after consideration of their whole life cycle assessments, besides their structural and thermal properties. The load-bearing façades and timber galleries are the first of their kind in Finland, made possible by recent changes in fire regulations. External steel components, such as handrails, railings and staircases, are galvanised. Timber window-frames were ruled out for maintenance reasons; instead a composite system was developed, with timber frames clad externally with powder-coated aluminium. The façades are clad in laminated composite panels

made from recycled paper and resin. In the stairways, the choice of cladding in sound-absorbent rubber removed the need for a layer of mineral wool in the ceiling.

ENERGY AND CLIMATE CONTROL

The high thermal mass of the concrete floors and walls, the additional insulation, the integrated glazed conservatories and argon-filled, low-emissivity double glazing all work towards natural temperature control. These measures are combined with an innovative air circulation system. Each apartment is mechanically ventilated, with a heat exchange system which is particularly effective in Scandinavian climates; air is brought in at the north façade in summer, and at the south façade in winter. In the latter case, incoming air is heated in the conservatories by an inversion of the ventilation system, effected by maintenance personnel. The façades are coloured in accordance with this energy strategy: the south façade is grey, helping optimise solar gain in the cooler seasons while not overheating in summer; the north façades are white to favour incident natural light. The floor-based low temperature heating system was selected as a function of the thermal mass of the concrete; it makes use of the warm-water return network from the urban heating plant. A total of 63 solar collector panels produce 60 % of hot water needs. Energy consumption is metered individually in each apartment.

General view of the buildings.

**A small service building forms
the east side of the courtyard.**

General plan.

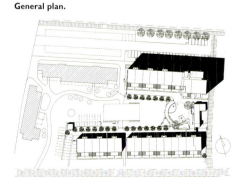

**West elevation. The landscaped
courtyard area is screened
to the north by the four-storey
block, while the lower south
building allows sun to enter.**

The terraced houses have
integrated glazed conservatories,
terraces and a hedged garden.

Part plan of the terraced
houses at ground and first
floor levels. A walkway links
the service building with
two first-floor studio flats.

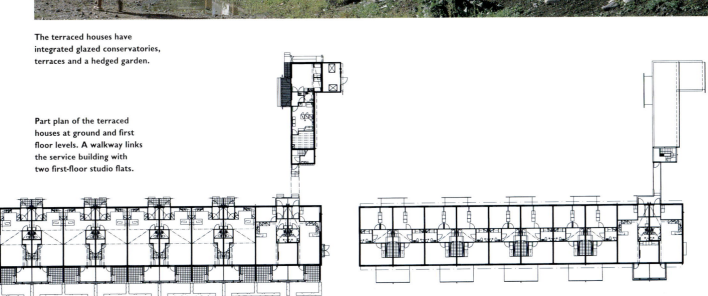

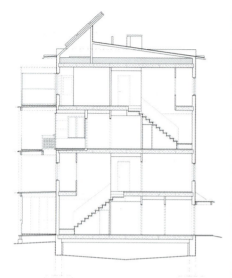

Transverse section through
the four-storey block, showing
two-level apartments one
above the other. Solar panels
are discreetly integrated.

Garden floor plan of the four-storey
block. Living areas are extended
by the glazed conservatories, external
terraces and small private gardens.

The walkways, terraces and glazed
boxes add interest to the façade;
the spaces between them become
social areas.

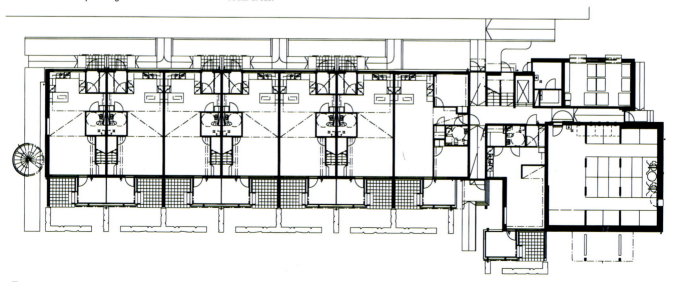

Section through the façade and walkway of the four-storey building.

1 external wall
(U = 0.21W/m²K)
- 6mm laminated panel
- 22mm vertical batten
- 9mm plasterboard wind barrier
- vertical frame with 148mm mineral wool
- 0.2mm damp-proof membrane
- 48mm vertical frame
- 13mm plasterboard finish

2 ceiling (U = 0.23W/m²K)
- 6mm laminated panel
- 22mm horizontal batten
- 9mm plasterboard wind barrier
- 196mm mineral wool
- 265mm hollowcore slab
- 50mm screed
- floor finish

3 external wall
(U = 0.26W/m²K)
- 6mm laminated panel
- 22mm horizontal batten
- 9mm plasterboard wind barrier
- vertical frame with 98mm mineral wool
- 0.2mm damp-proof membrane
- 48mm vertical frame
- 13mm plasterboard
- finish

4 door (U = 0.21W/m²K)

5 floor (U = 0.36W/m²K)
- decking
- 4mm bituminous waterproofing
- 25mm LVL board
- 80mm polyurethane insulation
- 265mm hollowcore slab
- finish

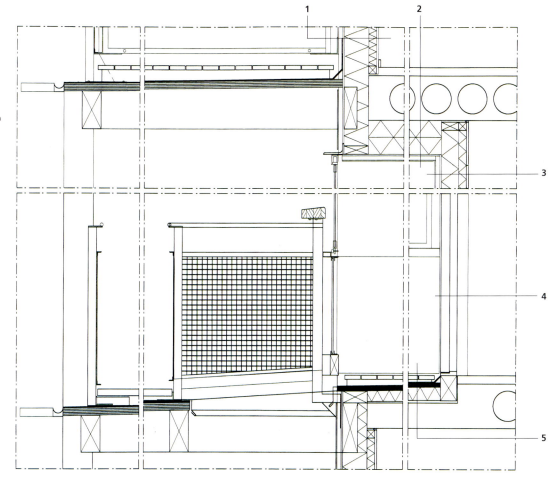

The second-floor apartments are accessed by an external timber walkway.

Address: Tilanhoitajankaari 20, Helsinki, Finland.
Project brief: 44 municipal rental apartments.
Client: Helsinki city property department (ATT), Pihlajiston Kiinteistöt Oy.
Architect: Arrak Architects, Kiiskilä, Rautiola, Rautiola Ltd., Helsinki; Hannu Kiiskilä, Mari Koskinen, Marja Nissinen, Olli Sarlin.
Engineers: structure: Engineering Office K. & H., Hämeenlinna; fluids: Calor, Helsinki; electricity: Projectus Team, Espoo.
European co-ordinator: Helsinki University of Technology, Research Institute for the Built Environment.
Landscape designers: MA Architects, Helsinki.
Timetable: design begun 1997; completed 2000.
Area: total area 4,797m².
Main contractor: Seicon, Helsinki.
Cost: €4.62 million excl. tax.
Funding: Sunh, EU Thermie programme; Tekes; loan from ARA state housing fund.

SALVATIERRA BUILDING IN RENNES, FRANCE

Jean-Yves Barrier

ENVIRONMENTAL FEATURES

▪ *Bioclimatic features*
Compact shape; passive and active use of solar energy; airtight envelope; hemp insulation; argon-filled double glazing; use of natural materials and non-hazardous finishes.

▪ *Materials and construction*
Concrete, earth and timber structure; structural walls and columns in situ concrete, floors solid fair-faced concrete slabs; east, west and north façades in timber-framed panels with hemp insulation; south façade in clay blocks; external window-frames in mengkulang; cladding in Silberwood spruce and Eternit Eterclin; roofing in coated steel sheet, terraces in waterproof flat roof system.

▪ *Finishes*
Interior paints: Pantex by La Seigneurie.

▪ *Technical features*
Two-way ventilation with heat recovery via heat exchanger, additional air intake heating by urban heating plant; solar hot water heating.

▪ *U-values*
- Timber-framed walls with hemp insulation 0.21W/m²K;
- earth walls 0.75W/m²K;
- roof 0.2W/m²K;
- glazing 1.3W/m²K;
- ground level floor plate 0.19W/m²K.

▪ *Energy consumption*
- Heating 14.9kWh/m²/year;
- total consumption 40kWh/m²/year.

The Salvatierra apartment block combines advanced technology and energy conservation measures with the use of natural materials to produce a warm, healthy environment. It applies a pragmatic and effective approach whose primary aim is user comfort.

CONTEXT AND SITE
The Salvatierra building is the only French project in the EU's Cepheus Passive Housing programme (*see p. 100*). Located in the Beauregard development area (*see pp. 88-89*), the project was initiated by the Rennes city authorities and a developer-builder co-operative. The Beauregard site, on the city's upper slopes, is designed to promote environmental quality, with large green areas, buildings laid out as a function of wind direction, and a waste management system.

FUNCTION AND FORM
The building is the largest Cepheus project, with 40 apartments ranging from two- to six-rooms. The layout, shape and orientation of the rooms, and the choice of materials, are designed to give best use of sunlight for both heating and natural lighting purposes. Apartments on the four lower floors are compact, limiting heat loss and making for simpler construction, while the two top floors contain two-level apartments with south-facing terraces. To avoid dark stairwells, the upper apartments are accessed from external walkways on the north façade, looking onto a courtyard garden.

STRUCTURAL PRINCIPLES
Besides its energy aspects, Salvatierra represents the integration of contemporary technology with traditional materials. Jean-Yves Barrier, who is widely experienced in bioclimatic projects, uses a mix of materials to make best use of the properties of each. The economical concrete structure contributes both lateral stability and thermal mass. The north and end façades are framed in timber, whose insulating properties reduce thermal bridging. The south façade is in unbaked earth, formed off-site by compression into blocks, 700 × 500mm in section and 600-1000mm long. The use of this traditional local technique in such a project puts a high value on local craftsmanship, raising hopes of its possible renaissance.

MATERIALS AND FINISHES
The building is distinguished from other Cepheus projects by its emphasis on the use of natural, non-hazardous, renewable and recyclable materials. The timber-framed walls are insulated between uprights by two 80mm layers of fibrous hemp, whose thermal properties are similar to mineral wool. The upper part of the building is clad in overlapping pre-painted spruce planks, and the lower floors in Eterclin, a combination of wood fibres and cement which has good fire resistance (class M0 to the French regulations). The use of painted timber

South façade.

for cladding and window-frames recalls the traditional housing of the region. The clay blocks have an earth- and chalk-based finish coat on internal and external faces. Floors are tiled or finished in wood, and paints are environmentally certified, reflecting the construction co-operative's decision to emphasise quality and user comfort.

ENERGY AND CLIMATE CONTROL

To meet Passive Housing criteria, a building must achieve temperature and climate control without conventional heating systems. Annual heating energy consumption is limited to $15kWh/m^2$, and total energy consumption (heating, hot water, lighting, domestic appliances) to $42kWh/m^2$, around 75 % less than average values for conventional new housing. These figures are achieved through a combination of bioclimatic measures, with careful design of the building envelope and technical systems. The thermal mass of the earth blocks contributes to temperature regulation in summer and winter, while the windows are in 4-16-4 high-transmission, low-emissivity double glazing, with argon infill to increase insulation. Careful detailing, particularly of the floor-to-façade connections, aims to reduce heat loss by ensuring air impermeability. In addition to these bioclimatic features, the two-way ventilation system is equipped with an 80 % efficient heat exchanger. Heat recovered from used air, taken from the kitchens and bathrooms, is used to warm fresh intake air, which is distributed via outlets in the corners of the main rooms. Remaining requirements are met by the district heating plant, which can also supply any hot water requirements not met by the $100m^2$ of solar collector panels on the roof. Future residents were kept informed of the project's progress, and provided with information on passive housing; their commitment to the aims of the project should ensure the building's continuing economical management.

Plan of a typical floor.

The two-level apartments above are set back from the lower floors.

Right:
The north façade is clad in pre-painted spruce.

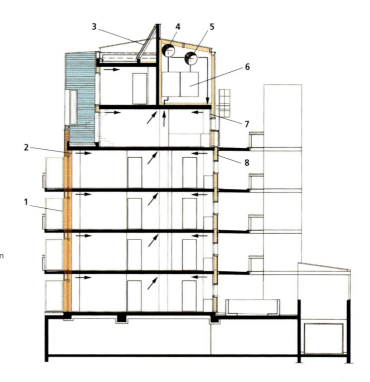

Transverse section showing ventilation principles.
1 50mm thick earth blocks
2 pre-heated fresh air
3 solar panels
4 air outlet
5 fresh air intake
6 services area
7 pre-heated fresh air
8 150mm hemp fibre insulation

Plan of a three-room apartment. Ventilation outlets are in the corners of the rooms.

The upper apartments have a timber frame.

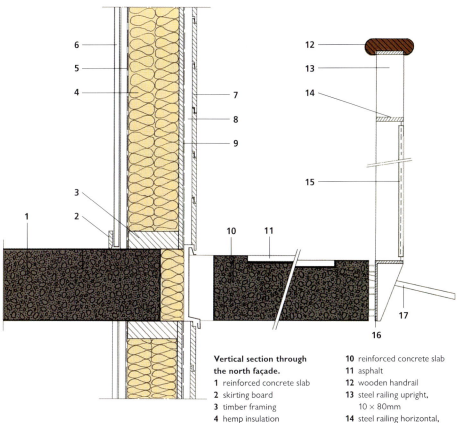

**The earth blocks are
500 × 700mm in section.**

**Vertical section through
the north façade.**
1 reinforced concrete slab
2 skirting board
3 timber framing
4 hemp insulation
5 damp-proof membrane
6 13mm plasterboard fixed to rail
7 cladding in painted spruce
8 battens
9 weatherproofing
10 reinforced concrete slab
11 asphalt
12 wooden handrail
13 steel railing upright,
10 × 80mm
14 steel railing horizontal,
10 × 80mm
15 steel grille with 62 × 30mm
mesh
16 5mm steel plate
17 water drainage pipe

**Horizontal section through
the corner of the south and
west walls.**
1 spruce cladding
2 weatherproofing
3 batten
4 timber cover joint
5 waterproof joint
6 finish coating
7 hemp insulation
8 timber framing
9 damp-proof membrane
10 13mm plasterboard fixed
to rail
11 reinforced concrete column
12 unbaked earth block
13 timber upright
14 timber window-frame.

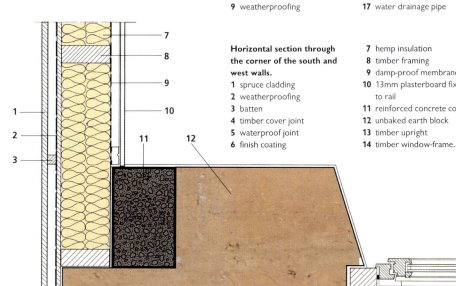

Address: Zac Beauregard, 35000 Rennes, France.
Project brief: 40 experimental, two- to six-room
apartments, plus three conventional apartments.
Client: Construction co-operative, Jean-Claude Allain
& Thierry Wagner, Rennes.
Architect: Jean-Yves Barrier, Tours.
Engineers: energy: Oasiis, Aubagne; structure: BSO,
Saint-Brieuc.
Timetable: design begun 1998; construction on site
November 1999 - March 2001.
Area: habitable area 3,100m²; four typical floors,
plus two-level apartments above; basement car park.
Contractors: Concrete works: Beltrame; earth
construction: Guillorel; timber: Ceb 35; paintwork:
Goni; heating and plumbing: Grosdoigt; insulation:
Lenain; external fittings: Février; solar panelling:
Clipsol.
Cost: FF16 million (€2.439 million) excl. tax.

KINDERGARTEN IN STUTTGART, GERMANY

Joachim Eble Architektur

ENVIRONMENTAL FEATURES

▮ *Bioclimatic features*
Structure in solid timber; additional thermal insulation; use of untreated local timber and non-hazardous materials and finishes; active use of solar energy; rainwater recovery system.

▮ *Materials and construction*
Prefabricated spruce panelling used for internal and external walls, floors and roof; glulam beams and columns in spruce. Linoleum floor covering; cladding in spruce planking and triple-layer board; roof cladding in titanium zinc.

▮ *Finishes*
Auro transparent coating Lasur 130 to internal panels and cladding; Auro Lack-Lasur opaque coating to window-frames.

▮ *Technical features*
Solar panels for water heating.

▮ *Site*
Low impact construction due to use of prefabricated structural elements.

In the late 1990s, new German legislation, guaranteeing a nursery school place for every child at the age of three, led to the construction of a large number of new kindergartens. In common with many others, the Stuttgart-Heumaden kindergarten creates a healthy and pleasing environment whose warmth is partly due to the use of timber throughout the structure and fittings.

CONTEXT AND SITE

The Heumaden kindergarten is set at the centre of a green space close to the housing blocks of one of Stuttgart's southern districts. The designer Joachim Eble, a pioneer of environmental architecture in Germany, and the client, the Stuttgart youth department, were united in their wish to use non-hazardous materials and products throughout the building (*see pp. 63-68*).

FUNCTION AND FORM

The building contains seven classrooms, a hall, a few dedicated rooms, a social assistance office, offices, a cafeteria and building services areas. As is usual in Germany, all classrooms comprise a large room for whole-class activities and a smaller area for group work; the seven units are therefore divided into different volumes, clearly differentiated by shape and colour. The irregular, organic plan allows the total area of 1,390m² to be visually broken down into more manageable parts, helping children identify more easily with their own group. Three external staircases, accessed from the first floor gallery, give children direct access to the garden.

STRUCTURAL PRINCIPLES

The structure is in solid timber, with a clearly defined structural logic. Walls, floors and roof structure are made from prefabricated panels composed of planks of second-grade local spruce, nailed together through their thickness to form slabs. Floor panels are 160mm thick, 1m wide and long enough to span across the rooms at around 5.5m. External wall panels are 100mm thick, internal walls 80mm; wall panels are 3m high and a maximum of 9m wide, this dimension being limited by transport con-

straints. Roof panels are 120mm thick. Thanks to the commitment of all involved, sustainable principles were rigorously applied throughout the project: the spruce is from the nearby Schönbuch forest so as to reduce transport, and all contractors selected were local.

Acoustic insulation between floors is provided by a 20mm sound absorption layer of coconut fibre, topped by a 50mm floating cement screed. Floor coverings are linoleum, and the soffits of the spruce panels are left exposed.

MATERIALS AND FINISHES

In some areas, internal wall panels are planed on both sides and left exposed. Those forming external walls are exposed on their inside face. The façades are clad in 24mm unplaned spruce planking, interspersed with panels of 12mm triple-layer board, with planks set horizontally or vertically. The distinction between different volumes is accentuated by the use of colour. Vibrant tones of yellow and orange-red, symbolising the earth, contrast with two shades of blue, used on the three classroom blocks and some first-floor façade areas, which evoke the air and sky.

Finishes are based on natural materials, using linseed oil and mineral pigments in a solvent based on orange oil. The timber panels have a base coat, then several coats – two for internal panels, three for external cladding – of Auro Lasur 130, a transparent finish which leaves the grain of the wood visible. Window-frames have a base coat and two coats of Auro Lack-Lasur, an opaque coating containing a higher proportion of pigment and linseed oil. The colours used on the external cladding, lit up by the sun, are slightly darker than those used inside. The

colours chosen for the linoleum floor coverings are in the same palette: red, orange or yellow in the classrooms, blue in corridor and services areas.

ENERGY AND CLIMATE CONTROL

For some years, all new public buildings in Stuttgart have been built with 25 % more thermal insulation than current regulations required. The additional costs of this policy are recouped over a period of around twelve years, through an estimated 30 % reduction in energy consumption. In the Heumaden kindergarten, insulation is provided by the thermal properties of the solid timber, plus 160mm of sprayed cellulose in the gap between the laminated panels and the 19mm fibreboard behind the external cladding. Solar panels for hot water heating, and a rainwater recovery system, add to the project's environmental credentials.

The kindergarten's organic form and use of colour recall the anthroposophic principles of the Austrian educationalist Rudolf Steiner.

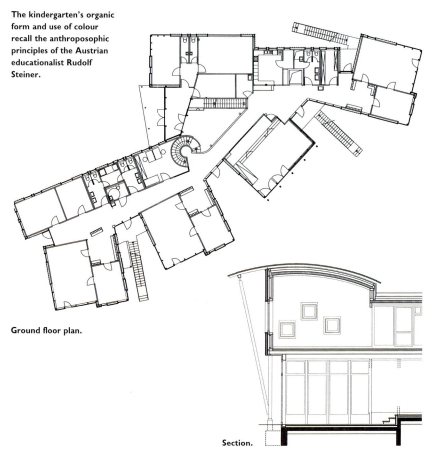

Ground floor plan.

Section.

On the façades, warm earth tones contrast with sky blues.

The main entrance, on the rear façade, is friendly and welcoming.

The different volumes are emphasised by the alternating use of horizontal and vertical timber cladding. Vertical planks are fixed to triple-layer board.

Irregular window positioning makes for a lively, interesting façade.

**Vertical section
through the façade.**

1 roof
 - titanium zinc sheet
 - 32mm timber planking
 - ventilated air gap
 - 19mm timber planking
 - waterproof membrane
 - 2 × 100mm cellulose insulation
 - damp-proof membrane
 - 120mm nailed-laminated spruce
  panel
2 100 × 60mm rafters
3 solid façade
 - 100mm nailed-laminated spruce
  panel
 - damp-proof membrane
 - 80 × 60mm horizontal battens
 - 2 × 80mm cellulose insulation
 - 80 × 60mm vertical counter-
  battens
 - waterproof membrane
 - 19mm timber planking
 - 40 × 60mm battens, ventilated air
  gap
 - cladding in 24 × 140mm unplaned
  spruce planks
4 floor
 - 0.3mm linoleum
 - 50mm cement screed
 - 2 × 20mm coconut fibre sound
  insulation
 - 160mm nailed-laminated spruce
  panel with acoustic profiling

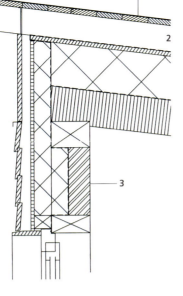

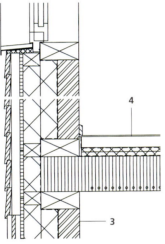

**The façades are finished
in Auro natural coatings.**

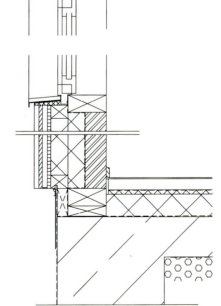

Address: Pfennig-Äcker 27, 70619 Stuttgart-Heumaden, Germany.
Project brief: kindergarten with seven classes, plus social assistance
office.
Client: Stuttgart city authority, youth department.
Architect: Joachim Eble Architektur, Tübingen.
Structural engineers: Schneck & Schaal, Tübingen.
Timetable: design begun January 1995; construction on site
July 1996-January 1998.
Area: useable area 1,088m²; Ground and first floors, with mezzanine
in first-floor classrooms.
Timber contractors: Gaia Nouva with Holzbau Schüle, Böblingen.
Cost: DM3.742 million (€1.913 million).

KINDERGARTEN IN PLIEZHAUSEN, GERMANY

D'Inka + Scheible

ENVIRONMENTAL FEATURES

▌ *Bioclimatic features*
Thermal buffer formed by services areas on north side; active and passive use of solar energy; additional thermal insulation; glazed double skin on south wall; use of non-hazardous and recyclable materials and naturally durable timber; rainwater recovery system; green roof.

▌ *Materials and construction*
Prefabricated panels with solid spruce frame; insulating double glazing with glulam framing; internal cladding in plywood with pine veneer; linoleum floor covering; cladding, sun-screens and decking in larch; ZinCo Floradrain 60 extensive green roof system.

▌ *Technical features*
Solar panels for water heating; photovoltaic modules.

▌ *U-values*
- Walls 0.16W/m²K;
- roof 0.21W/m²K;
- curtain walling 1.2W/m²K;
- double glazing 0.84W/m²K;
- ground level floor plate 0.17W/m²K.

▌ *Site*
Rapid construction due to the use of prefabrication, with structure in standard timber elements.

In 1978, Baden-Württemberg was the first German Land to elect Green representatives to its regional parliament. Since then, facilities for children and young people have been built according to an economic and environmental rationale, based on well-judged choices of structural and building services systems.

CONTEXT AND SITE
The Pliezhausen kindergarten is on the edge of a group of educational and sports facilities, close to residential bungalows and reached via a pathway, shaded by a pergola, running alongside a car park. At the north edge of the complex, it gives onto a garden planted with fruit trees.

FUNCTION AND FORM
The building is divided clearly into three identical blocks, with an equally clear differentiation between the classrooms and service areas. Each classroom block contains a spacious, 3.5m high space for whole-class activities, with floor-to-ceiling glazing on the south wall looking onto the orchard. A beech staircase leads up to a quiet play area on a mezzanine, looking down onto the classroom areas and hallway; beneath this, a smaller, shaded area is reserved for work in small groups. Beside each classroom, a terrace in larch decking leads to steps down to the garden. A circulation area separates the classroom blocks from the service areas to the north, where offices, studio, cafeteria, lavatories and storage are housed in three lower

blocks directly behind the classrooms. The communal space is designed to have several functions; near the entrance, it forms a broad playground, while smaller areas beside the classrooms are used as cloakrooms.

STRUCTURAL PRINCIPLES
The design is a result of a combination of economic and environmental concerns. The structural frame is based on a repeating grid of 1.25m between uprights. This facilitated both prefabrication and erection, bringing down costs and reducing construction time to six months. Vertical structure consists of 200 × 90mm glulam columns, timber framed walls and curtain-wall façades. Structural beams are in glulam spruce, and are 300 × 80mm sections for the 6.5m spans in the classrooms, and 400 × 80mm sections for the 8.25m spans in the entrance hall. The roof is insulated by 180mm of rockwool between the beams; additional insulation is provided by the green roof. Column and beam sections have 30 minutes of fire resistance. To meet this requirement elsewhere, the wall between the hall and the service areas is lined with plasterboard on the corridor side, behind its plywood facing.

MATERIALS AND FINISHES
Local spruce is used for the structural framing: solid sections for the wall framing, and glulam for the curtain-walling. Internal walls are faced with 19mm plywood panelling with Polish pine veneer. Some are perforated to improve their acoustic properties. External cladding is in overlapping 26mm planed larch planks; sun-screens and external decking are also in planed larch, without preservative treatment or coating. The green roof is planted with colourful sedums,

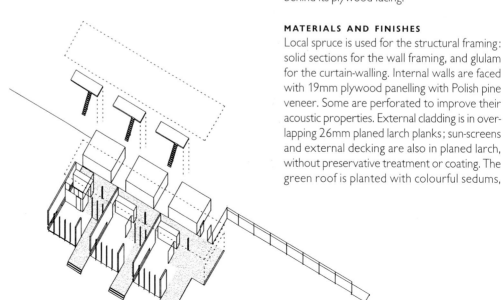

which require only minimal maintenance; its 70mm substrate is laid in drainage elements made from recycled polyethylene. This is laid over a multi-layer bitumen waterproofing system, protected by an absorbent mat and root barrier layer.

ENERGY AND CLIMATE CONTROL

The solid walls are insulated by a double layer of rockwool: 180mm between uprights, and a further 50mm on the outside of the structure. To the south, best use is made of solar gain by means of a ventilated double skin: an internal skin of 70mm double-glazed units is separated by a 300mm air gap from the outer skin of 12mm single glazing, supported by a lightweight structure in galvanised steel angles. To allow natural ventilation to the classrooms, a handle system enables the small lower glazing panels to be opened. Blinds within the air gap prevent over-heating in summer. Hot water for washbasins and the cafeteria is heated by 20m^2 of solar panelling on the roof, while 5m^2 of photovoltaic modules provides the kindergarten's electricity supply. Rainwater is collected in a tank and is used for toilet flushing and irrigation, via a pump. Overflow from this tank flows into a biotope area which is used as an educational tool, bringing environmental awareness from an early age.

The three classrooms face south onto the garden.

Ground floor plan.

Access to the kindergarten is along a pergola.

External cladding,
sun-screens and
decking are in larch.

The south façades have
a glazed double skin.

A hallway separates
the classrooms from
the service areas.

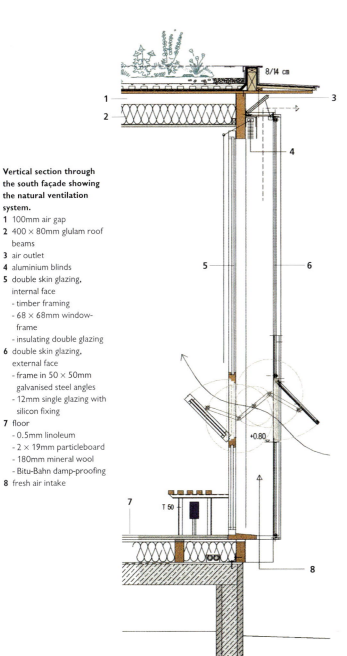

Vertical section through the south façade showing the natural ventilation system.

1 100mm air gap
2 400 × 80mm glulam roof beams
3 air outlet
4 aluminium blinds
5 double skin glazing, internal face
 - timber framing
 - 68 × 68mm window-frame
 - insulating double glazing
6 double skin glazing, external face
 - frame in 50 × 50mm galvanised steel angles
 - 12mm single glazing with silicon fixing
7 floor
 - 0.5mm linoleum
 - 2 × 19mm particleboard
 - 180mm mineral wool
 - Bitu-Bahn damp-proofing
8 fresh air intake

Vertical section through a solid wall.

1 roof
 - sedum
 - 70mm substrate
 - profiled drainage element
 - absorbent protective mat
 - multi-layer bitumen waterproofing
 - plywood in Polish spruce
 - 180mm mineral wool
 - damp-proof membrane
 - plywood in Polish spruce
2 air gap
3 300 × 80mm glulam roof beams
4 solid façade panel
 - 19mm Polish spruce plywood
 - damp-proof membrane
 - 180mm mineral wool
 - 2 × 50mm mineral wool
 - 12mm particleboard
 - Buzi-Bahn waterproof membrane
 - 48 × 48mm battens
 - cladding in overlapping 25 × 180mm Douglas fir planks

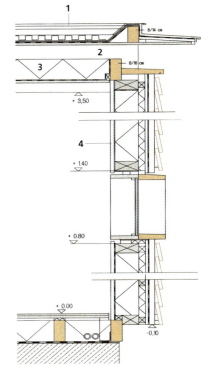

Details of the double skin façade.

Address: Karlstrasse, 72124 Pliezhausen, Germany.
Project brief: kindergarten, with 3 ground-floor classrooms plus mezzanines.
Client: Pliezhausen town council.
Architect: D'Inka + Scheible, Fellbach
Structural engineers: H. Siewert, Pliezhausen.
Timetable: competition October 1998; construction on site March - August 1999.
Area: useable area 593m².
Main structure contractor: Holzbau Rieg, Schwäbisch Gmünd.
Cost: DM1.9 million (€971,500).

NOTLEY GREEN PRIMARY SCHOOL, UK

Allford Hall Monaghan Morris

ENVIRONMENTAL FEATURES

■ *Bioclimatic features*
Compact plan form with flexibility of use; natural lighting and ventilation; temperature and humidity control; green roof; use of recycled materials.

■ *Materials and construction*
Block walls, timber beams, timber framing and cladding; cellulose insulation; external cladding in plywood and red cedar; Erisco-Bauder green roof on plywood support; floor coverings in linoleum, bamboo and rubber.

■ *Other technical features*
Heated floors; innovative ventilation system.

■ *U-values*
- Walls 0.21W/m²K;
- linoleum floors 0.37W/m²K;
- wood floors 0.38W/m²K;
- roof 0.32W/m²K;
- glazing 1.5W/m²K.

■ *Energy consumption*
Heating 142kWh/m²/year.

■ *Sound insulation*
Office walls, 35-40dB; circulation and washroom walls, 40dB.

Notley Green primary school, in Essex, is illustrative of the county's recently-adopted policy of using solar technologies and energy-saving measures in public buildings such as schools and hospitals. It is also a good example of the multi-disciplinary approach to design. Close co-operation between different disciplines within the design team led to production of a new specification for future Essex schools.

CONTEXT

The competition brief for this project was concerned as much with overall approach as with details of design and construction, aiming as it did to produce a new prototype "green" school. Much emphasis was put on community consultation. The building is set within a new garden village, itself still under development, so during the early design stages there was little local community to consult. However, the idea of maximising the use of school buildings outside school hours was retained.

FUNCTION AND FORM

The triangular shape was selected from four alternatives, whose environmental qualities were studied and assessed after discussion with future users. As well as making a strong architectural statement within the site, this shape has an optimum ratio between useable floor area and building envelope area, thus reducing heat loss. The efficient layout of internal space allowed total floor area to be reduced by 10 %, leaving more money available for environmental measures. A central atrium provides natural light and ventilation, functions as a circulation space and may also be used as an extension of the hall and other adjacent areas. The six classrooms, which face south-east, are warmed by the morning sun during spring and autumn. They give onto external terraces which have electricity and running water and form an integral part of the teaching areas. The technical teaching rooms look onto the playground areas to the south-west, while on the street side, facing north-north-east, the offices and services areas are grouped behind a more urban façade. The hall is used outside school hours by community and other groups. At the north-western point of the triangle is a covered external courtyard designed as a small amphitheatre.

STRUCTURAL PRINCIPLES

The impact on the site was reduced by minimising excavation, with any excavated earth re-used for landscaping within the site. For the same reason, precast slabs constructed on ground beams over a void were used in preference to in situ concrete. Block walls up to 5m high, founded on the ground beams, support Masonite timber I-beams spanning 6m. A 15mm plywood skin supports the roof system and transfers horizontal loads to the external walls. External cladding is in red cedar tongue-and-groove, chosen for easy maintenance, with horizontal glazing bands interspersing windows with marine ply panels. The timber beams carrying the projecting eaves are propped by a steel structure, allowing sections to remain slender.

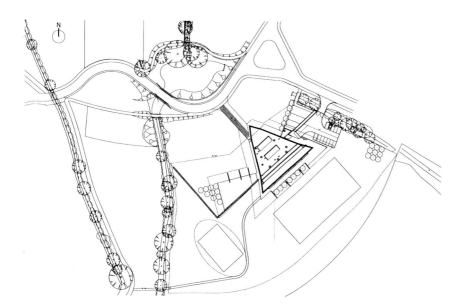

MATERIALS AND FINISHES

The choice of materials attempts to balance concerns of recyclability, embodied energy, advantages in use, maintenance, quality, cost and availability. Window-frames are in isothermal wood and aluminium, rather than solid wood, for lower maintenance. Floors use boards in compressed bamboo, a rapidly renewable material, and natural linoleum. Recycled materials are widely used: the Warmcell insulation is made from old newsprint; the entrance hall has rubber matting from reclaimed tyres; the Made of Waste polyethylene wall coverings are made from recycled plastic bottles. Water pipes and cable casings contain no PVC. The green roof system, which requires only a shallow substrate, helps create a microclimate and absorb CO_2; it also functions as an educational tool, with a demonstration element on display in the playground. The plant species need minimal maintenance and provide a carpet of green whose aspect changes with the seasons.

ENERGY AND CLIMATE CONTROL

For both budget reasons and ease of use, simple, manually-controlled systems were installed, operable by both teachers and pupils. The proportion of glazing was determined using a computer model, to give optimum natural light while preventing excessive heat loss. The green roofs slope upwards to form clerestory rooflights, bringing north light into the classrooms, while the central courtyard and hall reduce the need for artificial lighting.

Except for the kitchens and lavatories, the building is naturally cross-ventilated via openings in the façades and overhead. The central areas use a ventilation system recalling those used in Roman baths, whereby fresh air circulates under the floor in 450mm clay pipes, is blown into the library and extracted at high level through the clerestory windows. Windows on the south and west walls are shaded by metal sun-screens, with internal blinds allowing incident sunlight to be adjusted. The use of a heated floor system reduces temperature gradients and allows temperature to be regulated by zone.

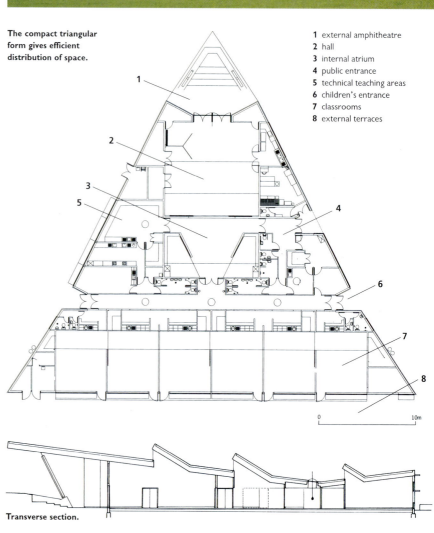

The compact triangular form gives efficient distribution of space.

1 external amphitheatre
2 hall
3 internal atrium
4 public entrance
5 technical teaching areas
6 children's entrance
7 classrooms
8 external terraces

0   10m

Transverse section.

South-east façade.
The classrooms extend
onto external terrace
areas.

Different-coloured doors
distinguish
the different classes.

The clerestory
roof-lights bring
a comfortable level
of natural light.

Sliding doors open
to combine the hall
and internal atrium into a
single space.

The roof projects over an external amphitheatre area which may be used as an extension of the hall.

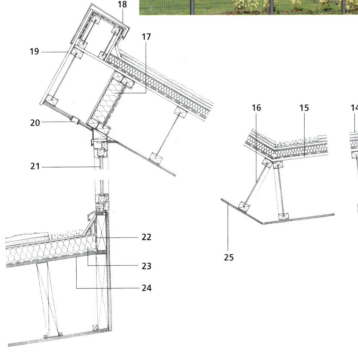

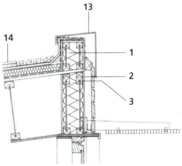

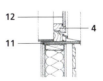

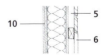

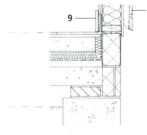

Section through the roof and external wall.

1 Warmcell insulation
2 battens
3 Masonite beam
4 isothermal wood and aluminium window-frame
5 ventilation
6 19mm marine ply
7 225mm timber framing with Warmcell insulation infill
8 red cedar cladding on 75 × 50mm battens
9 plywood skirting
10 double-thickness plasterboard
11 mastic joint
12 double glazing
13 powder-coated coping
14 Erisco-Bauder green roof
15 15mm plywood skin
16 400mm Masonite beam
17 60mm mineral wool insulation
18 powder-coated coping
19 painted marine ply
20 ventilation grille
21 Velux opening window-frame
22 Damp-proof membrane
23 Mineral wool insulation
24 15mm plywood skin
25 beech-veneered plywood

Address: Blickling Road, Black Notley, Braintree, Essex, UK.
Project brief: primary school with six classes.
Client: Essex County Council.
Architects: Allford Hall Monaghan Morris, London (Simon Allford, David Archer, Scott Batty, Ceri Davies, George Dawes, Johnathan Hall, Paul Monaghan, Peter Morris, Demetra Ryder Runton, John Thornberry).
Engineers: structure Atelier One, London; environmental engineering Atelier Ten, London.
Quantity surveyors: Cook & Butler.
Landscape designers: Jonathan Watkins Landscape, London.
Timetable: design begun December 1997; construction on site October 1998-September 1999.
Area: 1,044m².
Main contractor: Jackson Building, Ipswich.
Cost: €1.95 million

SECONDARY SCHOOL IN MÄDER, AUSTRIA
Baumschlager & Eberle

ENVIRONMENTAL FEATURES

▌ *Bioclimatic features*
Simple and compact form; passive and active use of solar energy; additional thermal insulation; acoustic insulation in wool; glazed double skin; polyurethane pipes; PVC-free cabling; solvent-free adhesives and coatings.

▌ *Materials and construction*
Structure in standard elements; reinforced concrete columns, precast reinforced concrete slabs; prefabricated wall panels with solid spruce framing; rockwool insulation; walls lined with cellulose gypsum boards; larch window frames; cladding in larch-veneered plywood.

▌ *Other technical features*
Earth cooling tubes; two-way ventilation with heat recovery via heat exchanger; computer-controlled heating, ventilation and electric lighting; solar water heating; photovoltaic modules.

▌ *U-values*
- Walls 0.15W/m²K;
- roof 0.15W/m²K;
- glazing 0.6W/m²K.

▌ *Energy consumption*
Heating 20kWh/m²/year.

Carlo Baumschlager and Dietmar Eberle, pioneers of the Vorarlberg "building artists" group, here remain true to their minimalist principles. Austria's first eco-school is based on a sufficiency of form and function, along with a balance between economic and environmental concerns.

CONTEXT AND SITE
Baumschlager & Eberle have built several buildings around the new centre of Mäder, all of high environmental quality (*see pp. 60-62*). Arranged to create a public square, the school buildings use contrasting materials and styles: a double-skin cube of glass and wood for the main school, and horizontal lines of concrete and glass for the adjacent sports hall.

FUNCTION AND FORM
The four-storey school building is based on a 28m × 28m square plan, a compact form which reduces total built area and brings down energy costs. A sober and precise design is complemented by well-thought-out detailing. On each floor, the rooms are arranged around a central recreation space, lit by a light well and by glazed bands along the top of the partitions. The ground floor houses a common room and workshops, with the stairs and washrooms in the north-west corner. Each of the three upper floors is divided into seven areas of 65-70m², whose plan, lighting and fittings are identical and which may be used for general or specialist teaching, administration or as staff rooms. This flexibility is designed to allow the school to adapt to changes in teaching practice and requirements.

STRUCTURAL PRINCIPLES
The structural system makes best use of the properties of the materials used. The primary structure consists of 750mm wide precast reinforced concrete floor slabs, spanning 9m onto concrete columns. Internal and external walls use prefabricated timber-framed panels, while the glazed curtain-walling is framed in glulam larch. The repeating grid allowed a rationalisation of fabrication and construction, reducing cost.

MATERIALS AND FINISHES
The building's four façades are all identical. They are glazed across two-thirds of their width, and encased throughout in an outer skin of non-jointed glass. Outside the glazed areas, this protects the cladding, in 19mm larch-veneered plywood, from the weather, providing a screen which slows its rate of weathering and removes the need for chemical treatment to the wood. The use of a double-skin system thus creates new possibilities for the external use of timber products.

Environmental logic has been applied with rigour. Floor coverings are linoleum; paints, coatings and adhesives use no chemical solvents; electric cables are PVC-free; water pipes are polyurethane, a less harmful substance than

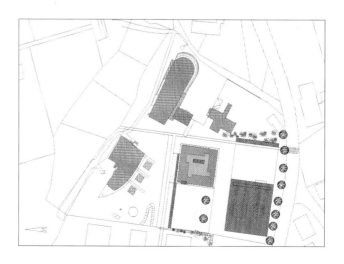

PVC. Walls and ceilings are clad in walnut-veneered plywood, perforated in some areas to improve acoustic qualities. Behind this, a layer of sheep's wool replaces the more generally-used absorbent mineral layer, avoiding potential health risks from fibre inhalation.

ENERGY AND CLIMATE CONTROL

The double skin system allows the building to benefit from solar gain while ensuring temperature regulation in summer. The vertical panes making up the external skin overlap at their edges, with a gap of 80mm for natural ventilation. In the glazed façade areas, the 530mm air gap between the two skins houses white cotton roller blinds. To reach the target set by the local authority of annual energy consumption below 20kWh/m^2, additional insulation is provided by two layers of rockwool, 140mm and 120mm thick, in the timber-framed walls.

Outside air, naturally warmed in 837m of earth cooling tubes, then passes through the heat exchanger in the ventilation system before being blown into the classrooms. If further heating is needed, it is provided by the biomass heating plant which also supplies the town's other public buildings. On the roof, 28m^2 of solar panels are connected to a 3000-litre water tank, and provide around 50 % of annual hot water requirements. The 90m^2 of photovoltaic modules on the roof of the sports hall supply the school with 10,000kWh each year. Energy consumption is optimised by a computer-controlled lighting and ventilation system using motion detectors in each classroom.

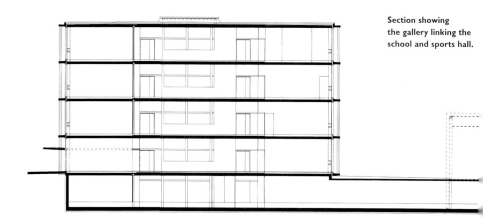

Section showing the gallery linking the school and sports hall.

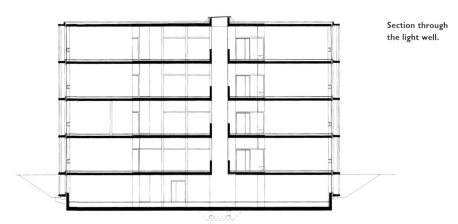

Section through the light well.

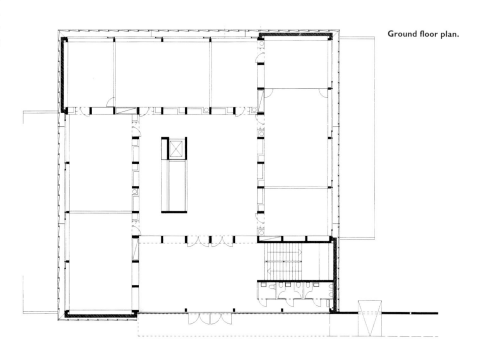

Ground floor plan.

All four façades are
encased in an outer skin
of storey-height sheets
of glass.

The four façades are identical.

The outer glazing panes overlap, with an 80mm gap providing natural ventilation.

Vertical sections through the double skin façades.

1 Solid wall panel
  - 12.5mm plasterboard
  - damp-proof membrane
  - 12.5mm plasterboard
  - 120mm mineral wool
  - waterproof membrane
  - 24mm air gap
  - 19mm larch plywood
2 overlapping glazing
3 insulating triple glazing
  in larch frames
4 typical floor
  - 4mm linoleum
  - 30mm particleboard
  - timber supports
  - 220mm reinforced
    concrete slab
5 ground floor
  - 4mm linoleum
  - 30mm particleboard
  - damp-proof membrane
  - timber supports
  - 350mm reinforced
    concrete slab
  - 120mm polystyrene

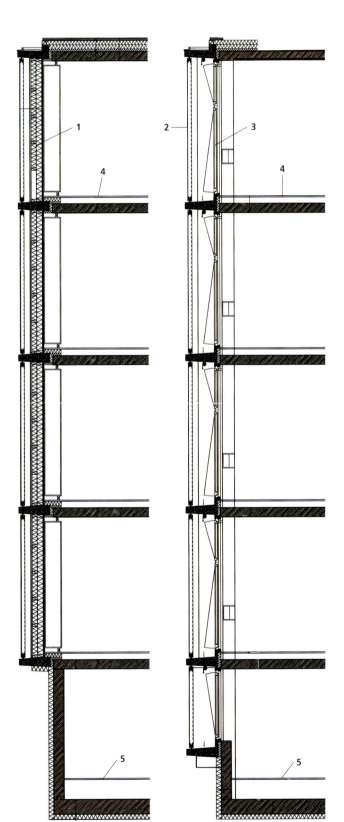

Automatically-operated blinds
between the two glazed skins
shade the classrooms in summer.

Address: Alte Schulstrasse 7, 6841 Mäder, Austria.
Project brief: secondary school with eleven classes.
Client: Mäder town council.
Architect: Baumschlager & Eberle, Lochau
(project architect Rainer Huchler).
Engineers: statics: Rüsch, Diem + Partner,
Dornbirn; environmental engineering: Spektrum,
Dornbirn.
Timetable: design begun May 1994; construction
on site November 1996 - August 1998.
Area: useable area 3,728m². Basement, ground
floor and three upper storeys.
Cost: ATS 88 million (€6.395 million).

LEONARDO DA VINCI SECONDARY SCHOOL IN CALAIS, FRANCE

Isabelle Colas and Fernand Soupey

ENVIRONMENTAL FEATURES

■ Bioclimatic features
Form and siting adapted to prevailing wind direction; optimum natural lighting; use of local materials and European timbers; low-emissivity insulating double glazing; use of renewable energy.

■ Materials and construction
Reinforced concrete frame; solid reinforced concrete floor slabs, some on permanent concrete formwork; double external walls in insulating clay blockwork, added insulation and external brick skin; circulation area walls in fair-faced perforated blocks; Placostyl partitions; framing in glulam timber or trusses; floor coverings in linoleum or ceramic tiles; green flat roofs; external walkways in oak decking.

■ Technical features
Programmable heating and air-conditioning; two-way ventilation with heat recovery system; gas co-generator; gas boilers with condenser; Héliopac solar water heating system for kitchens; photovoltaic panels; wind turbine; rainwater recovery system.

■ U-values
Ground floor slab above void 0.53W/m²K;
- walls 0.49W/m²K;
- roof 0.30W/m²K;
- glazing 1.94W/m²K.

■ Energy consumption
Total gas use (heating and hot water) 65.6kWh/m²/year (measured in 2000).

■ Sound insulation
Airborne noise, walls: between circulation areas and classrooms 26dB; between stairs and classrooms 44dB; between two practicals rooms 52dB; between two offices, 44dB.

■ Site
Waste sorting and recycling (pilot "green site" project).

The Leonardo da Vinci school is the first in a series of HQE school projects planned by the Nord-Pas-de-Calais region. Its design and construction are based on the HQE target system. For an additional cost of around 8 % compared to its conventional equivalent, energy and water consumption have been reduced by around 30 % by a number of sophisticated systems: a wind turbine, a co-generator, solar panels, photovoltaic modules and a rainwater recovery system.

CONTEXT AND SITE
The school is designed for 1,700 pupils, studying both general and technical subjects up to higher education level. It is set in the Beau-Marais district, on low-lying land criss-crossed by dykes between marshland and dunes. Water became a theme of the design; the site is bordered by canals, and crossed by trenches which channel rainwater to the pool along the main building's west side. The lines of these trenches, running east-west, are emphasised by lines of willow, ash and alder trees and by lighting, helping structure the external areas of the site. On the banks, traditional techniques are used, with local stone and mesh gabions alternating with plaited willow faggots. The terraces, planted with native plants, form a variety of natural habitats and serve as an educational tool. Excavated material was re-used on site in the landscaping around the car park at the eastern edge of the site.

FUNCTION AND FORM
The buildings are set out to give maximum shelter from the prevailing on-shore wind. The layout allows the façades to benefit from sunlight all year round, increasing internal comfort and reducing energy consumption. Grouped from the south-west corner of the four-hectare site, the five buildings' different shapes and façade treatments are designed to suit their different functions. An oak footbridge over the canal leads to a main block in the form of a quarter-circle, where offices and a documents centre are set either side of an internal street, lit from above.
From this building, a wing extends to the east housing the scientific teaching areas, and another to the north housing general teaching areas, the canteen and kitchens. Specialist teaching takes place in a lower building in the courtyard. At the east of the site, a terrace provides nine staff houses.

STRUCTURAL PRINCIPLES
The low bearing capacity of the soil, with the water table at or near ground level, led to the use of 20m deep piled foundations. The structure is a reinforced concrete frame, with in situ floor slabs, cast on permanent concrete formwork in the rectangular buildings. Lateral stability is provided by reinforced concrete shear walls. Timber framing is glulam or trusses. Internal corridor walls are in fair-faced perforated brickwork, using dense 110mm, three-hole bricks to provide sound insulation. Walls between classrooms are in Placostyl plaster partitions, allowing them to be removed in the future if need be. The double-skin external walls have a 190mm inner skin of insulating clay brick, painted on the internal face, backed by 50mm of mineral wool. The outer skin is in 110mm fair-faced blocks on the lower façades, with ceramic cladding above.

MATERIALS AND FINISHES
Materials were analysed systematically according to three main criteria: appearance, durability, and whole-life environmental impact, from fabrication to demolition and disposal. To limit cost and transport, local raw materials and products were used where possible: Boulonnais sand and stone for concrete, gabions and external landscaping; clay for the walls; untreated oak for decking. The green roofs have a 200mm substrate planted with grasses, forming accessible terraces which help control thermal gradients and stormwater. The range of plants is similar to those growing on the nearby dunes, with the same constraint of superficial drying out in summer. Various steps were taken to reduce site nuisance: waste was sorted into seven categories and recycled; naturally-based mould oil was used for formwork; decantation basins were installed below the concrete batching plant, along with wheel-washing facilities for site traffic.

ENERGY AND CLIMATE CONTROL

The project's energy concept aims to make the school as autonomous as possible in terms of water, light, heating and ventilation. Measures to reduce water consumption, such as low-volume flush toilets and taps with flow limiters, are combined with a system which collects rainwater from the 3,000m² of roofs, storing it in a 200m³ pool. After filtration, this water is pumped back into the non-drinking water network; the 2,000m³ of water collected each year covers requirements for toilet flushing and irrigation. The optimisation of natural lighting is another important element of the design. The orientation of the glazed areas, reflection from internal walls, a light well, the colours of the walls and the shape of the false ceilings are all designed to maximise the diffusion of natural light. Running costs are kept to a minimum by a computer-controlled heating and ventilation system based on building occupation. Heating is supplied by high-yield gas boilers with condenser, with low nitrogen oxide emission. Other installations use renewable energy sources: photovoltaic panels, solar collector tubes linked to a heat pump, and a wind turbine.

CO-GENERATOR AND WIND TURBINE

A proportion of the school's electricity needs are met by a 135kW Seewind turbine, with a 22m diameter three-blade rotor on a 35m mast. The turbine functions when the wind speed is between 10km/h and 90km/h, with any production surplus to requirements sold to EDF, the national electricity distributor, via a link to the grid. A 165kW gas co-generator, fed by mains gas, is connected to an alternator to provide the remainder of electricity needs. The motor and its exhaust are water-cooled via heat exchangers, thereby recovering energy which is then used in the heating network. The 320kW recovered in this way represents around 20% of energy requirements.

The site is bordered on all sides by canals and pools.

Part of the school's energy needs are met by a wind turbine.

Rainwater is collected in a pool which runs alongside the main building.

Diagrammatic summary of the energy concept.

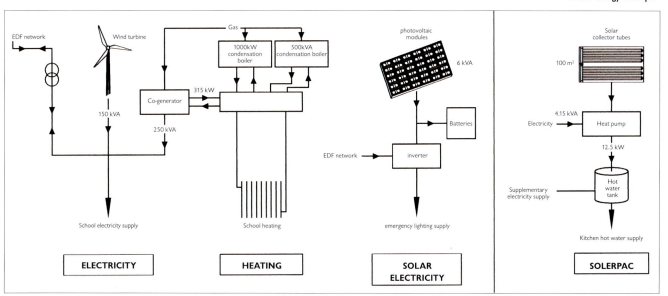

SOLAR COLLECTORS
AND PHOTOVOLTAIC MODULES

The low-voltage electricity required for the security lighting and alarm systems is supplied by 75m² of photovoltaic panels, mounted on an aluminium structure on the roof. This is made up of 136 modules with capacity 50Wp (peak watts), giving total capacity of 6,800Wp. Annual production is over 5,100kWh; electrical power produced is stored in an array of batteries. Hot water for the kitchens is heated by a Héliopac solar heating system. 100m² of solar collector tubes on the kitchen roof form the primary loop, filled with glycolated water; two 25kW heat pumps then transfer solar heat to the water in the secondary circuit, heating it to 55°C. Hot water is stored in two 5,000 litre tanks.

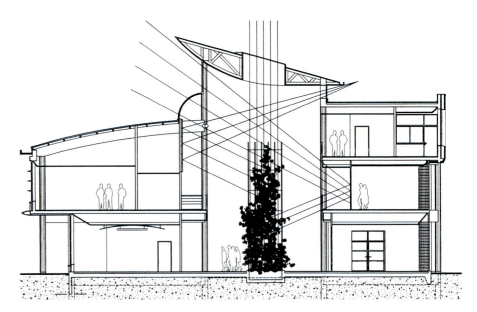

Section through the internal street.

The internal street area is lit from above to give comfortable lighting levels.

Address: rue Martin Luther King, 62100 Calais, France.
Project brief: secondary school for 1,700 pupils, with three teaching sections.
Client: Nord-Pas-de-Calais regional authority.
Architect: Isabelle Colas and Fernand Soupey, Calais.
Engineers: energy: Jacobs Serete; fluids: Berim.
Landscaping: Empreinte, Roubaix.
Environmental consultants: François Septier, Nord Ingénierie, Lille; Serge Sidoroff, Intakta, Paris.
Timetable: competition December 1995; construction October 1996 - September 1998.
Area: total area 21,852m²; net useable area 20,452m²; ground, first and second floors.
Contractors: Norpac and Thelu.
Cost: FF132 million (€20.123 million) excl. taxes.

The school offices and
documentation centre give
onto the internal street.

SPA POOL IN BAD ELSTER, GERMANY

Behnisch & Partner

ENVIRONMENTAL FEATURES

■ Bioclimatic features
Passive use of solar energy; glazed double skin façades and roof; insulating double glazing; ceiling in fritted glass to limit glare and solar gain.

■ Materials and construction
Main structure, steel frame; walls, insulating double glazing in stainless steel framing; roof, insulating double glazing in aluminium framing.

■ Technical features
Automatically-opening façade panels for fresh air entry in summer.

■ U-values
Walls and roof, insulating double glazing 1.2W/m²K.

Until now, the maintenance of a comfortable environment within indoor swimming pool buildings has required intensive use of energy-hungry systems. With its "smart" glazed roof, the Bad Elster spa shows how reliance on such equipment can be reduced.

CONTEXT AND SITE
Bad Elster, in Saxony, has been a spa since 1848, specialising in "mud bath" cures. The Albert Baths, which have now been completely renovated with the addition of up-to-date facilities, were built in 1910 in a decorative, Art Nouveau style and were the centrepiece of the resort. Set around a rectangular courtyard, the buildings presented a monumental façade to the town beside them. The newly refurbished courtyard itself now houses the spa's new attractions, including an information pavilion, a massage and therapy centre and outdoor pools. Alongside them is the new covered pool, whose transparent envelope blurs the distinction between indoor and outdoor space.

FUNCTION AND FORM
With their formal minimalism and use of innovative technology, the modern additions form a contrast with the historic buildings which sets both off to advantage. The new bath-house has a free-form, playful composition, its structure almost vanishing amid the play of light and bright, vibrant colour. The internal space is bathed in natural light, with the surrounding buildings, and the wooded hills beyond, clearly visible through the glazed walls and roof.

STRUCTURAL PRINCIPLES
At an early stage of the design process, the architects and engineers developed an energy concept to suit the brief, the site and its climate. This was checked by models, and influenced both the form and structure of the building. The steel frame supports a transparent envelope formed by a glazed double skin system designed to reduce energy consumption; this principle was applied to both walls and roof. The two skins are around 1m apart, shaping a sort of pedestrian gallery around the building perimeter at ground level.

On the façades, a stainless steel structure supports the outer skin of insulating 10/16/10mm double glazing, with laminated internal panes. The inner skin of fixed single glazing is 20mm thick in the accessible lower areas, and 10mm thick elsewhere. Sun shading is provided by highly reflective aluminium blinds. The roof system comprises an outer skin of 10/14/16mm double glazing, held in aluminium frames, with a louvred ceiling of pivoting glass panels. These panels, 10mm thick, are screen-printed (fritted) on their upper surface with a pattern of white dots over 45 % of their area to reflect a proportion of incident light. On their lower surface, a brightly-coloured composition in red,

blue, green and yellow by the artist Erich Wies-ner gives a lively and welcoming feel.

MATERIALS AND FINISHES

Throughout the spa, the emphasis is on the use of non-hazardous materials and their compatibility with environmental sustainability. As design progressed this became a central theme, linked to the reduction of the maintenance budget. The glazed roof of the pool slopes by 3 % to allow rainwater to run off. The underside of the roof's outer skin is accessible for cleaning when the glass louvres below are fully open.

ENERGY AND CLIMATE CONTROL

The ideal internal temperature for the spa pool is 30°C, with relative humidity of 65 %. This puts particular constraints on the design of the double skin system. Optimum performance, in terms of both energy and cost, was achieved through a series of short term and long term measures, including the setting out of the building within the site, the use of high-performance insulating glazing, the controlled use of solar gain, and the positioning of openings in the façade to allow natural ventilation in summer.

The cost of the roof system came to around FF10,000/m^2 (€1,525/m^2). However, the roof performs a number of functions, including some which are generally met by specific systems, such as climate control and solar protection. Natural convection eliminates the need for a large-scale mechanical ventilation system with its bulky, unsightly ductwork.

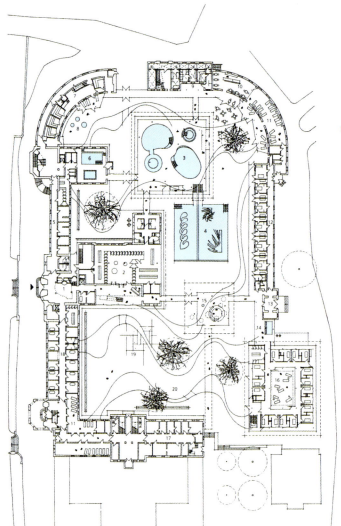

Plan of the spa centre.

The walls and roof of the bath-house have a glazed double skin.

The transparent envelope
is set beside the original
Art Nouveau buildings.

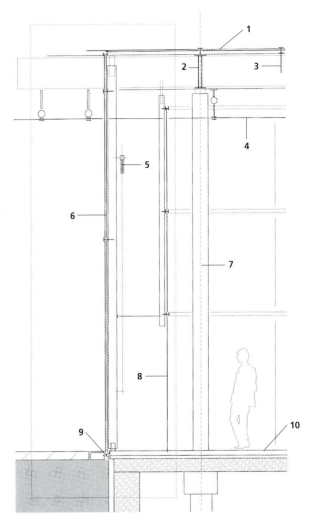

**Detail view and vertical section
through the double skin system.**
1 insulating double glazing
2 steel beams
3 secondary steel structure
4 fritted glass louvres
5 sun-blinds
6 double glazing
7 steel column
8 single glazing
9 expansion joint
10 floor
  - tiles
  - cement screed with integral
    heating
  - concrete slab

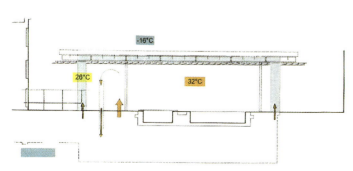

In winter and by night.

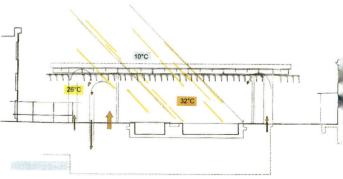

In spring and autumn.

In winter and by night, the ceiling louvres are horizontal; the ventilated air space thus created acts as a buffer, reducing heat loss by transmission and preventing condensation on the steel structure and glazing. In summer, the louvres are inclined at right angles to the sun's rays, giving maximum protection via their reflective frit. Excess heat is vented naturally by automatically-opening shutters at the top of the north and south façades.

Address: Kurmittelhaus, Badstrasse, Bad Elster, Germany.
Project brief: renovation of existing spa; construction of new covered pool, therapy centre and information centre; refurbishment of external courtyard space with outdoor pools.
Client: Sächsische Staatsbäder, Bad Elster.
Architect: Behnisch & Partner, Stuttgart (Günter Behnisch, Manfred Sabatke); project architect: Christof Jantzen, with Michael Blank, Dieter Rehm, Richard Bessler, Nicole Stuemper, Thorsten Kraft.
Engineers: structure: Fischer + Friedrich, Stuttgart; energy: Transsolar Energietechnik, Stuttgart.
Landscape designers: Luz & Partner, Stuttgart.
Colourist: Erich Wiesner, Berlin.
Timetable: competition 1994; construction on site December 1996 - December 1999.
Area: net useable area 71,093m², of which pool building 690m².
Cost: DM100 million (€51.129 million), of which indoor and outdoor pools DM23.1 million (€11.811 million).

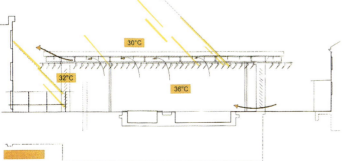

In summer.

CULTURAL AND VISITOR CENTRE AT TERRASSON, FRANCE

Ian Ritchie Architects

ENVIRONMENTAL FEATURES

▌ *Bioclimatic features*
High thermal inertia; optimised solar gain; natural ventilation.

▌ *Materials and construction*
Gabion wall; reinforced concrete slabs; laminated glazing on steel frame, separated from perimeter walls.

▌ *Technical features*
Cooling by water evaporation.

▌ *U-values*
- Roof 5.6W/m²K;
- floor 0.4W/m²K.

Cleverly integrated into its themed garden surroundings, this building makes good use of bioclimatic principles to control solar gain and allow natural ventilation in summer – not easy to achieve in a greenhouse.

CONTEXT AND SITE

The town of Terrasson-la-Villedieu (population 6,000) is at the head of the Vézère valley. The area, with its many prehistoric sites including the Lascaux caves, as well as the villages of Rocamadour and les Eyzies, is a Unesco world heritage site, and sees large numbers of tourists. Terrasson's *Jardins de l'Imaginaire*, designed by the American landscape architect Kathryn Gustafson, welcomes 35,000 visitors every year. This six-hectare contemporary park, set on a steeply-sloping site, presents an interpretation of garden design through the ages. Themed sequences set out symbols and myths from different civilisations: the sacred wood, the green tunnel, elemental gardens, theatre of plants, the "axis of the winds", perspectives, a water garden, a rose garden and a topiary garden. Ian Ritchie's greenhouse is the only building in the gardens, and functions as a stop-off point for visitors on their way round.

FUNCTION AND FORM

When first seen from above, the building appears as a flat horizontal surface, reflecting the sunlight, a virtual lake set amongst the park's other water features but which changes in aspect with the sky and the surrounding foliage. From below, the visitor sees the curving gabion wall which fits neatly into contours of the site, like the retaining walls which create the park's different levels. The building is designed as a public performance space for theatre, concerts, conferences and exhibitions, as well as a reference library and plant research centre. The plan form is derived from a sector of a circle combined with a right-angled triangle. A tiered theatre space set into the floor is overlooked by a mezzanine housing a café and souvenir shop. Along the curving north wall, citrus trees describe a walkway which adds to the ambiguous nature of the space, designed to be as much an extension of the gardens outside as a building in its own right.

STRUCTURAL PRINCIPLES

The curving gabion wall - a technique more often used in civil engineering projects than in buildings – is a free-standing cantilever. The floor slab, the gabion bases and the south wall, set into the hillside, are reinforced concrete. The glass roof, which has a 2° slope, is supported by a steel structure, painted white. This structure is independent of the perimeter walls, and consists of T-section beams spanning onto a tubular edge beam, supported by circular hollow section columns. An asymmetrical arrangement of cables braces the structure.

The roof was designed, fabricated and built by the German company Seele, and was erected in ten days by five people. Its innovative glazing support system, which required an Atex testing programme to gain approval, has stood the test of time well.

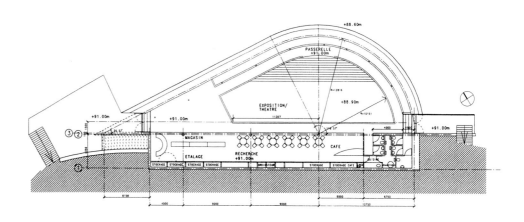

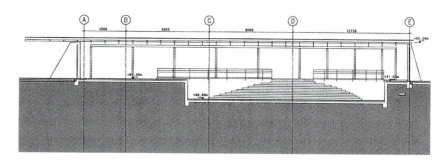

MATERIALS AND FINISHES

The curved gabion wall is made of unprocessed local stone in stainless steel mesh cages. The roof is in laminated glass, with two 8mm panes and four layers of polyvinylbutyral (PVB) film. The glass is supported on adjustable stainless steel point fixings which allow rotation. A 15mm diameter collar is fixed to the glass before laminating; its cylindrical part fits inside the lower pane, with a 3mm ring section within the PVB interlayer. The panes are 1.5m square, with a point fixing near each corner; edge panes are triangular, trapezoidal or part-circular. This system, allowing vertical adjustment of the fixing points, gives a completely smooth outer surface, with the glass plane uninterrupted except by the 15mm silicone joints between panes. To the right of the building, the drainage channel is bordered by a rainwater basin which also prevents visitor access to the roof.

ENERGY AND CLIMATE CONTROL

The areas at the edge of the glasshouse are designed as covered spaces, protected from the wind and seasonal temperature extremes. In winter, direct sunlight warms the internal face of the gabion wall and parts of the floor slab, raising the internal temperature by around 8°C relative to the outside. The air gap between the walls and the glass roof helps ventilation, reducing the risk of condensation. In summer this gap, with the side doors, allows natural ventilation via the ever-present wind. The mass of the concrete and stone, cooled at night, increases the building's thermal inertia. Water evaporates from the gabions and the adjacent trees, producing the effect of a cool radiation. The site is only open to the public in spring, summer and autumn, the seasons when the climate control system works best. On hot summer days, retractable blinds in the roof ensure that inside temperatures are close to those outside.

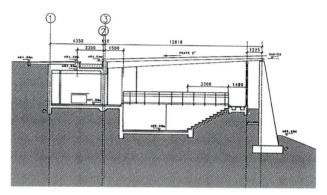

Longitudinal and transverse sections. The internal spaces set into the ground benefit from its high thermal inertia.

Seen from above, the glass roof resembles a lake, reflecting the sky.

From the path below, the gabion wall emphasises the slope of the hill.

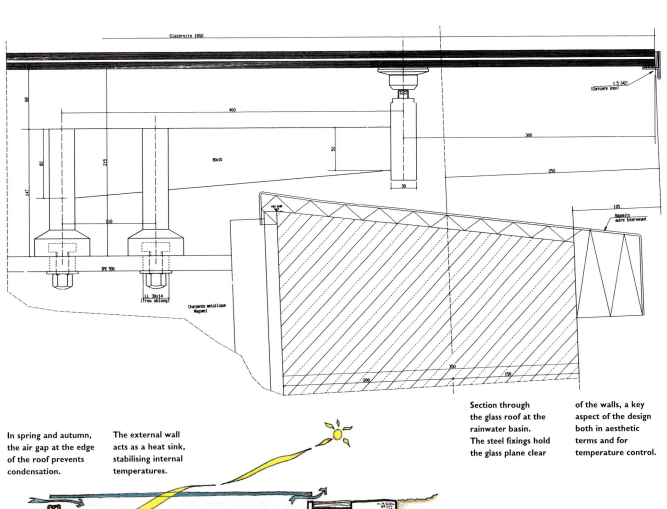

Section through
the glass roof at the
rainwater basin.
The steel fixings hold
the glass plane clear

of the walls, a key
aspect of the design
both in aesthetic
terms and for
temperature control.

In spring and autumn, the air gap at the edge of the roof prevents condensation.

The external wall acts as a heat sink, stabilising internal temperatures.

In summer, blinds prevent direct sunlight from causing overheating. Evaporation cools

the wall, producing "cold radiation" which improves internal comfort.

Address: 24120 Terrasson-la-Villedieu, France.
Project brief: glasshouse housing cultural and visitor centre.
Client: Terrasson-la-Villedieu town council.
Architect: Ian Ritchie Architects, London;
Ian Ritchie, S. Conolly, E. Wan.
Engineers: steel structure: Ove Arup & Partners, London; concrete and fluids: ARC, Brive.
Landscape designer: Kathryn Gustafson, Paysage Land, Paris.
Timetable: design begun October 1992; construction August 1993 - July 1994.
Area: 400m², within six-hectare park.
Contractors: glass roof: Glasbau Seele; glazing: Vegla.
Cost: FF4.16 million (€634,188) at 1994 prices.

DATAGROUP OFFICES IN PLIEZHAUSEN, GERMANY

Kauffmann Theilig

ENVIRONMENTAL FEATURES

■ Bioclimatic features
Compact volume, with circular shape around an atrium; passive use of solar energy; use of thermal mass of concrete walls and floors; air circulation floors; natural humidity control via flowing water; argon-filled insulating double glazing; indirect natural lighting.

■ Materials and construction
Structure in concrete, steel and timber; concrete floor slabs supported on concrete cores and irregularly-placed circular steel columns; timber-framed walls, cladding panels in coated Landes pine; partitions in birch-veneered plywood with glazed panels; elliptical glass roof with insulating double glazing and tensioned cable structure; oak and stone flooring; timber balconies.

■ Technical features
Two-way ventilation with heat recovery via heat exchanger; solar water heating; pre-heating and cooling of fresh air via earth cooling tubes.

■ U-values
Façade and roof glazing 1.3W/m²K.

■ Energy consumption
Heating 35kWh/m²/year (measured).

These offices, for a rapidly-expanding IT services company, provide 250 work-stations in an attractive and comfortable building environment, achieved at low cost due to the use of integrated design measures. The building's high transparency and innovative aspects are designed to reflect a forward-thinking company philosophy.

CONTEXT AND SITE
The Datagroup building stands like a signal beside the motorway from Stuttgart to Tübingen, on the outskirts of the small town of Pliezhausen. The 10,000m² site is accessed from the north side and falls steeply to the south, with a panoramic view over the Schwabian plain. With a relatively low budget available, the client wanted an office building which would facilitate day-to-day work and communication between staff.

FUNCTION AND FORM
The main entrance leads directly to the central atrium, encircled by three floors of open-plan offices. This circular form reduces both circulation area and façade area, hence reducing heat loss. It also makes the atrium, covered by a glazed roof, into a focal point, the functional and "emotional" heart of the building. Vertical and horizontal circulation routes pass through it, and it becomes a meeting-place, helping create a sense of community. On the upper floors, open-plan areas are interspersed with meeting rooms and separate offices for section leaders and secretaries. Deep wooden balconies and projecting eaves give integral shading, diminishing the effects of contrasting light levels and reflections on computer screens. The glazed partitions between the offices and gallery, and between sections, provide sound insulation while maintaining a visual link with the adjacent work area. The 6m drop in ground level across the building allows the canteen and seminar rooms, building services areas and a car park to be located at lower ground level.

STRUCTURAL PRINCIPLES
Three reinforced concrete cores, containing stairs, lifts and washrooms, provide lateral stability. Electricity and telecommunications cables and fresh air ducts are set out on an orthogonal grid within the concrete floor slabs.

Above the atrium, an elliptical glazed roof, 21m long by 13m across, covers the main circular space, plus several smaller circular openings in the slab. The cable net structure, developed with the glazing systems company Seele, can be likened to a tennis racquet, with cables on a 1.3m orthogonal grid tensioned against a steel ring beam. The roof envelope itself is in argon-filled insulating double glazing, connected to the cables at the structural nodes by a circular steel element.

MATERIALS AND FINISHES
The concrete cores are unclad, allowing full use to be made of their thermal mass. As for the roof, façade glass is in insulating double glazing. The internal décor and fittings mix materials, colours and shapes with a deconstructivist freedom: partitions are in glass and birch-veneered ply; hand-rails along the gallery combine steel, glass and solid beech. Besides serving various functional purposes, the irregular form of the façade breaks up the volume of the building as seen from the surrounding countryside.

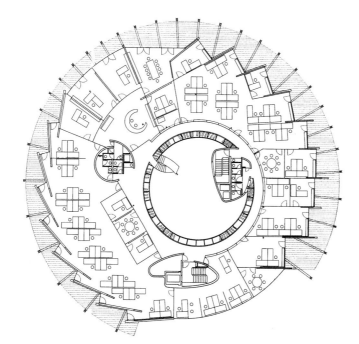

ENERGY AND CLIMATE CONTROL

To avoid problems with sunlight on computer screens, natural light is brought into the offices indirectly: from the atrium roof, via the glazed partitions around the gallery; and through the façades, whose windows are oriented to avoid direct lighting, as well as being shaded by the eaves and balconies. In winter, the building's compact form and insulated walls, together with the heat generated by numerous computer terminals, electric lights and body heat, almost completely remove the need for heating during working hours.

Energy requirements are therefore mainly associated with air-conditioning during hot weather. In summer, cooled air from earth cooling tubes is blown into the space each morning to cool the concrete elements, creating a low-temperature reservoir. Used air is removed below slab level. In winter, used air passes through a heat exchanger, warming the fresh intake air before being evacuated at roof level. In the atrium, water flowing along a concrete wall helps maintain a comfortable level of air humidity.

Combined with high levels of thermal insulation, these essentially passive, simple and low-cost measures limit annual energy consumption by heating and air-conditioning to 35kWh/m². Performance was optimised using computer simulation software TRNSYS and Adeline, and checked against measurements on a physical model. Annual savings on heating and ventilation costs are estimated at € 10,000.

The circular plan gives an optimum ratio between façade area and office area.

Deep projecting eaves and balconies shade the offices from direct sunlight and prevent overheating in summer.

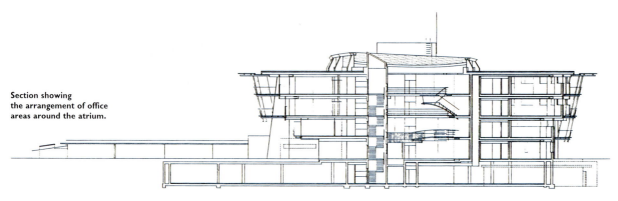

Section showing the arrangement of office areas around the atrium.

The arrangement of offices around a central atrium reduces the length of circulation routes.

The glass roof is
supported by a cable net.
The atrium is shaded by
a fabric screen made up
of alternating triangular
yellow and white panels.
When fully opened,
it resembles a flower;
when the sun goes down,
a suspended weight furls
the fabric into a steel
ring, and the flower
closes.

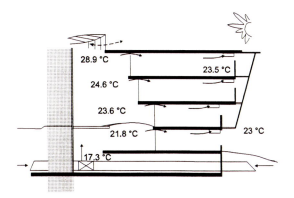

28.9 °C
23.5 °C
24.6 °C
23.6 °C
21.8 °C   23 °C
17.3 °C

In summer, fresh air arrives in the atrium after flowing through 130m of earth cooling tube, which cools it by around 7°C.

It then passes through 100mm diameter plastic pipes, cast into the 300mm floor slabs, before being blown into the offices.

Right: The external fresh air intake.

Air ducts cast into the floor slabs, oriented towards the atrium.

Fresh air outlet in an office floor.

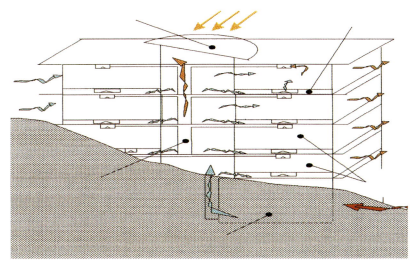

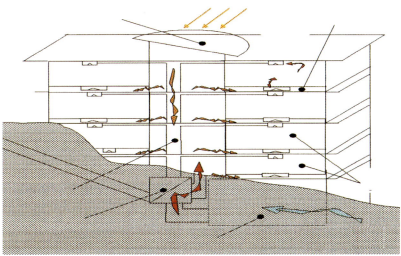

Address: Wilhelm Schickard Strasse 7, 72124 Pliezhausen, Germany.
Project brief: IT offices for 250 people.
Client: Grundstücksgesellschaft Gniebel, Herr Schaber, Pliezhausen.
Architect: Kauffmann Theilig, Ostfildern; project partner: Wolfgang Kergassner.
Engineers: structure: Pfefferkorn & Partner, Stuttgart; energy: Transsolar, Stuttgart; building physics: Horstmann, Altensteig; fluids: Schreiber, Ulm.
Timetable: design begun June 1993; construction December 1993 - February 1995.
Area: total area 7,500m², net useable area 5,600m².
Cost: DM17 million (€8.692 million) excl. taxes.

RESEARCH CENTRE IN WAGENINGEN, NETHERLANDS
Behnisch, Behnisch & Partner

ENVIRONMENTAL FEATURES

▮ *Bioclimatic features*
Compact shape; passive use of solar energy via two glazed atriums; use of high thermal mass materials; natural ventilation; use of local materials and naturally durable timbers; atrium planting and water features; green flat roofs; rainwater recovery system; re-use of contaminated agricultural land.

▮ *Materials and construction*
Structure in concrete, timber and steel; reinforced concrete floor slabs and circular columns; laboratory façades in steel-framed curtain-walling, insulating double glazing and fibre cement spandrels; external cladding and decking in robinia; atrium façades in larch framing and panels with insulating double glazing; atrium roof in single glazing on steel structure; stairs and walkways in galvanised steel; use of mass-produced components.

▮ *Technical features*
Automatic sun shading in roof, activated by light meters.

▮ *U-values*
- Ground level floor plate 0.9W/m²K.
- roof 0.9W/m²K;
- fixed glazing 1.35W/m²K;
- fibre cement spandrels 0.9W/m²K;
- timber spandrels 1.1W/m²K;
- window-frames 1.7W/m²K;

▮ *Site*
Rapid construction due to use of prefabricated elements.

For some decades, Günter Behnisch and his associates have taken a humanist environmental approach, with the focus on user well-being. Working with drawings and models, they produce lively designs, often bathed in light, whose deliberate inclusion of apparently haphazard elements has the effect of putting users at their ease.

CONTEXT AND SITE
The competition for the Forest and Nature Research Institute at Wageningen aimed to produce a European pilot project, on the theme of "building for man and his environment", within a standard budget. Behnisch, Behnisch & Partner's proposal gave future users, experts on ecology, the opportunity to suggest measures to achieve a harmonious relationship between the building and the natural environment around it. Land at the site, a former wheat-field at the northern edge of the university town of Wageningen, had been exhausted and contaminated by intensive agriculture. This apparently unlikely site for an environmental project will be gradually revitalised. The introduction of landscape elements such as dry-stone walls, ponds and ditches, hedges and trees, the regeneration of the natural water cycle and the creation of contrasting natural conditions – damp and dry, hot and cold, sunny and shady, windy and sheltered – together allow nature to regenerate itself.

FUNCTION AND FORM
In plan, the building is in the shape of a capital E: from the rectangular north wing, containing the laboratories, spring three linear office blocks, separated by glazed atriums. The south gable areas house a library, conference room and restaurant. The formal simplicity of the composition arises for both economic and environmental reasons. The building is limited to three storeys to give better communication and visual contact between those working in the building. The office and service areas giving onto the internal courtyards are accessed via walkways and bridges, giving the impression of crossing a garden. The atriums, which were not part of the original brief, offer a variety of atmospheres, giving workers a choice of relaxation area. The first, with its luxuriant vegetation, has a more private atmosphere. The second, set with ponds and sculptures, is more formally designed.

STRUCTURAL PRINCIPLES
For cost reasons, the building frame is in reinforced concrete, with circular columns supporting solid slabs. To make best use of the concrete's thermal mass, false ceilings were only used in areas where fire protection or acoustics made them necessary. The structure and hand-rails of the stairs and walkways serving the offices are in steel.

MATERIALS AND FINISHES
Materials were chosen as a function of both intended use and environmental impact. A number of criteria were taken into account,

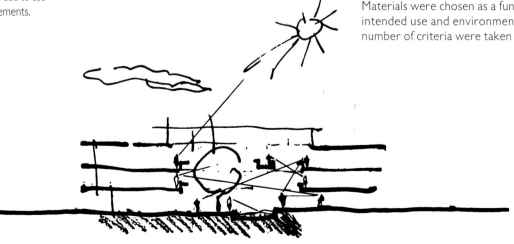

including energy used in manufacture, renewability and recyclability, transport, maintenance and design life. The façades looking onto the atriums are protected from wind and rain by the glass roofs, and are framed and clad in larch, a locally available species requiring no applied treatment in this context. These façades use glued small-section planks, a technique which makes best use of rough timber offcuts. The internal walls are 60 % glazed, with windows positioned so as to achieve optimum natural lighting in the offices. Walls exposed to the weather have a steel structure, with fibre cement spandrels and external cladding in robinia, the only native timber to be naturally durable to biological hazard class 4. External and internal façades have insulating double glazing, while the glass roofs are single glazed.

ENERGY AND CLIMATE CONTROL

The building's design, while using contemporary technology to meet contemporary needs, is also based on the time-honoured principles of natural lighting and use of local materials.

The basic elements of the energy concept are the two glazed atriums. They help regulate solar gain, while their very large volumes even out temperature differences. In winter, diffuse sunlight warms the air and heat is stored in the massive structural elements. In summer, the gardens are cooled by evaporation from the pools and plants. A system of blinds, inspired by those used in commercial greenhouses, provides shading in summer, and helps insulate the envelope against heat loss in winter. Hot air and smoke is extracted via electrically-operated valves, allowing intensive natural ventilation, cooling the building mass at night. This system reduces running costs considerably. Occupants can ventilate their own offices as they wish by opening the sliding and pivoting French windows or frameless panes. Only the kitchen and library have automatic mechanical ventilation. The water cycle is controlled by green roofs together with a rainwater recovery system, which feeds the atrium pools as well as being used for toilet flushing.

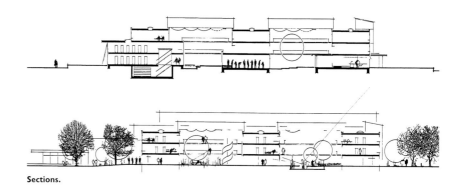

Sections.

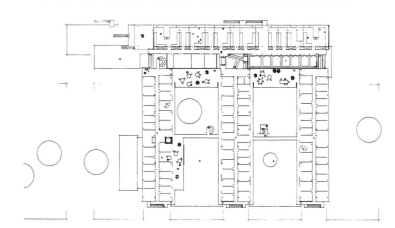

Office floor plan.

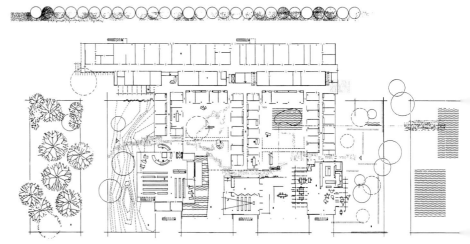

Ground floor plan.

External landscaping creates
contrasting natural areas.

The extensive green roofs
are planted with sedums.

The sun blinds were inspired
by commercial greenhouses.

**Occupants can ventilate
their own offices as they wish.**

**Solar gain by day,
natural ventilation by night.**

**Green roofs and external
landscaping help regulate
the natural water cycle.**

**The atriums allow
natural ventilation.**

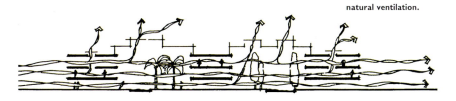

Address: Wageningen, Netherlands.
Project brief: research institute for approx.
300 people with laboratories, offices,
library, conference room, kitchen and
canteen.
Client: Rijksgebouwdienst Direktie Oost,
Arnhem.
Architect: Behnisch, Behnisch & Partner
(Günter Behnisch, Stefan Behnisch, Günther
Schaller); project leader: Ton Gilissen,
with Ken Radtkey, Brook Müller, Andreas
Ditschuneit, Yianni Doulis, Michael Schuch,
Martin Schodder.
Engineers: structure: Aronsohn VOF,
Amsterdam; building physics: Fraunhofer
Institute, Stuttgart; fluids: Deerns RI,
Rijkswijk.
Sculptors: Michael Singer, USA; Krijn
Giezen, France.
Landscaping: Behnisch, Behnisch & Partner,
with Copijn, Utrecht (atriums) and
Van Hees, Gouda (external landscaping).
Timetable: competition August 1993;
design begun October 1993;
construction October 1996 - April 1998.
Area: total area (excl. atriums) 11,250m².
Main contractor: Thomasson Dura
(Dura Bouw), Houten BV.
Cost: DM 43.5 million (€22.241 million)
approx., including external landscaping.

AVAX HEADQUARTERS BUILDING IN ATHENS, GREECE

Meletitiki / A. N. Tombazis and Associates Architects Ltd.

ENVIRONMENTAL FEATURES

■ *Bioclimatic features*
Use of thermal mass; double skin
to control solar gain; natural ventilation;
cold storage system.

■ *Materials and construction*
Structural frame and floors in concrete;
façade outer skin in pivoting fritted glass
fins.

■ *Technical features*
Individual air-conditioning with
automatic and manual controls.

■ *U-values*
- Walls $0.35W/m^2K$;
- roof $0.31W/m^2K$;
- glazing $2.8W/m^2K$.

■ *Energy consumption*
- Electricity $62.3kWh/m^2/year$;
- cooling $7.7kWh/m^2/year$;
- heat pump $27.4kWh/m^2/year$;
- lighting $9.3kWh/m^2/year$.

One of Greece's major construction groups, Avax is a young company. With its new headquarters building, the group sought to establish a dynamic image with both technological and environmental associations, while providing comfortable working conditions for its staff.

CONTEXT AND SITE
The building is in a dense urban district of central Athens, on the slopes of Mount Lycabettos around 100m above sea level. The $500m^2$ site is bordered by other buildings to its rear and sides, with the main, longest façade facing east. The building is part of the EU's Thermie 2000 programme (DG XVII), which provided funding for research and other costs associated with the project's energy-saving and other environmental aspects.

FUNCTION AND FORM
The building makes the most of the land use plan. Its $3,500m^2$ total area is spread over three basement car park levels, ground floor with double-height entrance hall, four typical office floors and an upper, administrative level with a roof garden. On the street side, large planters structure the external areas; the rear courtyard houses a small garden, and the entrance hall is surrounded by an extensively landscaped area. On the typical floors, the offices and meeting rooms along the main façade are separated by a corridor from the service zone containing washrooms, kitchens, stairs and lifts. The column-free space is designed to be readily adaptable to future needs, with interior fittings varying according to level. The

arrangement of the furniture and the moveable, glazed partitions maintain a feeling of openness.

STRUCTURAL PRINCIPLES
The 45 % glazed façade is divided into 7.2m bays by five 600mm diameter concrete columns, which support the floors. To the rear of the building, the concrete walls have only 10 % openings.
The glazed areas in the main façade comprise two framed panes, 1.7m high overall, above a solid spandrel panel; a large pane provides views, while the smaller, 500mm upper window can be manually opened to adjust lighting and ventilation. The columns are set in front of the façade, and linked at each spandrel level by steel trusses carrying vertical, pivoting fins of specially-made fritted glass. These form the outer layer of a double skin system which works as a diaphragm, controlling solar gain and natural lighting.

MATERIALS AND FINISHES
The offices have granite floor cladding above a false floor to give easy access to services. This also allows the floor slab soffits to remain exposed (they are painted only), enabling good use to be made of their thermal mass. The east wall also contributes to this effect; the 200mm concrete spandrel beams are inside the building envelope, with external insulation clad in steel panels. Windows are double glazed, with aluminium frames detailed to reduce cold bridging, and internal Venetian blinds. The west façades have a double skin of 100mm blocks with mineral wool insulation and internal plaster facing. At the ground floor and top level, shading is provided by external

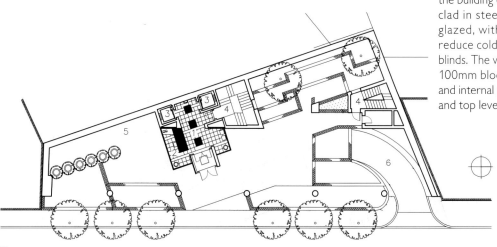

Venetian blinds. The flat roof is a concrete slab, with polystyrene insulation and raised marble paving. Internal walls are in plasterboard and fair-faced blocks.

NATURAL LIGHTING

The building's shallow plan, with offices only 3m deep, allows optimum natural lighting levels. The "smart" façade acts as a filter, whose density varies automatically according to temperature and amount of sunlight. This was modelled by computer simulations using Radiance and Superlite software. To make up the balance of lighting levels as necessary, artificial lighting is designed with both energy conservation and comfort in mind. Internal walls are painted white to help diffuse light, and a 200-250 lux indirect lighting system is completed by task lighting at each workspace. Motion detectors in the corridors and car park are linked to a control system which automatically adjusts light levels; this system can be manually overridden via infra-red controls.

ENERGY AND CLIMATE CONTROL

Air-conditioning requirements are reduced by a natural ventilation system. During the day, solar gain is filtered by the façade fins, and lighting generates only minimal heat. Manually-controlled, ceiling-mounted helical fans extend the comfort zone from 25°C to 29°C. Between 9.30p.m. and 7a.m. during the summer months, the building is pre-cooled by mechanical ventilation, with a central cooling plant in the basement operating during the night, when temperatures are lower, efficiency higher and energy cheaper. Air-conditioning is activated by motion detectors in each area; the false floor system allows installation of local cooling plants, as well as providing space for air ducts. The façade fins are adjusted and the night cooling system activated by a central building management system, designed as part of the Passport-Air project (part of the European energy programme Joule). Individuals participate nonetheless in energy management as they open their windows, turn their fans on and off and operate their own air-conditioning. A proportion of hot water needs are met by solar collector panels, while electricity for security and telephone systems and ground floor lighting is supplied by photovoltaic panels.

The main façade has an outer, "smart" layer which filters sunlight to give optimum internal conditions.

When the weather is cloudy, the glazing panels are fully open.

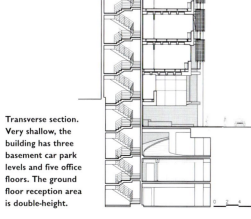

Transverse section. Very shallow, the building has three basement car park levels and five office floors. The ground floor reception area is double-height.

0   2   4   6M

The ground floor is open and accessible to passers-by.

The offices benefit
from natural light,
filtered by the fritted
glass façade fins.

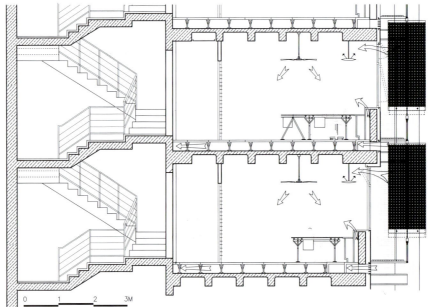

Section through
the office floors. Climate
control is achieved
by the combined effects
of windows, ceiling fans
and cooled air taken
in at floor level.

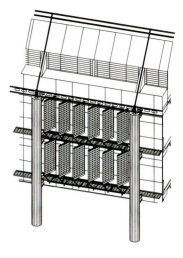

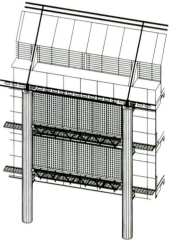

The "smart" façade filters sunlight according to internal temperatures, thus regulating solar gain and light effects. The automatically- controlled system may be manually overridden. The main structural columns support steel trusses which carry the fritted glass panels.

Address: 15 Koniari Street, Athens, Greece.
Project brief: headquarters building with reception, office and administration areas.
Client: Avax.
Architect: Meletitiki / A. N. Tombazis, assisted by Nikos Fletoridis, Athens.
Engineers: structure: Structural Design, Athens; electricity: M-E Consulting Engineers, Athens; energy: Society for Appropriate Technologies, Athens.
Timetable: design begun 1992; construction February 1994 - May 1998.
Area: total area 3,050m²; five storeys plus three basement car park levels.
Contractors: Avax, Athens.
Cost: €367,647 excl. taxes.

IGUZZINI HEADQUARTERS BUILDING IN RECANATI, ITALY

Mario Cucinella Architects

This building, with offices set around an atrium, is noteworthy for its efficient use of natural ventilation in a hot region of Italy. The lighting system was developed after laboratory tests which accurately simulated sunlight effects within the offices.

ENVIRONMENTAL FEATURES

■ *Bioclimatic features*
Efficient plan with flexibility of use; natural ventilation; comfortable temperature, humidity and light levels.

■ *Materials and construction*
Concrete frame and floor slabs; sun screening in aluminium panels; steel and glass staircases.

■ *Technical features*
Thermo-convectors.

CONTEXT AND SITE

The 90,000m² iGuzzini site is situated among the hills and valleys of the central Italian Marches. It brings together the group's industrial activities and administrative headquarters, with a total building area of 30,000m². Mario Cucinella has undertaken the remodelling of the whole site, including the construction of new management buildings, new production units, reorganisation of access routes and new landscaping, lighting and signage. This reorganisation has established a hierarchy of pedestrian and vehicle traffic and a clear distinction between industrial sectors, car parks and green space. From the main gate, a tree-lined avenue leads to the various buildings, as well as a public garden incorporating the excavated remains of a pre-Roman site.

FUNCTION AND FORM

The rectangular headquarters building is organised around an atrium which contains a garden, lifts and services, linked directly to the adjacent areas by a glass and steel staircase. The administrative offices occupy three mostly open-plan floors, with management offices on the top floor, complete with terrace. The atrium is 100m² in area, 13.8m high, and roofed by twelve 2.8m high skylights which bring overhead light and natural ventilation into the offices. This configuration maintains the ratio of useable to total net area at 0.83, which is within normal market ranges for this type of office and hence does not adversely affect profitability. The south façade is completely glazed; as outside temperatures can exceed 38°C in sum-

mer, sun shading is provided by a fixed canopy above the upper terraces, projecting 6.7m horizontally and extending down 3.7m vertically in front of the façade. At ground floor level, a grassy slope running the width of the building conceals a shaded external car park.

STRUCTURE, MATERIALS AND FINISHES

The site is in a seismic zone, and consequently the main structure and floors, with the ground floor constructed over a ventilated void, are in reinforced concrete. The north and south façades are clad in glazed curtain-walling, supported 780mm in front of the concrete structure by steel cantilever elements. The aluminium framing elements are detailed to avoid cold bridging, and the glass is low-emissivity 8-12-6mm double glazing. The east and west façades are opaque, clad in 1200 × 300mm matt black ceramic panels. The sun canopy consists of 330mm aluminium strips, supported on a steel I-beam structure. Positioned to shade the building completely from direct summer sun and 80 % in spring and autumn, the roof canopy strips are spaced at 400mm and set at 45° to the horizontal. Those in front of the façade are placed horizontally, 500mm apart, so as to allow direct winter sunlight and allow views from the building. The concrete frame, slabs and block walls are directly in contact with the internal space, and act as a thermal mass. A false floor, covered by ceramic tiles, was preferred to a suspended ceiling as it gave greater flexibility.

Longitudinal section.
The office floors
are arranged around a
central atrium.

View of the building showing the south façade. In the foreground, the car park is shaded by trees.

ENERGY AND CLIMATE CONTROL

The project makes use of active and passive elements, within a simple overall strategy which combines natural ventilation and thermal inertia with protection against the sun. The roof openings are half the area of the façade openings, and the roof-lights incorporate aluminium louvres which open for ventilation. The curtain wall façades comprise 6.6 × 3.2m frames, divided into nine glazed sections, of which four can be opened – two at the top, two at the bottom. This configuration, making use of the temperature gradient between ambient atrium air and fresh air entering via the façade, allows natural cross-ventilation. When there is no wind, the system works by a chimney effect, with layers of air forming in the atrium. The openings between the offices and atrium are small, and have little effect on air movements. A central control system ensures that all elements are functioning. The thermal mass of the structure works in conjunction with natural ventilation principles, cooling during the night and helping prevent overheating during the day. This results in a comfortable environment during 55 % of the year, with cooling by convectors being required during 10 % and heating during 35 %. Energy consumption is 70 % lower than for a conventional office block.

To achieve satisfactory internal lighting levels, tests were carried out using a heliodon (see p. 97). The results showed lighting levels of 565 to 1031 lux, highly satisfactory given that 350-500 lux is generally considered adequate for offices. The sun shading assumptions were also tested, and validated after some modifications: the central, most exposed windows had to be fitted with internal blinds, and reflectors installed to allow light to penetrate further into the offices.

Preliminary drawing showing energy principles. The sun canopy was subsequently modified to make it more efficient.

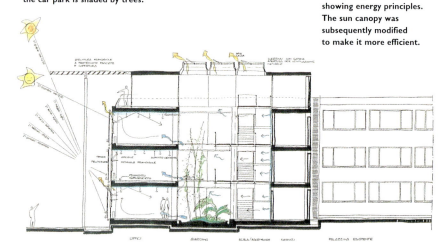

The central atrium allows natural ventilation.

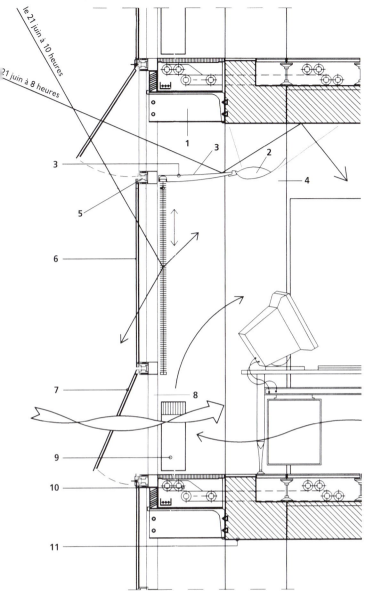

le 21 juin à 10 heures

21 juin à 8 heures

Section through the south façade.
1 200 × 100 × 5mm steel RHS
2 up-lighter
3 aluminium panel, 1mm thick
4 550 × 550mm concrete column
5 aluminium frame section
6 8/12/6mm low-emissivity double glazing
7 opening window
8 aluminium façade element
9 radiator
10 service duct
11 concrete floor slab

The east façade, with escape stairs.

Detail showing the sun canopy.

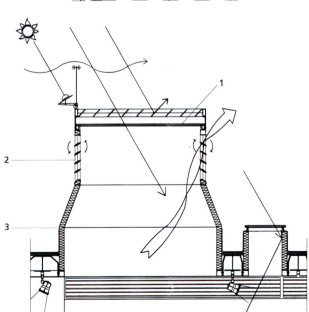

Section through the atrium roof-lights.
1 12/12/10mm double glazing
2 aluminium strips
3 80mm aluminium sandwich panel

Address: iGuzzini Illuminazione, SS 77, km 102, Recanati, Italy.
Project brief: administrative and management headquarters.
Client: iGuzzini Illuminazione SRL.
Architect: Mario Cucinella Architects (MCA), Paris and Bologna; Mario Cucinella, Elizabeth Francis, Edoardo Badano, Simona Agabio, Francesco Bombardi, Elisabetta Trezzani.
Engineers: environment: Ove Arup & Partners, London; structure: Domella & Sabbatini, Recanati.
Daylight factor studies: Ecole polytechnique de Lausanne.
Landscape design: James Tynan, Lyon.
Timetable: design 1995-97; construction 1996-97.
Area: total area 3,000m².
Contractors: façade and steelwork, Promo SRL, Macerata.
Cost: €3.2 million excl. landscaping; landscaping €700,000.

TOTAL ENERGIE FACTORY AND OFFICES IN LA TOUR-DE-SALVAGNY, FRANCE

Jacques Ferrier

ENVIRONMENTAL FEATURES

■ Bioclimatic features
Integration into the landscape; compact volumes; additional insulation in office walls; active use of solar energy.

■ Materials and construction
Main structure in galvanised steel portal frames; end walls in blockwork; cladding and roof in profiled steel sheeting; window-frames integrated into flush aluminium panels; perforated aluminium canopies; gable cladding and sun shading in Prodema panels; use of standard catalogue components.

■ Technical features
Photowatt photovoltaic modules; reversible heat pumps; heat storing floor; hydrocarbon separator for car park surface water.

■ U-values
- Walls 0.4W/m²K;
- roof 0.49W/m²K.

■ Energy consumption
- 138,944kWh winter;
- 27,275kWh summer.

■ Sound insulation
Walls 48dB.

Sober and elegant, Total Energie's new production facility is also both economical and environmentally friendly, combining sensitive environmental treatment with structural efficiency. The key to this success lies in a close co-operation between client, architect, engineers and contractors from an early stage of the project.

CONTEXT AND SITE

Total Energie is a fast-growing company which manufactures solar photovoltaic cells, mainly for export to developing countries where they are used to power well pumps or for similar applications. Having outgrown its former Lyon site, the group decided to build a new facility at the edge of the city. The client specified economical construction and the integration of its own PV modules as a showpiece for the technology. The site is in a recently-built business park, set within rural surroundings close to the village of La Tour-de-Salvagny. The building is divided into several volumes whose scale and shape recall nearby barns, grouped in the north-west corner of the site so as to leave room for future expansion. It is partly built into the hillside to avoid rising higher than the adjacent trees, and thus fits discreetly into the surrounding landscape.

FUNCTION AND FORM

In keeping with the group's corporate philosophy, the office and workshop buildings use the same architectural language, with a clear, efficient structural system. There are two main buildings. In the north building, the main assembly area and warehouse are overlooked by a gallery housing the design office, research laboratory and after-sales department. The double width of the block is visually reduced by the longitudinal offset between its two volumes. Parallel with this building, and linked to it by a galvanised steel footbridge, the smaller block houses two levels of administrative offices and the sales departments. The entrance hall, on the line of the footbridge, extends into a display area overlooking the surrounding countryside to the south.

STRUCTURAL PRINCIPLES

The project's modest budget resulted, rather than in an everyday building, in a minimalist clarity. High-quality architecture has been achieved through a rigorous approach, with specific responses to specific needs using standard, mass-produced catalogue items. The steel portal frames are a structurally economical system, quick to erect, as used in warehouses and agricultural buildings. They span 12m on a 6m grid, giving a large column-free space with high flexibility of use. The building envelope can be easily dismantled, and has already been modified by the addition of a window in the office area.

MATERIALS AND FINISHES

The façades and roof are clad in pre-coated panels of profiled steel sheeting. In the factory building, the envelope consists of a steel sheet, two layers of insulation and an internal steel skin. In the offices, the 200mm block walls are insulated on their outer face behind the metal cladding, and lined internally with a further insulating layer. The uniformity of the internal envelope thus produced is deliberately pointed up

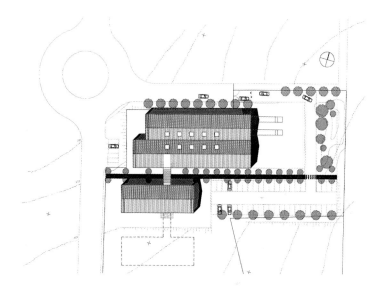

by a few details. The west gable walls are clad in Prodema, a wood-fibre product impregnated with heat-hardened resins, in panels or horizontal strips which provide shading to the windows. In front of each gable a perforated aluminium canopy, supported by a separate portal frame structure, provides a sheltered external storage area. To avoid costly cut-outs in the cladding, windows in the long façades are set within vertical bays clad in plane aluminium sheets. The quality of the whole arises from the careful detailing and treatment of the transitions between different standard elements.

ENERGY AND CLIMATE CONTROL

Total Energie's photovoltaic modules are used in the project in two ways. 120 500 × 1000mm Photowatt modules, inclined at 40°, are fixed in front of the glazed panels in the office building's south façade. The multi-crystalline silicon in the panels presents the eye with irregular patterns, highlighted in silver and blue; semi-transparent, they act as sun-screens as well as producing energy. Above the laboratory, a glazed area incorporates 36m² of PV modules, producing a bluish light below. Together, the panels produce around 20 % of energy requirements, as well as providing a full scale test facility. Heating is similarly adapted to the buildings' specific needs. Reversible heat pumps heat both the laboratory and the offices, where controls allow temperature to be regulated room by room. The factory areas are warmed by a heat storing floor system, which reaches a basic temperature of 10°C in winter, combined with radiators to provide the extra heat necessary. Heating is electronically controlled via an external thermostat.

The offset between the buildings helps their integration into the surroundings.

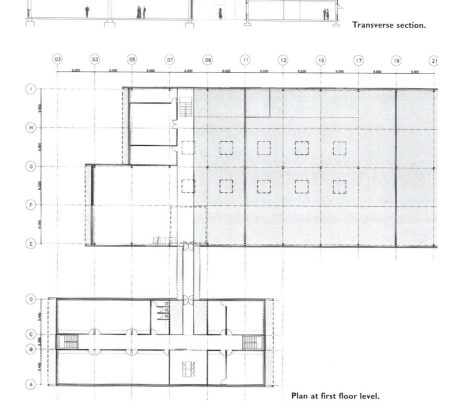

Transverse section.

Plan at first floor level.

A galvanised steel
footbridge links
the offices to
the factory.

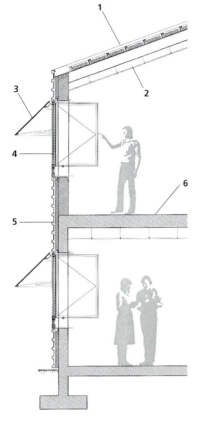

Left:
The gables are clad in
Prodema panels and louvres.

**Vertical section through
the office building.**
1 roof
  - steel cladding
  - double-layer insulation
  - internal steel skin
2 galvanised steel structure
3 inclined PV panels on coated steel
  fixings
4 windows with low-emissivity
  insulating glazing in aluminium
  frames with anti-cold bridge detail
5 typical façade
  - coated steel cladding
  - air gap
  - thermal insulation
  - damp-proof membrane
  - block wall
  - internal cladding with insulation
6 reinforced concrete floor

The translucent
PV panels work
as sun-screens
above the south
windows.

Each gable
is extended by
a perforated
aluminium canopy.

**Vertical section through factory
building.**
1 roof
  - steel cladding
  - double-layer insulation
  - internal steel skin
2 galvanised steel structure
3 upper façade
  - cladding in resin-impregnated
    wood
  - air gap
  - thermal insulation
  - damp-proof membrane
  - block wall
  - internal cladding with insulation
4 canopy in perforated coated
  aluminium on separate galvanised
  steel structure
5 windows with low-emissivity
  insulating glazing in aluminium
  frames with anti-cold bridge detail
6 fixed sun shading in
  resin-impregnated wood strips
7 lower façade
  - cladding in flush
    resin-impregnated wood panels
  - air gap
  - thermal insulation
  - damp-proof membrane
  - block wall
  - internal cladding with insulation
8 reinforced concrete mezzanine
  floor

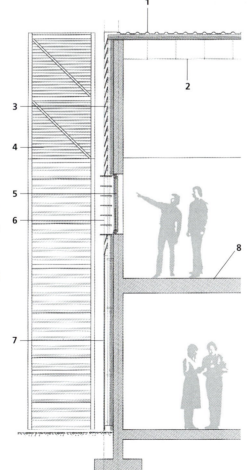

Address: 12, allée du Levant, 69890 La Tour-de-Salvagny, France
Project brief: factory and offices.
Client: Total Energie (chief executive Roland Barthez).
Architect: Jacques Ferrier, Paris (project architect Jean-François Irissou,
with Guillaume Saunier, Stéphane Giet).
Engineers: Pitance.
Installation of PV panels: Solarte, Yves Jautard.
Timetable: design begun January 1998;
construction June 1998 - March 1999.
Area: offices: net area 800m²; factory: net area 1,400m².
Main contractors: Pitance.
Cost: FF8.15 million (€1.242 million), including heating and ventilation
but excluding PV panels.

MOTORWAY SERVICE AREA AT LA BAIE DE SOMME, FRANCE
Bruno Mader

ENVIRONMENTAL FEATURES

▮ *Bioclimatic features*
Site landscaping; use of timber for structure, cladding and internal fittings; use of naturally durable timbers; use of local stones in concrete panels; deep projecting eaves to reduce direct sun in summer; upper roof skin to reduce roof heating; perimeter trench to collect rainwater.

▮ *Materials and construction*
Structural columns in glulam larch; timber framing; walls in precast concrete panels with exposed Hourdel pebbles on outer face; curtain-walling in Cekal Climalit double glazing with aluminium frames; flooring in grey reconstituted stone terrazzo; ceiling in okoume-veneered plywood; roof cladding in steel panels with upper skin in larch; decking and pontoons in ipe wood; belvedere façade in larch.

▮ *Technical features*
Two-way ventilation with heat recovery; hydrocarbon filter for surface water; wind turbine.

▮ *U-values*
- Walls 0.4W/m²K;
- roof 0.35W/m²K;
- curtain-walling 2.6W/m²K.

▮ *Site*
Rapid, low-impact construction.

The environmental approach may be applied to all types of building. In this project a motivated design team, supported by the client and technical and financial partners, have turned a run-of-the-mill service station into a lookout point linked to the surrounding landscape.

CONTEXT AND SITE
Situated between the Somme and the English Channel, this service area, with its lookout tower and wind turbine, rises gently from a 20-hectare site in the midst of a calm, open landscape. The buildings are laid out on an orthogonal grid, with landscaping to reduce the impact of vehicles on the surroundings: service access is at one end of the site to avoid interrupting the panoramic views, while the car parks, bordered by canals, are grouped together at a lower level to allow visual continuity between the site and the fields around. The three transverse canals running across the site take rainwater run-off from the service area and the adjacent motorway. One of them forms a pool, running alongside the pontoon adjacent to the building and around the circular belvedere, which is reflected in it. This pool also serves as a reservoir in case of fire.

FUNCTION AND FORM
The long, horizontal building is aligned with an avenue of four rows of ash trees, planted to line up with the structural timber columns. Its flat, slender roof plate shelters the various service areas. Opposite the fuel pumps, the shop, toilets and cafeteria are housed in three concrete blocks, the gaps between them framing a series of views over the plains of Picardy beyond. The café, boutiques selling regional products and an exhibition area are housed within a large, light, glazed building overlooking the adjacent marsh. Steps lead down to a pedestrian walkway, extended by the terrace

alongside the canal, leading to the belvedere. Inside the latter, a display presents the plant and animal life of the region. By night, lighting built into the floor and walls marks the way across the pools, floodlit from beneath the walkways and pontoons.

STRUCTURAL PRINCIPLES
The walls of the three service blocks are formed of large precast concrete panels, above which the main roof is visible through sections of glazing. The concrete walls, together with a single cross-braced bay, provide lateral stability to the glulam larch columns supporting the roof. These columns project upwards beyond the roof plane, recalling the rows of timber posts of the coastal mussel and oyster beds. The shallow roof structure, in glulam timber, is concealed by plywood ceiling panels, veneered in okoume, so that it appears as a thin plate.

MATERIALS AND FINISHES
In a nod to the vernacular, a layer of local grey pebbles placed in the concrete formwork gives the walls a roughness which contrasts with the smooth veneered ceiling. The ceiling panels are perforated in some areas to improve acoustics. The belvedere has a concrete core, and an open-work outer wall in unplaned larch, reminiscent of hunting lodges, which is gradually acquiring a patina in shades of grey. The pontoons and walkways are in ipe hardwood, whose density and natural durability enable it to withstand large changes in moisture levels. Lighting and ventilation plant are placed above

The service area sits well within its surroundings.

the concrete blocks, and rainwater pipes concealed within the roof thickness, allowing a purity of line which sets the surrounding landscape off to advantage. To ensure a homogenous whole, the rest of the service area was built to a precise specification setting out requirements for form, materials and signage.

ENERGY AND CLIMATE CONTROL
With ceiling heights of over 5m, the building benefits greatly from natural lighting. The curtain-walling is in double glazing with a 12mm air gap, framed in aluminium sections detailed to avoid cold bridging. The deep projecting eaves limit direct sunlight into the space, thus avoiding overheating. A two-way ventilation system recovers heat from used air; air is blown in at the foot of the glazed façade, avoiding condensation and contributing to comfort in summer. The steel cladding of the main roof, visible from the belvedere, is covered by an upper layer of larch planking, promoting air circulation and avoiding excessive temperatures in summer.
The site is very exposed and highly suitable for the installation of a wind turbine. The single turbine supplies 500,000kWh each year, enough to cover electricity and air-conditioning requirements. Since energy production is variable and cannot be stored, it is sold to EDF, the national distributor, and bought back at favourable rates.

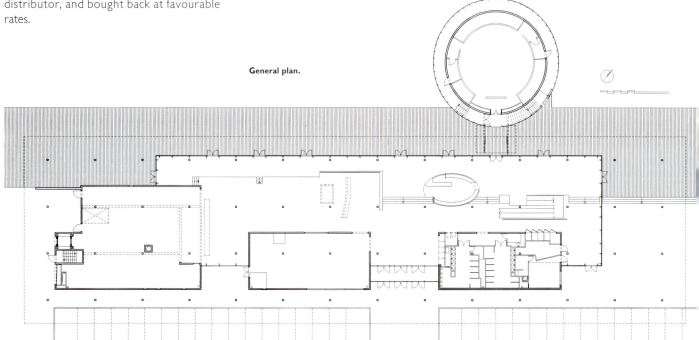

General plan.

Landscaping includes a water treatment system; after passing through a hydrocarbon separator, surface water is filtered by reed beds in the pools.

The three service blocks are grouped under a single timber roof.

The roof is protected
by an upper skin in larch.

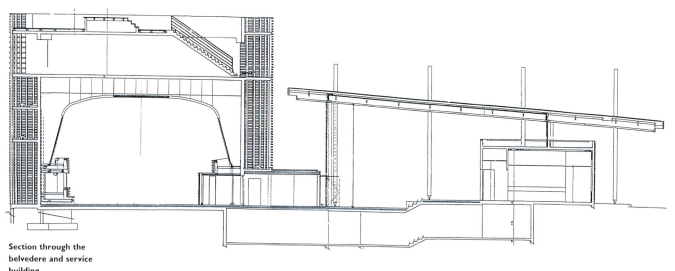

Section through the
belvedere and service
building.

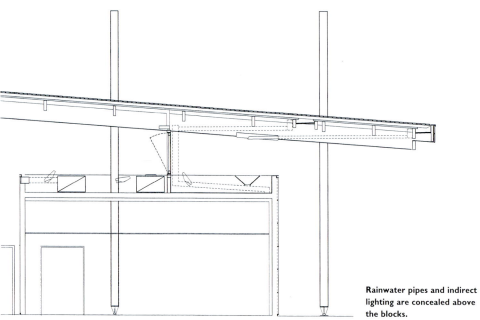

Rainwater pipes and indirect
lighting are concealed above
the blocks.

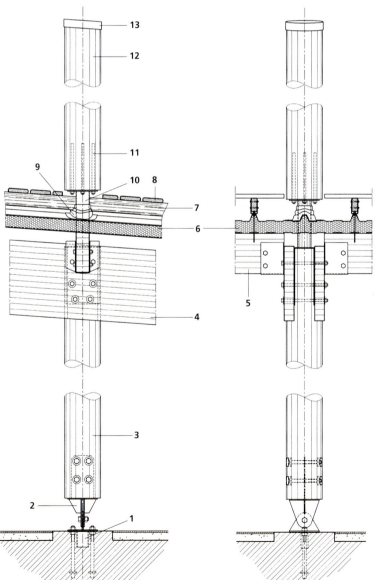

**Details are designed to ensure
the long-term durability of the timber.
Steel connections protect the column
bases, projecting timbers are capped,
and connections detailed to prevent
water traps.**

Left:
**Details showing column
and roof beam connections.**

1 cast-in base-plate and bolts.
2 pinned steel connection
3 240mm diameter glulam
  column.
4 glulam primary roof beam
5 glulam secondary beam
  with bolted steel connection
6 120mm double-skin steel
  cladding panel
7 solid timber batten fixed
  to cladding via steel riders

8 upper skin in 25mm larch
  planks
9 Pipeco type waterproofing
  joint
10 steel column connection
  element
11 16mm threaded rods,
  screwed and glued into
  column and bolted to steel
  connector
12 240mm diameter glulam
  column
13 zinc capping piece

Address: near Abbeville on the A16 motorway, France.
Project brief: service station with restaurant, display
and sales areas, toilets, exhibition and belvedere.
Client: building, Somme regional authority; external areas:
Sanef.
Architect: Bruno Mader; assistant architect Pascal Boisson.
Engineers: timber structure: Sylva conseil; fluids: Inex,
Cegef; quantity surveyor: Michel Ducroux.
Landscape design: Pascale Hannetel.
Timetable: competition December 1995;
design March 1996 - February 1997; site September 1997-
May 1998.
Area: total area 4,828m².
Contractors: main contractor Quille; timber: Mathis.
Cost: building plus external areas FF19.7 million
(€3.003 million) at 1997 prices; scenography, FF2.5 million
(€381,120).

CAR PARK IN HEILBRONN, GERMANY

Mahler Günster Fuchs

The work of the German architectural practice Mahler Günster Fuchs, driven by both stylistic and technical innovation, often makes extensive use of timber with a view to its environmental advantages. The Heilbronn car park bears their hallmarks of optimum use of materials, purity of form and clarity of line.

ENVIRONMENTAL FEATURES

■ *Bioclimatic features*
Integration into the surrounding site; use of local timber; natural lighting and ventilation; landscaping around building.

■ *Materials and construction*
Steel H-section frame; reinforced concrete floors cast on permanent concrete formwork; façade in open-work Douglas fir.

CONTEXT AND SITE

The building is designed to provide car parking for people visiting the town centre, as well as the nearby swimming pool and ice hockey stadium. To protect the mature trees at the rear of the site, the car park is set alongside the main road. Standing close to a stone tower, all that remains of the town's fortifications, the building's distinctive shape signals the visitor's arrival in the town.

FUNCTION AND FORM

There are six car park levels, 137.5m long by 18.5m wide, with semi-cylinders at each end containing the access ramps. The building's aspect varies with angle of view, weather and light. From a distance, approaching drivers perceive it as monolithic, fortress-like; from close to, the gaps in the façade let through vertical beams of light.

STRUCTURAL PRINCIPLES

Several materials are used, with best use made of the qualities of each. The steel frame, set out on a 4.6m grid, consists of 300mm H-section columns and 450mm H-section beams. This supports 50mm thick precast panels, 2.5m wide, which act as permanent formwork for the 150mm reinforced concrete floor slabs. Lateral stability is provided by the concrete walls around the ramps. The façades are composed of chevron sections in Douglas fir, 40 × 60mm wide and 15.2m long, fixed 25mm apart on a timber fame to form 2.5m wide prefabricated panels. These are fixed to the concrete slabs via steel connections. The swing doors giving pedestrian access to the different levels are also in Douglas fir and are integrated into the façade.

MATERIALS AND FINISHES

The grey-ochre tones of the unplaned Douglas fir match the colours of the stone in the old ramparts. In front of the east ramp and the road side façade, a galvanised steel grillage on circular glulam columns stands 1.2m outside the

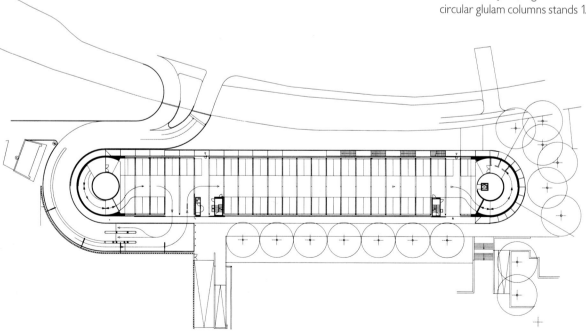

façade line, linked back to the structure by horizontal steel struts. The visual superposition of this arrangement with the façade behind creates combinations of vertical and horizontal lines, bringing animation to the whole. Any suggestion of an improvised solution is dispelled by the high quality of the details.

ENERGY AND CLIMATE CONTROL

The gaps between the timber chevrons ensure natural light and ventilation within the car park, resulting in a rare sense of comfort and security, as well as bringing considerable savings in running costs. The free flow of outside air across the building also meant that no fire protection was required. On the façade facing the town centre, the concrete access staircase lies in the space between timber façade and steel grillage, protected by an outer mesh skin. This creates a safe, buffer zone, reminiscent of the galleries at the top of the old fortified towers. The building is surrounded by green; existing trees have been retained, shrubs have been planted to restructure the areas leading to the sports facilities, and the surrounding grass runs almost up to the car park itself. Only the access roads and footpaths are paved, in concrete blocks. At night, external lighting along the façades lights up the building and its immediate area, adding to the subtle interplay of vertical and horizontal lines.

The 137m long car park runs alongside a park.

The semi-open cladding in timber chevrons ensures natural light and ventilation.

Address: Mannheimer Strasse, 72024 Heilbronn, Germany.
Project brief: 500-space car park.
Client: Heilbronn municipal authority.
Architect: Mahler Günster Fuchs, Stuttgart, with Karin Schmidt-Arnoldt.
Structural engineers: Fischer & Friedrich, Stuttgart.
Timetable: design begun 1996; construction December 1997 - December 1998.
Area: net area 13,500m²; ground floor plus five levels, including roof parking.
Timber contractors: Holzbau Müller, Blaustein-Ditingen.
Cost: DM10.8 million (€5.522 million).

The external stairway
is protected by a mesh skin
on a galvanised steel
structure.

The 18.5 × 2.5m
façade panels were
prefabricated off-site.
Transverse sections.

Transverse
sections.

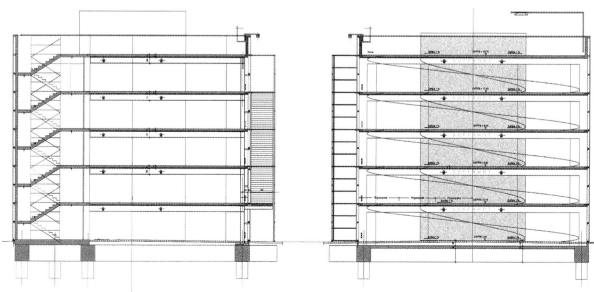

Appendix

Useful Addresses

ADEME
27, rue Louis Vicat
F - 75015 Paris
Tel.: + 33.1.47.65.20.00
Fax: + 33.1.46.45.53.36
www.ademe.fr

ADPSR – Architects,
Designers and Planners
for Social Responsability
P.O. Box 18375
Washington, DC 20036-
8375
USA
information@adpsr.org

AECB – Association
for Environment Conscious
Building
P.O. Box 32
UK – Llandysul SA44 5ZA
admin@aecb.net
www.aecb.net

Agence d'urbanisme
et de développement de la
région Flandre - Dunkerque
38, quai des Hollandais
F - 59140 Dunkerque
Tel.: + 33.3.28.58.06.30
Fax: + 33.3.28.59.04.27
doc@agur-dunkerque.org

AICVF
(Association des ingénieurs
en climatique, ventilation
et froid)
66, rue de Rome
F - 75008 Paris
Tel.: + 33.1.53.04.36.10
Fax: + 33.1.42.94.04.54
www.aicvf.asso.fr

Arbeitsgemeinschaft
Holz e.V.
Postfach 30 01 41
D - 40401 Düsseldorf
Tel.: + 49.211.47.81.80
Fax: + 49.211.45.23.14
www.argeholz.de
argeholz@argeholz.de

Association HQE
Villa Pasteur
83, boulevard Mac Donald
F - 75019 Paris
Tel.: + 33.1.42.05.45.24
Fax: + 33.1.42.05.64.69

Austrian Energy Agency
(E.V.A.)
Otto-Bauer-Gasse 6
A – 1060 Wien
Tel. + 43.1.586.15.24
eva@eva.ac.at

BREEAM
Tel.: + 44.1923.664.462
Fax: + 44.1923.664.103
breeam@bre.co.uk

CIDB
(Centre d'information et de
documentation sur le bruit)
14, rue Jules Bourdais
F - 75017 Paris
Tel.: + 33.1.47.64.64.64
Fax: + 33.1.47.64.64.65
www.cidb.org

Cler
(Comité de liaison énergies
renouvelables) 28, rue Basfroi
F - 75011 Paris
Tel.: + 33.1.46.59.04.44
www.cler.org

CNDB
6, avenue de Saint-Mandé
F - 75012 Paris
Tel.: + 33.1.53.17.19.60
Fax: + 33.1.43.41.11.88

CORDIS – Community
Research & Development
Information Service
Rue Montoyer 40
B – 1000 Brussels
Tel. + 32.2.238.17.36
Fax + 32.2.238.17.98
Press@cordis.lu

CSTB
4, avenue du Recteur Poincaré
F - 75782 Paris Cedex 16
Tel.: + 33.1.40.50.28.28
Fax: + 33.1.45.25.61.51
www.cstb.fr

CTBA
Allée Boutaut
F - 33300 Bordeaux
Tel.: + 33.5.56.43.63.00
Fax: + 33.5.56.39.80.79
www.ctba.fr

Deutsche Energie-Agentur
Chausseestrasse 128a
D - 10115 Berlin
Tel.: + 49.30.726.16.56
Fax: + 49.30.726.16.56-99
info@deutsche-energie-
agentur.de

Ecole d'architecture
de La Villette
Formation continue à la HQE
144, avenue de Flandre
F - 75019 Paris
Tel.: + 33.1.44.65.23.55
Fax: + 33.1.44.65.23.56

Enstib
27, rue du Merle Blanc
BP 1041
F - 88051 Epinal Cedex 9
Tel.: + 33.3.29.81.11.50
Fax: + 33.3.29.34.09.76

Environmental Law
Network International
(elni)
c/o Öko-Institut e.V.
Elisabethenstr. 55-57
D – 64283 Darmstadt
Tel. + 49.6151.819.131
Fax + 49.6151.819.133
unruh@oeko.de

Fraunhofer-Institut für
Solare Energiesysteme ISE
Heidenhofstr. 2
D - 79110 Freiburg im
Breisgau
Tel. + 49.761.45.88 - 0
Fax + 49.761.45.88 - 9000
info@ise.fhg.de

Freiburg Futour
Wipperstrasse 2
D - 79100 Freiburg im
Breisgau
Tel.: + 49.761.400.26.40
Fax: + 49.761.400.26.50
info@freiburg-futour.de
www.freiburg-futour.de

Gemeinde Mäder
Alte Schulstrasse 7
A - 6841 Mäder
Tel.: + 43.55.23.52.860
Fax: + 43.55.23.52.860-20
Gemeinde.maeder@vol.at

Gepa
26, boulevard Raspail
F - 75007 Paris
Tel.: + 33.1.53.63.24.00
Fax: + 33.1.53.63.24.04

Geschäftsstelle Vauban
Technisches Rathaus
Fehrenbachallee 12
D - 79106 Freiburg im
Breisgau

Ifen
(Institut français
de l'environnement)
61, boulevard Alexandre-
Martin
F - 45058 Orléans Cedex 1
Tel.: + 33.2.38.79.78.78
Fax: + 33.2.38.79.78.70
www.ifen.fr

Institute of Environmental
Technology
Fachhochschule beider Basel
Fichtenhagstr. 4
CH – 4132 Muttenz
Tel. + 41.61.467.45.05
Fax + 41.61.467.42.90
ifuinfo@fhbb.ch

Istituto Nazionale
di Urbanistica
Piazza Farnese 44
I – 00186 Rom
Tel. + 39.06.688.01.190
Fax + 39.06.682.14.773
inunaz@tin.it

Landeshauptstadt Stuttgart
Hochbauamt
Dorotheenstrasse 4
D - 70173 Stuttgart
Tel.: + 49.711.216.66.84
Fax: + 49.711.216.74.30

Minergie
Steinerstrasse 37
CH - 3000 Bern 16
Tel.: + 31.352.51.11
Fax: + 31.352.42.06
info@minergie.ch

Ministère
de l'Aménagement
du territoire et de
l'Environnement
20, avenue de Ségur
F - 75302 Paris 07 SP
Tel.: + 33.1.42.79.20.21
Fax: + 33.1.42.19.14.67
www.environnement.gouv.fr

Observ'ER
(Observatoire des énergies
renouvelables)
146, rue de l'Université
F - 75007 Paris
Tel.: + 33.1.44.18.00.80
Fax: + 33.1.44.18.00.36
Observ.er@wanadoo.fr

Österreichisches Ökologie-
Institut für angewandte
Umweltforschung
Seidengasse 13
A – 1070 Vienna
Tel.: + 43.1523.61.05
Fax: + 43.1523.58.43
oekoinstitut@ecology.at

Passivhaus Institut
Rheinstrasse 44-46
D - 64283 Darmstadt
Tel.: + 49.61.51.826.99-0
Fax: + 49.61.51.826.99-11
Passivhaus@t-online.de
www.passiv.de

Proholz-Holzinformation
Österreich
Uraniastrasse 4
A - 1011 Vienna
Tel.: + 43.222.712.04.74.31
Fax: + 43.222.713.10.18

Roy Prince, Architect
Sustainable ABC
P.O. Box 30085
Santa Barbara, CA 93130
USA
Tel.: + 1.805.898.9660
Fax: + 805.898.9199
royprince@sustainableabc.com

Stern
Schwedterstrasse 263
D - 10435 Berlin
Tel.: + 49.30.443.636.30
Fax: + 49.30.443.636.31

Swiss Priority Programme
Environment
Programme Management
(SPP)
Länggassstrasse 23
CH - 3012 Bern
Tel.: + 41 31 307 25 25
Fax: + 41.31.307.25.26
info@sppe.ch

Ville de Rennes
Direction de l'architecture,
du foncier et de l'urbanisme
71, rue Dupont des Loges
Hôtel de Ville
F - 35031 Rennes
Tel.: + 33.2.99.28.57.18
Fax: + 33.2.99.28.58.51

Zentrum für Energie
und Nachhaltigkeit im
Bauwesen (ZEN)
c/o EMPA Dübendorf
CH - 8600 Dübendorf
Fax: + 41.1.823.40.09
zen@empa.ch

Zürcher Hochschule
Winterthur
Zentrum für nachhaltiges
Gestalten, Planen und
Bauen
Prof. Hansruedi Preisig
CH - 8401 Winterthur
Tel.: + 41.52.267.76.16
Fax: + 41.52.267.76.20
hansruedi.preisig@zhwin.ch

BIBLIOGRAPHY

References

A Green Vitruvius. Principles and Practice of Sustainable Architectural Design, University College Dublin, Architects' Council of Europe, Softech and the Finnish Association of Architects/James & James, London, 1999.

Ecological Architecture. Bioclimatic Trends and Landscape Architecture in the Year 2001, Loft, Barcelona, 2000.

Stadterweiterung: Freiburg Rieselfeld, avedition, Stuttgart, 1997.

Sophia and Stefan Behling, Sol Power. The Evolution of Sustainable Architecture, Prestel, Munich, London, New York, 2000.

Beierlorzer, Boll, Ganser, Siedlungskultur, IBA Emscher Park, Vieweg, Braunschweig/Wiesbaden, 1999.

G. Z. Brown and Mark DeKay, Sun, Wind and Light. Architectural Design Strategies, John Wiley & Sons, New York, 2001.

Bund Deutscher Architekten (ed.), Umweltleitfaden für Architekten, Ernst & Sohn, Berlin, 1995.

Daniel D. Chiras, The Natural House. A Complete Guide to Healthy, energy-efficient, natural homes, Chelsea Green Publication, 2000.

Andrea Compagno, Intelligent Glass Façades. Material, Practice, Design, 5th edition, Birkhäuser, Basel, Berlin, Boston, 2002.

Norman Crowe, Richard Economakis and Michael Lykoudis (ed.), Building cities: Towards a civil society and sustainable environment, Artmedia Press, London, 1999.

Klaus Daniels, The Technonlogy of Ecological Building. Basic Principles and Measures, Examples and Ideas, Birkhäuser, Basel, Boston, Berlin, second enlarged edition, 1997.

Klaus Daniels, Low Tech, Light Tech, High Tech. Building in the information Age, Birkhäuser, Basel, Boston, Berlin, 2000.

Deutsches Architekturmuseum Frankfurt am Main, Ingeborg Flagge and Anna Meseure (ed.), DAM Annual 2001, Prestel, Munich, London, New York, 2001.

Brian Edwards, Towards a Sustainable Architecture. European directives and Building Design, Architectural Press, Oxford, 1996, 1999.

Brian Edwards and David Turrent, Sustainable Housing. Principles and Practice, E & FN Spon, London, 2000.

Dr. Wolfgang Feist, Das Niedrig-Energie-Haus, C. F. Müller, Karlsruhe, 1996.

Dora Francese, Architettura bioclimatica. Risparmio energetico e qualità della vita nelle costruzioni, Utet, Torino, 1996.

Dominique Gauzin-Müller, Construire avec le bois, Le Moniteur, Paris, 1999.

Anton Graf, Das Passivhaus. Wohnen ohne Heizung, Callwey, Munich, 2000.

Mary Guzowski, Daylighting for sustainable Design, Mc Graw-Hill, New York, 2000.

Susannah Hagan, Taking shape. A new contract between Architecture and Nature, Architectural Press, Oxford et al., 2001.

Ekhart Hahn, Ökologische Stadtplanung, Haag & Herchen, Frankfurt am Main, 1987.

S. Halliday, Green Guide to the Architects Job Book, Riba Publications, London, 2000.

S. Robert Hastings, Solar Air Systems. Built Examples, Solar Heating and Cooling Executive Committee of

the International Energy Agency, James & James, London, 1999.

Dean Hawkes, The Environmental Tradition: Studies in the Architecture of Environment, E & FN Spon, London, 1996.

Dean Hawkes and Wayne Forster, High Efficiency Buildings, Calman & King Ltd., London, 2002.

Thomas Herzog, Solar Energy in Architecture and Urban Planning, Prestel, Munich, London, New York, 1996, 1998.

Othmar Humm and Peter Toggweiler, Photovoltaik und Architektur/ Photovoltaics in Architecture, Birkhäuser, Basel, Boston, Berlin, 1993.

Jean-Louis Izard, Architectures d'été: construire pour le confort d'été, Edisud, Aix-en-Provence, 1993.

David. D. Kemp, The environment dictionary, Routledge, London, New York, 1998.

Eric Labouze, Enjeux écologiques et initiatives industrielles, Puca, Paris, 1993.

Craig Langston, Sustainable Practices in the Built Environment, Architectural Press, Oxford, 2001 (second edition).

Pierre Lavigne, Paul Brejon and Pierre Fernandez, Architecture climatique: une contribution au développement durable, vol. 1: Bases physiques, Edisud, Aix-en-Provence, 1994.

Philip Jodidio (ed.), Green Architecture, Taschen, Cologne, New York, 2000.

David Lloyd Jones, Architecture and the Environment. Bioclimatic Building Design, Laurence King, London, 1998.

Amerigo Marras, Eco-tec: Architecture of the In-between, Princeton Architectural Press, New York, 1999.

Ed Melet, Duurzame Architectuur/Sustainable Architecture. Towards a Diverse Built Environment, NAI, Rotterdam, 1999.

Walter Meyer-Bohe, Energiesparhäuser, Deutsche Verlags-Anstalt, Stuttgart, 1996.

Jürg Minsch, Institutionelle Reformen für eine Politik der Nachhaltigkeit, Springer, Berlin, Heidelberg, New York, 1998.

H. R. Preisig, W. Dubach, U. Kasser, K. Viriden, Ökologische Baukompetenz, Handbuch für die Kostenbewusste Bauherrschaft von A bis Z, Werd, Zürich, 1999.

Anna Ray-Jones, Sustainable Architecture in Japan, the Green Buildings of Nikken Sekkei, John Wiley & Sons, New York, 2000.

Sue Roaf, M. Hancock, Energy Efficient Building, Blackwell Scientific Publications, 1992.

Sue Roaf, Manuel Fuentes, Atephanie Thomas, Ecohouse. A Design Guide, Architectural Press, Oxford et al., 2001.

Richard Rogers, Philip Gumuchdjian, Cities for a Small Planet, Faber and Faber, London, 1997.

Miguel Ruano, Ecourbanismo. Entornos humanos sostenibles: 60 proyectos/Ecourbanism. Sustainable Human Settlements: 60 Case Studies, Gustavo Gili, Barcelona, 1999.

Thomas Schmitz-Günther, Eco-Logis, Könemann, Cologne, 1998.

Astrid Schneider (ed.), Solararchitektur für Europa, Birkhäuser, Basel, Boston, Berlin, 1996.

Ansgar Schrode, Niedrigenergiehäuser, Rudolf Müller, Cologne, 1996.

Catherine Slessor, Eco-Tech, Umweltverträgliche Architektur und Hochtechnologie, Gerd Hatje, Ostfildern-Ruit, 1997.

Peter F. Smith, Architecture in a Climate of Change. A guide to sustainable design, Architectural Press, Oxford et al., 2001.

Ross Spiegel and Dru Meadows, Green Building Materials, a Guide to Product Selection and Specification, John Wiley & Sons, New York, 1999.

Fred A. Stitt, Ecological design handbook. Sustainable strategies for architecture, landscape architecture, interior design and planning, Mc Graw-Hill, London, New York, 1999.

Jean Swetchine, Ambiances et équipements, first part: Thermique, Editions de la Villette, Paris, 1983.

Randall Thomas, Environmental design. An introduction for architects and engineers, E & FN Spon, London, 1999.

UIA Berlin 2002 (ed.), Resource Architecture, Birkhäuser, Basel, Boston, Berlin, 2002.

Anke Van Hal, Ger de Vries, Joost Brouwers, Opting for Change. Sustainable Building in the Netherlands, Aeneas, AJ Best, 2000.

Ernst Ulrich von Weizsäcker, Amory B. Lovins, L. Hunter Lovins, Factor Four. Doubling Wealth, Halving Resource Use, Earthscan, London, 1998.

B. Vale and R. Vale, The New Autonomous House, Thames and Hudson, London, 2000.

Andy Wasowski and Sally Wasowski, Building inside nature's envelope. How new construction and land preservation can work together, Oxford University Press, Oxford, New York, 2000.

James Wines, Green Architecture, Taschen, Cologne, New York, 2000.

Tom Woolley and Sam Kimmins, *Green Building Handbook*, vol. 1 and 2, E & FN Spon, London, 2000.

Wuppertal Institut and Planung-Büro Schmitz Aachen, *Energiegerechtes Bauen und Modernisieren. Grundlagen und Beispiele für Architekten, Bauherren und Bewohner*, Birkhäuser, Basel, Boston, Berlin, 1996.

Ken Yeang, *Designing with Nature: the Ecological Basis for Architectural Design*, Mc Graw-Hill, New York, 1995.

Ken Yeang, *The Green Skyscraper. The Basis for Designing Sustainable Intensive Buildings*, Prestel, Munich, London, New York, 1999.

Surveys

Bâtiment et haute qualité environnementale. Mode d'emploi à l'usage des maîtres d'ouvrage, Strasbourg.

A.E. Cakir, *Licht und Gesundheit*, Institut für Arbeits- und Sozialforschung, Berlin, 1990.

Ökologischer Stadtumbau, Theorie und Konzept, Ekhart Hahn, FS II 91-405, Wissenschaftszentrum Berlin für Sozialforschung, Berlin, 1991.

Ökologischer Stadtumbau, ein neues Leitbild, Ekhart Hahn and Udo E. Simonis, FS II 94-403, Wissenschaftszentrum Berlin für Sozialforschung, Berlin, 1994.

Symposiumsbericht Solararchitektur, Symposium at Glashaus Herten, 27-28 October 1995, Verein für grüne Solararchitektur, Tübingen, 1995.

Bauen für eine lebenswerte Zukunft. Niedrigenergie-Bauweise in Freiburg, Freiburg im Breisgau, 1996.

Holzschutz, Bauliche Empfehlungen, Informationsdienst Holz, Düsseldorf, 1997.

TriSolar. Leben mit der Sonne, Installa Totherm GmbH, Bau- und Haustechnik, Issum, 1997.

Bauen mit Holz ohne Chemie, Informationsdienst Holz, Düsseldorf, 1998.

Ecological Building Criteria for Viikki, Helsinki City Planning Department Publications, Helsinki, 1998.

Evaluation de la qualité environnementale des bâtiments, CSTB, PCA, Paris, 1998.

Intégrer la qualité environnementale dans les constructions publiques, CSTB, Paris, 1998.

Mémento des règles de l'art pour une bonne qualité environnementale à l'intention des architectes, Tribu, Paris, 1998.

F. Allard, P. Blondeau, A. L. Tiffonnet, *Qualité de l'air intérieur. Etat des lieux et bibliographie*, Puca, Paris, 1998.

Guide de recommandations pour la conception de logements à hautes performances énergétiques en Île-de-France, Cler, Montreuil, 1999.

Projet urbain de Rennes, Rennes, 1999.

Ville et écologie, bilan d'un programme de recherche (1992-1999), Puca, Paris, 1999.

Projects around the World of Expo 2000, Expo 2000 Hannover GmbH, 2000.

Sustainable Buildings 2000, Proceedings, Colloquium Maastricht, 22-25 October 2000.

Une charte pour l'environnement, Rennes, 2000.

Weltbericht zur Zukunft der Städte Urban 21, Bundesministerium für Verkehr, Bau- und Wohnungswesen, Berlin, 2000.

INDEX

Illustration credits